Baudelaire's Prose Poems

Baudelaire's Prose Poems

The Practice and Politics of Irony

SONYA STEPHENS

OXFORD
UNIVERSITY PRESS

OXFORD
UNIVERSITY PRESS

Great Clarendon Street, Oxford OX2 6DP

Oxford University Press is a department of the University of Oxford.
It furthers the University's objective of excellence in research, scholarship,
and education by publishing worldwide in

Oxford New York

Athens Auckland Bangkok Bogotá Buenos Aires Calcutta
Cape Town Chennai Dar es Salaam Delhi Florence Hong Kong Istanbul
Karachi Kuala Lumpur Madrid Melbourne Mexico City Mumbai
Nairobi Paris São Paulo Singapore Taipei Tokyo Toronto Warsaw

and associated companies in Berlin Ibadan

Oxford is a registered trade mark of Oxford University Press
in the UK and certain other countries

Published in the United States
by Oxford University Press Inc., New York

© Sonya Stephens 1999

British Library Cataloguing in Publication Data
Data available

Library of Congress Cataloging in Publication Data
Data available
ISBN–0–19–815877–7

1 3 5 7 9 10 8 6 4 2

Typeset by J&L Composition Ltd, Filey, North Yorkshire
Printed in Great Britain on acid-free paper by
Bookcraft Ltd, Midsomer Norton, Somerset

For Jon

Preface

THERE IS A tradition in criticism on Baudelaire's prose poetry to begin by justifying one's choice of this text. This is perhaps not surprising, given that another tradition within Baudelaire studies characterized the reader who did prefer the prose poems to *Les Fleurs du mal* as 'généralement dépourvu d'oreille' and 'mal initié aux subtilités de la prosodie'. The fact is, though, that now the choice needs no justification, for the *Petits Poèmes en prose* are no longer neglected by scholars and their interest and diversity are reflected in an ever growing number of studies devoted, either partly or exclusively, to the work.

The aim of this book is to consider the different manifestations of irony in Baudelaire's *Petits Poèmes en prose* and to demonstrate the centrality of these ironies to the theory and functioning of the new genre. The discussion of these takes different forms in the different stages of this account but, even when irony, or related concepts, are not being discussed directly, their significance should be clear in the inflections of the argument. The first chapter concentrates on Baudelaire's choice of genre and the way in which he seeks to define it, both by his careful consideration of titles and in the letter addressed to Arsène Houssaye, now attached as a form of preface to editions of the work. The threshold of Baudelaire's work is thus placed at the threshold of mine as an informing text. Although it is almost de rigueur amongst critics to cite aspects of this letter, it has not so far received the sort of detailed attention which properly promotes it to the status of a text in its own right. I have sought to redress this by subjecting it to close scrutiny in the light of broader discussions of the role of the paratext. When considered in this light, it reveals the dualities of the text as well as the duplicities of the author. The threshold of the *Petits Poèmes en prose* is, therefore, seen to be suggestive of the conflicting and duplicitous discursive modes of the poems themselves and to prefigure other sorts of thresholds which they represent. The second chapter builds on the forms of doubleness uncovered to show how the poetic texts are representative of a continuity between thematic and formal planes. Lyricism is here shown to be irreconcilably other, in its conjunctions with the prosaic, in its relation to past models, and in the fictions and figurations of the poetic subject. In this poetics of openness, the encounters with the other are born of productive interaction with the crowd and the lyric subject becomes *dédoublé*. This phenomenon is also discernible in the narrative strategies which the prose poems explore and is shown to betray an ironic separation. In the third chapter the consequences of this are examined in more closely referential terms. The politics are here to be understood principally in the sense of manoeuvring and intriguing, although this does not exclude consideration of the ideological implications of this in the specific context of nineteenth-century France, particularly with respect to power (both literary and social) and dominant discourse. In exploiting such discourse, the prose poems parody its truth and explode its hegemony and offer, in its place, moral ambiguity. By engaging with the dominant discourse in this way, the prose poem asserts its status as 'low' art. It is through an application of Baudelaire's theories of comic art to the prose poem that the full significance of this is revealed. The final chapter accordingly demonstrates how the *Petit Poèmes en prose* exploit comic forms and combine Baudelaire's notion of the *comique significatif* and the *comique absolu*. These forms of the comic depend, like irony, not only on superiority and *dédoublement*, but also on reception for, as Baudelaire says, 'c'est spécialement dans le rieur, dans le spectateur, que gît le comique'.

The risks of an argument built on irony are high and, in elaborating such an argument, one is always confronted with inescapable complexities, other unspoken beliefs, inferential processes, and their conclusions. I make no claim to the superiority of total vision that ironic interpretation necessarily implies, but instead offer here 'une série d'applications des principes ci-dessus énoncés', 'un échantillon sous chaque titre de catégorie'.

Acknowledgements

I WOULD LIKE to express my gratitude to those who played a part in shaping this book and who offered friendly advice at various stages of its development. Rosemary Lloyd is particularly to be thanked for her scholarly advice and support, as well as for the interest and enthusiasm she has shown, in official and unofficial capacities, for this and other projects. Robert Lethbridge also offered advice on an earlier version of this book and has followed its development with interest. Both colleagues and friends, they have given a great deal over the years and this brief mention cannot do justice to the countless ways in which they have enabled me to bring this work to fruition. I should also like to thank Jim Hiddleston and Graham Chesters, both of whom also saw early drafts and offered valuable commentary.

I am grateful to Royal Holloway, University of London for granting me leave to complete this project and to friends and colleagues in the Department of French, and in the College, who make it possible to take full advantage of such leave and who create a climate of academic interest and debate. I should also like to acknowledge the editorial team at Oxford University Press, especially Sophie Goldsworthy and Matthew Hollis, for their enthusiasm and their professionalism.

Finally, it is a pleasure to record here my gratitude to my parents for all their support and to thank Jon who provided, and in considerable measure, daily encouragement, interest, and understanding. He showed, in ways too numerous and too trivial to mention, how important this project was to him, too.

Contents

Abbreviations

FOR REFERENCES TO all Baudelaire's texts (unless otherwise stated), I have used Baudelaire, *Œuvres complètes*, edited by Claude Pichois, Bibliothèque de la Pléiade, 2 vols. (Paris: Gallimard, 1975–6), henceforth designated by *OC*, followed by the volume and page number. For his correspondence, references are made to Baudelaire, *Correspondance*, edited by Claude Pichois, Bibliothèque de la Pléiade, 2 vols. (Paris: Gallimard, 1973), henceforth designated as *C*, followed by the volume and page number.

I

Thresholds

Il n'est de seuil qu'à franchir.
Genette

[handwritten margin note: b1930 French critic + theorist. Structuralist approach]

BAUDELAIRE'S *Spleen de Paris* (*Petits Poèmes en prose*) invites an exploration of genre, not just because its title signals genre (the only genre with an oxymoron for a name) but because Baudelaire here offers a text with no real generic precedents. The way in which these prose poems present Baudelaire's consciousness of boundaries and of the contours of different literary landscapes figured in the hybrid requires further exploration since, in operating on the boundary between genres, and between different modes of discourse, Baudelaire makes choices which deliberately uphold or subvert existing literary models.

   The lack of any significant precursory models lends an indeterminacy to the text, especially as, despite earlier pioneering attempts at something approaching the prose poem, it was only with the posthumous publication of *Le Spleen de Paris* (*Petits Poèmes en prose*) in 1869 that any sort of generic blueprint can be said to have been established.[1] But if it is generally agreed that Baudelaire's prose poems constitute the model which was to determine the parameters of the genre and validate all such literary enterprises in the future, establishing expectations and conditioning the reader's response to such texts, the nature of that

[handwritten margin note: no precedents]

---

[1] See Suzanne Bernard *Le Poème en prose de Baudelaire jusqu'à nos jours* (Paris: Nizet, 1994 [1959]), 19–93 and more especially Nichola Ann Haxell, 'The Name of the Prose: A Semiotic Study of Titling in the Pre-Baudelairian Prose Poem', *French Studies* 44 (1990), 156–69.

model remains sketchy, little more elaborate on the subject than Baudelaire's *lettre-dédicace* to Houssaye.

This letter is, of course, significant, for not only does it make reference to the need for an authenticating precursory text, it is very much a part of the paratext, what Gérard Genette refers to as the 'contrat (ou pacte) générique',[2] or elsewhere as the threshold of the text, the *seuil*, that indeterminate zone between the outside of the text and the inside, 'une zone non seulement de transition mais de *transaction*: lieu privilégié d'une pragmatique et d'une stratégie, d'une action sur le public au service, bien ou mal compris et accompli, d'un meilleur accueil du texte et d'une lecture plus pertinente'.[3] The questions of titling and precedents, both of which constitute elements forming a part of the threshold, or paratext, of Baudelaire's prose poems are an appropriate place to start in a study which sets out to uncover the textual strategies of a new genre and to show these to be predicated on duality, and sometimes even duplicity.

The title of the work, Baudelaire's other major poetic collection, is itself highly problematic. We know that *Les Fleurs du mal* was the title Baudelaire settled on for his first collection only after several alternatives and much hesitation,[4] and there is similar evidence of long reflection and measured alternatives in relation to the collected prose poems. The very first prose poems were published in 1855 alongside verse poems and under no specific collective title.[5] From 1857 to 1861, Baudelaire used the collective title of *Poèmes nocturnes*, which recurs several times in his correspondence, but as a title accompanying the publication of prose poems only once.[6] From 1861 to 1866 the publications in various newspapers and reviews consistently give the titles *Poëmes en prose* or *Petits Poëmes en prose*, with *Le Spleen de Paris. Poèmes en prose* occurring twice in 1864.[7] There is only one other title used, *Petits poèmes lycanthropes*,

---

[2] G. Genette, *Palimpsestes: La Littérature au second degré* (Paris: Seuil, 1982), 9.

[3] Genette, *Seuils* (Paris: Seuil, 1987), 8.

[4] See Pichois's 'Notice' for further details, esp. *OC* i. 796ff.

[5] 'Le Crépuscule du soir' and 'La Solitude' appeared together without any other title in *Hommage à C.F. Denecourt, Fontainebleau. Paysages, légendes, souvenirs, fantaisies* (Paris: Hachette, 1855).

[6] In *Le Présent* (24 Aug. 1857) as a collective title for 'L'Horloge', 'La Chevelure', 'L'Invitation au voyage', 'Le Crépuscule du soir', and 'Les Projets'.

[7] For *Petits Poëmes en prose / Poëmes en prose*, see, in chronological order: *Revue fantaisiste* (1 Nov. 1861); *La Presse* (26 Aug., 27 Aug., and 24 Sept. 1862); *Revue nationale et étrangère*

which appears suddenly in June 1866,[8] only a matter of days before another newspaper prints a poem under the heading of *Le Spleen de Paris*.[9] The first collection of the prose poems in volume form is posthumous and appears in 1869 as the fourth volume of Baudelaire's *Œuvres complètes: Petits Poèmes en prose. Les Paradis artificiels*.[10]

A certain critical reflection is behind these titles, all of which have the status of *official* titles, that is to say titles agreed or used by Baudelaire (and/or his editors), in his lifetime and in the context of a publication of one or more prose poems.[11] Other titles exist, *La Lueur et la fumée*, *Le Promeneur solitaire*, or *Le Rôdeur parisien*, for example, but these cannot be considered official,[12] since they never accompanied a publication of the prose poems and occur only in private correspondence which, despite a growing awareness of the private document as destined for public consumption,[13] can only be considered part of the 'epitext' and as *officieux*.[14] The hesitation and reflection that these changes and the correspondence suggest lead us to attach significance to them, although they are, independently of all hesitation, textual items which invite analysis and speculation.

The role of the title of any work is to identify it, to designate its

---

(10 June 1863); *Le Boulevard* (14 June 1863); *Revue nationale et étrangère* (10 Oct. and 10 Dec. 1863); and *L'Artiste* (1 Nov. 1864). For *Le Spleen de Paris. Petits Poèmes en prose* or [*Petits Poèmes en prose*], see: *Figaro* (7 and 14 Feb. 1864); *La Revue de Paris* (25 Dec. 1864); and *Œuvres*, iv (Paris: Michel Lévy frères, 1869).

  [8] *Revue du XIXe siècle*, 1 June 1866 ('La Fausse Monnaie' and 'Le Joueur généreux').

  [9] 'La Corde' in *L'Événement* (12 June 1866).

  [10] Published by Michel Lévy frères. This first edition in volume form was established by Asselineau and Banville, although they are not named, and is considered by Claude Pichois to be one of two publications which reflect Baudelaire's intentions. The title-page preceding the prose poems bears an inversion of the volume's title: LE SPLEEN DE PARIS [*Petits Poèmes en prose*].

  [11] Genette clarifies: 'Est officiel tout message paratextuel ouvertement assumé par l'auteur et/ou l'éditeur, et dont il ne peut esquiver la responsabilité. Officiel, ainsi, tout ce qui, de source auctoriale ou éditoriale, figure au péritexte anthume, comme le titre ou la préface originale', *Seuils*, 14–15.

  [12] These are considered part of the 'épitexte' and are unofficial inasmuch as they are private, may never have been intended for public consumption, and only form part of the 'paratext' as a result of recent scholarly editions; ibid. 15.

  [13] As indeed Baudelaire's title *Mon cœur mis à nu* suggests.

  [14] 'Est officieuse la plus grande part de l'épitexte auctorial [. . .] dont il peut toujours dégager plus ou moins sa responsabilité par des dénégations du genre: "Ce n'est pas exactement ce que j'ai dit", "C'étaient des propos improvisés", ou: "Ce n'était pas destiné à la publication."' Genette, *Seuils*, 15.

contents, and to seduce the public into reading the work in question. The title might also indicate the form of the text. It can be considered significant, then, that Baudelaire chose variations on a similar theme and also that he selected titles offering the complete range of possibilities (title, subtitle, and generic indicator). Most of Baudelaire's titles for the publication of the prose poems belong to the class of *titres rhématiques*, titles which designate the text itself, or which designate the text as object. Genette takes the title of the prose poems, at one point, as illustrative of the very distinction he is elaborating:

> Si le thème du *Spleen de Paris* est bien (admettons-le par hypothèse) ce que désigne ce titre, le rhème en est [. . .] ce que Baudelaire en dit (en écrit), et donc ce qu'il en fait, c'est-à-dire un recueil de petits poèmes en prose. Si Baudelaire, au lieu de l'intituler par son thème, l'avait intitulé par son rhème, il l'aurait nommé par exemple *Petits poèmes en prose.*[15]

This recognizes that Baudelaire did indeed do this and sees the poet's hesitation as resolved only after his death, with the decision of Banville and Asselineau in favour of the *rhème*.[16] This distinction, however, indicates a central problem facing critics of the prose poems: how to designate the work? A glance at the critical editions published since 1869 suggests a clear preference for the *rhématique*,[17] but it is a position opposed by Claude Pichois in his edition for the Bibliothèque de la Pléiade, who insists that *Le Spleen de Paris* is 'le seul titre attesté avec certitude durant les dernières années de la vie de Baudelaire' and that '*Petits poèmes en prose* est trop peu attesté pour qu'on puisse retenir cette expression comme un titre qui correspondrait à l'intention de Baudelaire'.[18]

The solution to this thorny problem is not to be found in Genette's discussion of titles, although some elements can usefully be pressed into service. There is, for example, the question of timing. Pichois refers mainly to the later years, justifiably, since it is probably at this point that clear plans for presenting the prose poems as a collected volume are forming in Baudelaire's mind.

---

[15] Genette, *Seuils*, 75–6.   [16] Ibid. 76, n. 1.

[17] Examples include *Poëmes en prose* (*Revue fantaisiste*, 1 Nov. 1861, and *Le Boulevard*, 14 June 1863) and *Poëmes en prose* (*Le Boulevard*, 14 June 1863); *Petits Poëmes en prose* (*La Presse*, 26 Aug., 27 Aug., and 24 Sept. 1862, *Revue nationale et étrangère*, 10 June 1863, and *L'Artiste*, 1 Nov. 1864); and *Le Spleen de Paris. Petits Poëmes en prose* (*Figaro*, 14 Feb. 1864, and *La Revue de Paris*, 25 Dec. 1864).

[18] See 'Notice' to *Le Spleen de Paris* (*OC* i. 1299).

Genette, on the other hand, suggests that the title is born with the first publication, although he admits that hesitations may persist and titles may change after that point. The official status of the title is, however, restricted to those appearing (the last appearing?) 'du vivant de l'auteur et avec son aveu'.[19] Both of these positions raise further problems. Since the titles appearing in Baudelaire's lifetime are in newspapers and accompany a variable number of poems, they might be said to constitute a very different publication from a collection in volume form. In this context, there are also questions to be raised about authorial and editorial choice, for although the same can be true of other editions, it is unquestionably the case that Baudelaire was largely at the mercy of newspaper editors at the time of publication of these prose poems. The problem with the title of *Le Spleen de Paris* is that it occurs less frequently in the peritext (though more frequently in the epitext) and, most importantly, it does not appear in isolation, with one exception (and accompanying only one poem), in Baudelaire's lifetime. Pichois offers what seems like a way out of this impasse of official and unofficial titles when he says that 'deux publications seulement reflètent la volonté de l'auteur' (*OC* i. 1305), those of *La Presse* and the posthumous *Œuvres complètes*, both of which paradoxically offer *Petits poèmes en prose* as the title.

The purpose of this discussion is less to open a debate about which is the correct title than to demonstrate the prevalence of what is often seen to be only a descriptive superscription, a generic indicator appended to the title. *Petits Poèmes en prose* often stood alone as a title and accompanied an overwhelming majority of the publications in the press, and indeed is the title given to most editions since (where it is *Le Spleen de Paris* which has appeared as subtitle). It seems perfectly reasonable to speculate, however, that Baudelaire might well have changed the title for publication in volume form, particularly given his predilection for 'les titres mystérieux ou les titres pétards',[20] and the correspondence very much points in that direction.[21]

There is, moreover, an article accompanying the first publication of three prose poems in the *Figaro*, which, in the view of Robert

[19] Genette, *Seuils*, 66.
[20] Letter to Poulet-Malassis, 7 Mar. 1857 (*C* i. 378).
[21] See letters to Ancelle (*C* ii. 566, 581, and 615); and the letter to his mother (*C* ii. 625).

Kopp, although it may not have been written by Baudelaire, was almost certainly heavily influenced by his view of the work (not to mention by his vocabulary) and is worth, therefore, quoting in full:

Le Spleen de Paris est le titre adopté par M. C. Baudelaire pour un livre qu'il prépare, et dont il veut faire un digne pendant aux Fleurs du mal. Tout ce qui se trouve naturellement exclu de l'œuvre rythmée et rimée, ou plus difficile à y exprimer, tous les détails matériels, et, en un mot, toutes les minuties de la vie prosaïque, trouvent leur place dans l'œuvre en prose, où l'idéal et le trivial se fondent dans un amalgame inséparable. D'ailleurs, l'âme sombre et malade que l'auteur a dû supposer pour écrire Les Fleurs du mal est, à peu de choses près, la même qui compose Le Spleen de Paris. Dans l'ouvrage en prose, comme dans l'œuvre en vers, toutes les suggestions de la rue, de la circonstance et du ciel parisiens, tous les soubresauts de la conscience, toutes les langueurs de la rêverie, la philosophie, le songe et même l'anecdote peuvent prendre leur rang à tour de role. Il s'agit seulement de trouver une prose qui s'adapte aux différents états de l'âme du flâneur morose. Nos lecteurs jugeront si M. Charles Baudelaire y a réussi.

Certaines gens croient que Londres seul a le privilège aristocratique du spleen, et que Paris, le joyeux Paris, n'a jamais connu cette noire maladie. Il y a peut-être bien, comme le prétend l'auteur, une sorte de spleen parisien; et il affirme que le nombre est grand de ceux qui l'ont connu et le reconnaîtront.[22]

Here the generic indicator is missing, but the first paragraph elaborates not only the relationship with the earlier poetic volume,[23] it also offers an explanation of <u>the way in which Baudelaire's prose poetry form will embrace a range of other genres.</u> Having rehearsed the formal qualities and innovative shape of this new prose collection, the author—the article is signed Gustave Bourdin—proceeds to justify the title as it is given, linking the poetry of the street with the 'noire maladie' of Paris.

From this we can infer two things. If this article is the fruit of Baudelaire's mind in any way at all, we can read it as an explanation of his choice of titles and a conscious elaboration of the way in which he would hope the careful reader would apprehend the text. If it is solely the product of Bourdin's mind and pen, it is a perfect

---

[22] Quoted by Robert Kopp in Petits Poëmes en prose (Paris: Corti, 1969) and by Claude Pichois (OC i. 1297).

[23] Baudelaire elsewhere refers to the prose poems as complementing Les Fleurs du mal. See, for example, C ii. 615.

example of such apprehension of the text (or a gloss on the *lettre-dédicace* published in *La Presse* in 1862). In either case, we are compelled to see the titling of the work as a significant part of the peritext and as a threshold not to be crossed without some reflection. The same can be said to be true both of this Bourdin article and the letter to Houssaye, since at the time of publication (and, in the case of Houssaye, ever since) these form part of the peritext, or the *perigraphie* as Compagnon terms it,[24] and exercise a powerful influence over the way in which the text is both approached and appreciated.

We must, however, remain with titles for the moment, for these are the most public face of the text, that part of the work which will reach a wider audience than its readers, like headlines, and which may or may not seduce into further participation. Baudelaire's love of 'les titres mystérieux ou les titres pétards' is an avowed desire to seduce, or at very least to enter into some form of ludic relationship with the reader. There is, indeed, a paradox here, in that the mystery of a title (its refusal to yield concrete meaning and its suggestiveness) would seem to run counter to the descriptive function elaborated above.[25] The paradox is further compounded by the apparent reassurance of a generic description, for we are told we are dealing with prose poems, and the shock of the new, for prose poems have no precedent for the average reader.[26] What actually seduces is the epithet *petits* which, in its familiarity and unthreatening diminutive, appeals to the reader's indulgence. This is, of course, misleading, since there is nothing slight about the prose poems as a collection, although the lack of any authenticating precursory text might well have led Baudelaire to anticipate such a reaction. It is misleading, too, because it plays with the convention of the generic superscription which, by the mid-1850s was falling into disuse,[27] and suggests an ironic appropriation of an

---

[24] Antoine Compagnon, *La Seconde Main ou le travail de la citation* (Paris: Seuil, 1979), 328–56.

[25] Genette also highlights this as a problem. Quoting Lessing, he writes: ' "Un titre ne doit pas être comme un menu (*Küchenzettel*); moins il en dit sur le contenu, mieux il vaut". Pris à la lettre, ce conseil mettrait en totale opposition la fonction séductrice et la fonction descriptive. La vulgate entend plutôt ici un éloge des vertus apéritives d'une certaine dose d'obscurité, ou d'ambiguïté: un bon titre en dirait assez pour exciter la curiosité et assez peu pour ne pas la saturer.' *Seuils*, 87.

[26] For more on the significance of precursory texts, see Nichola Ann Haxell, 'The Name of the Prose', 160–2.

[27] 'Sauf ', as Genette puts it, 'recherche archaïsante'. *Seuils*, 91.

archaic tradition in the service of an innovative and experimental enterprise. In this respect, Baudelaire could be seen to be participating in a tradition to come where generic descriptions would suggest innovation with genre, and where there would be a blending of different literary forms and traditions, or at least their appellations, to create new hybrids of which the *poème en prose* would be but the first of many more elusive generic indicators.[28]

The past tradition, such as it is, is clearly invoked in the *lettre-dédicace* to Arsène Houssaye and in this dedicatory letter there is further evidence of the pre-eminence of the *rhématique* which serves, in some ways, to explicate, or at very least to amplify, the generic debate already present in the titling of the work. Indeed, the explicit function of the letter to Houssaye is precisely to set these prose poems in a generic context. In the case of earlier attempts at prose poetry (or what have been called 'poèmes en prose avant la lettre')[29] writers of prose poetry had linked their work to established verse models. This included both foreign-language originals, which prose poetry could translate, and literary transpositions of works from the plastic arts, so that the ends were seen to justify the means and distracted attention from form to content. This is, of course, the case with the secondary (or concealed primary) debt acknowledged in Baudelaire's letter to Houssaye where he refers to *Gaspard de la Nuit*, a work subtitled *Fantaisies à la manière de Rembrandt et de Callot*. Though known only to a few cognoscenti (only forty copies were sold), the text was, in fact, becoming increasingly renowned. The renown of the work is also explicitly, indeed rather heavy-handedly, referred to in Baudelaire's letter:

J'ai une petite confession à vous faire. C'est en feuilletant, pour la vingtième fois au moins, le fameux *Gaspard de la Nuit* d'Aloysius Bertrand (un livre connu de vous, de moi et de quelques-uns de nos amis, n'a-t-il pas tous les droits à être appelé *fameux?*) que l'idée m'est venue de tenter quelque chose d'analogue, et d'appliquer à la description de la vie moderne, ou plutôt d'*une* vie moderne et plus abstraite, le procédé qu'il avait appliqué à la peinture de la vie ancienne si étrangement pittoresque. (*OC* i. 275)

---

[28] Genette cites a range of such generic superscriptions and concludes, rather appropriately in the context of our discussion, that: 'Innover, c'est souvent marier deux vieilleries', ibid. 93–4.

[29] H. Fluchère, review of Maurice Chapelan, *Anthologie du poème en prose* (1946) in *French Studies*, 2 (1948), 188. Cited by Haxell in 'The Name of the Prose', 156.

Gaspard de la Nuit's poetic and artistic focus was to be the alibi for much of what succeeded as the prose poem continued to search for generic identity and the new prose poets' enlistment of Bertrand in their cause is a manifestation of the conventions of all dedicatory practice.[30] In other words, dedications of this public kind imply an acknowledgement of power, if not of influence. What is significant about the passage quoted above is that the dedication mimics an exchange of views, an aesthetic triangle in which Baudelaire seems to enlist Houssaye in a shared enterprise (prose poetry and aesthetic interest), a shared circle (*nos amis*) and a shared cultural inheritance in this domaine (Bertrand). The exchange is suggested through the interrogative parenthesis, which plays upon the celebrity of the work—with irony emblazoned in the italics. With a circulation of just forty copies, the work could hardly merit an epithet suggesting great celebrity or reputation, but it could justifiably be argued that, within a given literary circle, it might merit being held in esteem. But *fameux* precisely means something of great or poor reputation (even without italics) and there is subterfuge here in Baudelaire's feigned artistic association with Houssaye, who is, himself, treated to a helping of the same ambiguous recognition in a subsequent paragraph.

Indeed, when Baudelaire completes this aesthetic exchange, he refers to Houssaye's similar aspirations and efforts, in relation particularly to *La Chanson du vitrier*: 'Vous-même, mon cher ami, n'avez-vous pas tenté de traduire en une *chanson* le cri strident du *Vitrier*, et d'exprimer dans une prose lyrique toutes les désolantes suggestions que ce cri envoie jusqu'aux mansardes, à travers les plus hautes brumes de la rue?' (*OC* i. 276). The italics masquerade as integrated title, but what this mask barely conceals is Baudelaire's own 'désolante suggestion' that this *attempt* fell far short of poetry and what must surely be a deliberate intertext in his own titling of a prose poem treating a similar theme then begs the question: which of the two is truly the 'mauvais vitrier'?

It is in no way surprising that Baudelaire should seek to flatter

---

[30] Haxell asserts that this group of poets, 'by emulating the thematic and stylistic focus of this increasingly renowned work, hoped to gain prestige and kudos and to reinforce the poetic import of their own prose texts by indirect association with "un des saints de notre calendrier poétique", as Asselineau called Bertrand. This notion of a talisman of poeticity, of an authenticating precursory text, recurs throughout the evolution of the prose-poetry genre'.

Houssaye, who was, after all, *directeur littéraire* at *La Presse* in 1862 and the reference to *La Chanson du vitrier* as a precursory text, and indeed the dedication as a whole, is clearly ironic.[31] The acknowledgement of Bertrand must, then, also be ironic since, no sooner has Baudelaire referred to this than he insists upon the difference of his own enterprise.[32] It is a difference, moreover, to which the poet returns in relation to his own model as well as to Bertrand's:

Mais, pour dire le vrai, je crains que ma jalousie ne m'ait pas porté bonheur. Sitôt que j'eus commencé le travail, je m'aperçus que non seulement je restais bien loin de mon mystérieux et brillant modèle, mais encore que je faisais quelque chose (si cela peut s'appeler *quelque chose*) de singulièrement différent, accident dont tout autre que moi s'enorgueillirait sans doute, mais qui ne peut qu'humilier profondément un esprit qui regarde comme le plus grand honneur d'accomplir *juste* ce qu'il a projeté de faire.   (*OC* i: 276)

This apparently self-deprecating conclusion is already to be found in a more private letter to Houssaye (dating from Christmas 1861) in which Baudelaire expresses the view that Bertrand's work is *inimitable* and says: 'J'ai bien vite senti que je ne pouvais pas persévérer dans ce pastiche' (*C* ii. 208). Here again, Baudelaire's apparent self-deprecation creates a sense of unease and the reservations seem to attach themselves to the object of imitation rather than to himself as imitator. This 'malaise' appears justified by the questioning of form, by the experimentalism of any precursory texts, by all the suggestions of this new poetry as a 'low' art form. Bertrand himself describes his texts as 'bambochades romantiques' and 'fantaisies', while other 'precursors' use similarly unpretentious terms to designate their works, including 'ballades', 'chants', 'rhythmes primitifs', and 'fusains'.[33] Baudelaire's statement about

---

[31]   See Pichois's notes to this dedication where he describes the comparison as 'accablante pour Houssaye' (*OC* i. 1311) and also Chambers, 'Baudelaire's Dedicatory Practice', *Sub Stance*, 56 (1988), 5 and 16–17 n. 2.

[32]   Chambers sees this as the acknowledgement of a genuine debt, art. cit. 14, while Haxell notes Baudelaire's reference to Bertrand (and his subsequent denial of his influence); she does not, however, develop this point further to explain what sort of relationship to the precursory text this might imply, 'The Name of the Prose', 160.

[33]   See respectively Aloysius Bertrand, 'Bambochades romantiques', *Le Provincial* (May–Oct. 1828) and *Gaspard de la Nuit: Fantaisies à la manière de Rembrandt et de Callot* (Paris: Renduel, 1842); Jules Champfleury, 'Fantaisies et ballades', in *Chien-Caillou. Fantaisies d'hiver* (Paris: Martinon, 1847), Henry Mürger, 'Ballades', *L'Artiste* (12 July 1846), and Charles Monselet, 'Ballades parisiennes', *Le Figaro* (25 July 1857); Jules Claretie,

models in the *lettre-dédicace* reinforces a sense of poets in search of
a form, thereby providing an interface between the textual production of prose poems and the social and literary situation (between
text and context). Just as it situates itself, however, it draws away,
so that the ironic acknowledgement to precursors and the insincere
self-deprecation of the concluding paragraph and of the *Petits
Poèmes en prose* all become suspect. And just as pastiche seems to
apply to Bertrand rather than to Baudelaire, so the 'mystérieux et
brillant modèle' appears to remain the true outcome rather than
the expression of failure it purports to be.

Readers of Baudelaire have every reason to be cautious since, as
Ross Chambers has shown, his dedications 'have inspired suspi-
cion and raised questions concerning their sincerity and the degree
of opportunism, or possibly irony, they reveal'.[34] The *Salon de 1846*
('Aux Bourgeois'), Baudelaire's public dedication of *Les Fleurs du
mal* (to Théophile Gautier), this double (and doubly suspicious)
acknowledgement of Bertrand and Houssaye, not to mention the
dedications of individual poems all create a sense in which one
would not wish to trust the hand that dedicates. There is no doubt
that Baudelaire, in these dedications, is recruiting established
power in order to secure a better reception for his work than his
own reputation might otherwise enable, and for this reason he
settles on respectable figures of the period. He exploits, in other
words, their social prestige for his own ends and, at the same time,
generates an aesthetic context in which he is able to set his own
work apart from that of others. In so doing, he recruits through
intertextuality these favoured literary figures of the regime, but
with covert and self-interested oppositional ends. The dedicatee is
simultaneously both a presence and an absence, since his name is
his reputation (a cultural item) and his work is brought into relation
with Baudelaire's text *in absentia*. Where that absence is also figured
as difference, as it is in this case, and indeed as it might be said to
be in any intertext, what the dedication and the acknowledgement

---

'Chants du Limousin', *L'École du peuple* (1861), Louis de Lyvron, 'Chants du désert', *Revue
française*, 5 (1 July 1863), Paul-Ernest de Rattier *Chants prosaïques* (Paris: Dentu, 1861);
Arsène Houssaye, reprint of 'Poèmes antiques' as 'Rhythmes primitifs' in 'Fresques et bas-
reliefs. Tableaux et pastels', *Poésies complètes* (Paris: Charpentier, 1850); and Louis de
Lyvron 'Fusains', *Revue des lettres et des arts*, I (27 Oct. 1857). For a much fuller list of examples, see Haxell, 'The Name of the Prose', table II, 168–9.

[34] Chambers, 'Baudelaire's Dedicatory Practice', 5.

of Houssaye foreground is contrast and a deliberately duplicitous invocation and acknowledgement of influence.

This assertion of difference through such duplicitous discourse suggests also that both public and private discursive systems are simultaneously in operation. The public act of dedication moves here, in other words, towards the more private act of communication. This is an evolution which can be traced through the act of dedication itself, as Chambers has noted in respect of the increasingly common practice of the public dedication to a private person: 'Here the publicity given to the dedicatory gesture combines with the anonymity of the dedicatee so as to confuse the functions both of public dedication (whose dedicatee [. . .] is necessarily a public figure) and of the private *envoi* (an interpersonal gesture).'[35] This point is amplified by tracing the evolution of the dedication through four main periods—the classical or 'pious' dedication, the neo-classical or 'political' dedication, the 'esthetic' dedication (the category into which we can place Baudelaire), and the 'privatized' dedication—and by seeing the recruitment of established literary figures as a direct development of the 'political' (patronage) period. The 'privatized', Chambers argues, breaks with the tradition 'in that it seeks less to place the text under the protection of some source of power than to acknowledge a new type of social situation in which messages are by definition privatized, that is alienated.' He also elaborates two further categories in his classification of dedications: whether or not the dedication is *plain* or *motivated* and the extent to which it is integrated into the text it accompanies.[36]

Baudelaire's letter to Houssaye is clearly a *motivated* dedication, and one which displays all the rhetoric of ironic obsequiousness. His duplicity in presenting this as a dedication, or his insincerity, makes available a private message which, one can only assume, Houssaye did not receive, since it was undoubtedly his decision to preface the first publication of the prose poems in *La Presse* with this letter. This emphasizes the extent to which the covert implications of Baudelaire's writing were more difficult to perceive in their own age than they are now, so that even implausible dedicatees can function effectively in this process as 'screen-mechanisms' and even obvious 'noise' in the message can appear to

---

[35] Ross Chambers, 'Baudelaire's Dedicatory Practice', 6–7.   [36] Ibid. 15.

go unheard.[37] The function of this, then, goes well beyond the attempt to place the new text under the 'protection' of respectable figures; it goes further, even, than recruiting these respectable figures for oppositional ends. Like the dedication of the *Salon de 1846*, which has been described as a 'self-contradictory motivating text',[38] this implies cultural isolation more than it implies any sort of debt or influence. It is, in short, a parody of influence performed by a further parody of the prose poetry genre's referential practice.

Baudelaire uses the letter to Houssaye to launch the concerns of the prose poetry experiment (in the broadest sense) as well as the concerns of the text. As Chambers argues, 'if the prime function of a dedication is to tie the text as a structure to an address that situates it in a system of exchange, a corollary function is to make this system available in its historical specificity, as an indicator of the circumstances of production in light of which the text assumes it is most appropriately read.'[39] The insincerity of the dedication to Houssaye, particularly in the context of a literary debate, emphasizes Baudelaire's aesthetic isolation, and provides further evidence of a 'privatizing' effect of this dedicatory discourse, since the irony alienates him from it. Indeed, it is Baudelaire's truly 'private' dedication (that of the *Paradis artificiels* to J.G.F.) which suggests absolute isolation from any readership:

Il importe d'ailleurs fort peu que la raison de cette dédicace soit comprise. Est-il même bien nécessaire, pour le contentement de l'auteur, qu'un livre quelconque soit compris, excepté de celui ou de celle pour qui il a été composé? Pour tout dire, enfin, indispensable qu'il ait été écrit pour *quelqu'un*? J'ai, quant à moi, si peu de goût pour le monde vivant que, pareil à ces femmes sensibles et désœuvrées qui envoient, dit-on, par la poste leurs confidences à des amis imaginaires, volontiers je n'écrirais que pour les morts. (*OC* i. 399–400)

To this extent, one might argue that, apart from a desire to set his prose-poetry experiment apart from any precursor, the dedicatory act is spurious, a mere pretext for an elaboration of the concerns of the text and, as such, less a dedication than a preface, less a contextual-textual act than a purely textual one and, in the case of the prose poems, more akin to a liminary poem, such as 'Au Lecteur', than to a dedicatory letter. Like 'Au Lecteur', too, the

---

[37] Ibid. 12.   [38] Ibid. 16.   [39] Ibid. 13.

dedications to Houssaye and to J.G.F. (both of which are letters) are written in an apostrophic mode. This textual strategy implies an economy of exchange (of ideas, of favours, of language), but an exchange which is dysfunctional, because of the poet's cultural isolation in his historical moment.

Despite all this, the letter to Houssaye does address a reader, and significantly a reader who is other than the dedicatee, despite the apostrophe:

> Mon cher ami, je vous envoie un petit ouvrage dont on ne pourrait pas dire, sans injustice, qu'il n'a ni queue ni tête, puisque tout, au contraire, y est à la fois tête et queue, alternativement et réciproquement. Considérez, je vous prie, quelles admirables commodités cette combinaison nous offre à tous, *à vous, à moi et au lecteur. Nous pouvons couper où nous voulons, moi ma rêverie, vous le manuscrit, le lecteur sa lecture; car je ne suspends pas la volonté de celui-ci au fil interminable d'une intrigue superflue.* (*OC* i. 275, my italics)

Here Houssaye is addressed as editor, rather than reader and this can clearly be seen as further evidence of a *motivated* dedication. The reader, on the other hand, is a third party in the system of exchange, but one who is precisely significant in that it is he who is the true *destinataire*. So, although Chambers could be said to be right in suggesting that it is an error 'to read the dedicatee as a figure for the reader and to see the text–dedicatee relation as a model of the text–reader relation',[40] we can say that in this case the text–reader relation is *also* figured and independently of the dedicatee. In this respect, we might argue that the role of the reader in the dedication to Houssaye is to receive the text and that the role of Houssaye is merely to make the text, the generic context, and the reading strategy available. The dedication is, in other words, both a social and textual vehicle which ensures safe delivery of the *envoi*. It is a preface.

In this respect, too, we might say that the *lettre-dédicace* develops the generic superscription or the *titre rhématique* and that it amplifies the literary context of that superscription, so that the threshold of the text is an account of the text's objectives, and functions in a series of reciprocal relations. The act of dedication is, then, an amplification and explanation of the title, in its thematic focus—*Le Spleen de Paris* becomes 'c'est surtout de la

---

[40] Ross Chambers, 'Baudelaire's Dedicatory Practice', 13.

fréquentation des villes énormes que naît cet idéal obsédant'—but more significantly, in its generic invitation to (or confrontion with) the reader. Indeed the relationships are most carefully sustained by the way in which the *lettre-dédicace* seems to cross its own generic threshold in mimicking, through its very form, the text which it purports to describe. It is, in other words, a prose poem on the prose poem which provides a commentary on the title and the dedicatory act and, in form and function, speaks of genre.

If Houssaye is merely the intermediary in an indirect act of communication, with the reader, the *lettre-dédicace* is also properly a preface in that it postulates an imminent reading of the text it introduces. What is more, it suggests the kind of non-linear reading that the text requires. This indirect mode of communication with the reader not only reinforces the ironic distance between the named circle of readers (Houssaye and 'nos amis'), but also suggests, in fact, that it is only to an unknown reader (as in the J.G.F. preface), or a future reader that this *text* can be addressed whatever the letter might *appear* to say. Houssaye is a *destinataire-relais*[41] who has a role to play, but who is not, as is often the case in such instances, the reader's representative. And because the reading process figured in the prefatory *dédicace* is accomplished by another, Houssaye's role is limited to that of editor ('Nous pouvons couper où nous voulons [. . .] vous le manuscrit').

As a form of preface, then, this *lettre-dédicace* does all that it should. It situates the work in a context and offers some sort of genesis of it; it offers a commentary on the title of the work (although not explicitly); it offers a way, an order, of reading and raises questions of genre. All of these are, according to Genette's typology of the *préface originale*, functions of this kind of paratext.[42] The danger of such a preface is, of course, that it runs the risk of not being attached to the work, of not forming a part of the 'perigraphie' and, therefore, of not *completing* the text. But this is a danger most likely to occur in early, rather than later, editions of the work, since epitextual information moves increasingly into the peritext as editions become more complete. It is not, in any case, a situation which poses problems in this instance.

The dedicatory act, and the choice of dedicatee, enables

---

[41] The term is Genette's, *Seuils*, 180.
[42] See 'Les fonctions de la préface originale', ibid. 182–218.

Baudelaire to compose a preface which, while it does not specify the kind of reader it would like, contains an oppositional discourse which tells us the kind of reader to whom it is not addressed. In its *mimed* act of communication, it constitutes a structural entity which has meaning and it indissolubly associates specific historic conditions of textual production and questions of genre, which amount to ways of securing *une bonne lecture*. As a poetic text in its own right (a prose poem on the prose poem), indissolubility of poetic enterprise and generic debate, of literary and social context and textual reception, the *lettre-dédicace* is, as much as the text itself, an object of reading. The discursive function of the paratext would, then, appear to be the bringing into sharper focus of the lack of connection between dedicatee and intended reader and between text and precursor. By emphasizing this disconnection, this dysfunction, the *lettre-dédicace* foregrounds communicational failure (alienation) and prefigures the conflicting discursive, ideological, and generic modes of interaction of the prose poems themselves.

'L'Étranger' reflects just such a communicational failure. Despite the fact that we are told that we can begin where we like and read in any order, the convention of reading is such that any reader would be unlikely to 'skip' the first poem, and it is this text which is placed at the conventional head of the work.[43] The title of this prose poem is, of course, significant, too, and compounds the sense of alienation already present in the paratext, and indeed amplifies it by the disturbing intangibility of the exchange and, indeed, of the speakers, neither of whom are identified.

The questions asked in the poem would seem to represent the position of the socialized individual, the man who, by association with his suggestions of what might be important to his interlocutor, values family, friends, patriotism, faith, wealth, and beauty. All of these values are socially inscribed in an ideological, and by extension, a discursive system in which the stranger does not share, and would not want to share:

'Qui aimes-tu le mieux, homme énigmatique, dis? ton père, ta mère, ta sœur ou ton frère?

— Je n'ai ni père, ni mère, ni sœur, ni frère.

— Tes amis?

---

[43] It was, in fact, also one of the first group of poems to be published alongside the preface on 26 Aug. 1862 in *La Presse*.

— Vous vous servez là d'une parole dont le sens m'est resté jusqu'à ce jour inconnu.

— Ta patrie?

— J'ignore sous quelle latitude elle est située.

— La beauté?

— Je l'aimerais volontiers déesse et immortelle.

— L'or?

— Je le hais comme vous haïssez Dieu.

— Eh! qu'aimes-tu donc, extraordinaire étranger?

— J'aime les nuages . . . les nuages qui passent . . . là-bas . . . là-bas . . . les merveilleux nuages!' (*OC* i. 277)

The act of communication fails because the interlocutors do not recognize each other's cultural referents, they do not speak the same language. Even at points of contact, such as beauty, ambiguity is introduced by a response which defines a (no doubt very different) form of beauty and which specifies an inability to embrace this as a value because of the doubt over its existence introduced by the conditional form of *aimer* here. The response to the suggestion of gold is also significant for it elicits a more negative response, but one which is ultimately left ambiguous because of a lack of information regarding the faith of the questioner. This, too, then is an exchange characterized by indirectness which in its dysfunction signifies social and cultural alienation. It is, moreover, an alienation reinforced by the implied social disrespect for artistic values of the *tu* form used by the questioner, and an alterity which the artist desires since this is the mark of his benediction in a hostile environment. He, then, uses the *vous* form and dominates the exchange by his expression of incomprehension, his manipulation of the discourse of the other, and by the rejection of the interlocutor's code.

It has been shown that a similar, but inverted dynamic, is in operation in another of the poems which also occurs in proximity to this text, 'Chacun sa chimère', and which also expresses the displacement or desertion of meaning in the particular cultural and historical context.[44] Here, however, the exchange is reported, and

---

[44] This is number VI in the 1869 (and subsequent) editions and was also in the first ten to be published in *La Presse*. Jérôme Thélot sees this poem in a close relationship with 'L'Étranger': '[ils] s'expliquent l'un par l'autre: dans le même espace vacant, poète et communauté y intervertissent leur position respective, l'interrogé de "L'Étranger" devenant l'interrogateur de "Chacun sa chimère", pour un semblable dialogue de sourds'. For a full account of Thélot's argument, see 'Langage et autrui', in *Baudelaire: Violence et Poésie* (Paris: Gallimard, 1993), 71–111. The above quotation is on p. 75 n. 4.

only summarily: 'Je questionnai l'un de ces hommes, et je lui demandai où ils allaient ainsi. Il me répondit qu'il n'en savait rien, ni lui, ni les autres; mais qu'évidemment ils allaient quelque part, puisqu'ils étaient poussés par un invincible besoin de marcher' (*OC* i. 282). The exchange, as reported, does function. Communication occurs even if the experience of the force which motivates all parties is different (each having his own *chimère*).

In 'Le Miroir', on the other hand, there is an equivalent dialogue and one which expresses an equivalent opposition of discursive and ideological positions.

Un homme épouvantable entre et se regarde dans la glace.
    'Pourquoi vous regardez-vous au miroir, puisque vous ne pouvez vous voir qu'avec déplaisir?'
    L'homme épouvantable me répond: '—Monsieur, d'après les immortels principes de 89, tous les hommes sont égaux en droits; donc, je possède le droit de me mirer; avec plaisir ou déplaisir, cela ne regarde que ma conscience.'
    Au nom du bon sens, j'avais sans doute raison; mais, au point de vue de la loi, il n'avait pas tort.

Even before the exchange occurs, the position is fixed, since the narrative discourse unequivocally asserts a position which finds the interlocutor 'épouvantable'. The narrator challenges the man he considers ugly and receives a reasoned answer (that no self-justification is required). The exchange appears to function unproblematically, despite different ideological positions, but the delay in the articulation of the response (*I can look at myself if I like*) and the justification of the response, which is apparently at odds with the thrust of the challenge, allows a form of communicational dysfunction to occur anyway.

The narrator, a reasonable man, concedes the point and appears to accept the position as being no less valid than his own initial challenge. One man's response is considered from the point of view of authority—'la loi'—the other from the perspective of common sense—'le bon sens'. In a functional system—both communicational and political—one might reasonably expect these to be synonymous or, at very least, to be operative together. The poem uses a certain rhetoric to suggest the same kind of acknowledgement as the *lettre-dédicace* mimes. The more positive formulation couples common sense with reason (and an affirmation that the narrator *is right*); on the other hand, the *homme épouvantable* receives narrative treatment which negatively counterbalances the positive affirmation and gives him only ambiguous credence: from the point of view of the law, the man has done no wrong (which does not necessarily mean that he was not misguided in his belief). This text can be read, then, as a claim that equality is not a feature of existence and that justice and reason are not always compatible. And as an allegory of the kind of exchange economies that interest us here, it can be seen as a conflict of personal taste (or prejudice) and aesthetics, as well as a statement about public reception. By incorporating the rather facile statement of his interlocutor about the rights of all citizens, the accepted currency of speech act is called into question and consequently devalued.

The reader approaches the text with certain codes in mind and a willingness to respond to variants of those codes. Reception, or reader expectation of genre, implies recognition of certain modes of discourse, both literary and extraliterary, employed by the writer. The writer operates subtle shifts or modifications to codes to elicit different reader responses and in so doing to break out of generic and often ideological constraints. The complex narrative and linguistic strategies used to manipulate reader response also imply a rhetoric which could be seen to be the intersection of register and reception. All of these have their thresholds, because all have distinct identities.

Uncertainty about the generic identity of the prose poem means that a reader cannot be programmed by any historical conception of genre in its case, but rather proceeds to conceptualize the form based on the guidance of the paratext and on individual experience of the texts. It could be argued that the author's most important communicational act is his choice of type or genre which determines the text's meaning and that by reconstructing this genre the critic can make possible the representation of that meaning.[45] There is no

---

[45] This is a view of a number of critics in the fields both of generic theory and Baudelaire studies. See, for example, E. D. Hirsch, *Validity in Interpretation* (New Haven: Yale University Press, 1967), esp. ch. 3. Richard Terdiman in *Discourse/Counter-Discourse: The Theory and Practice of Symbolic Resistance in Nineteenth-Century France* (Ithaca and London: Cornell University Press, 1985) and Jonathan Monroe in *A Poverty of Objects: The Prose Poem and the Politics of Genre* (Ithaca and London: Cornell University Press, 1987) have explored the prose poem's significance as a socio-political genre, as a formal construction representing absolute counter-discourse; and Marie Maclean in *Narrative as Performance: The Baudelairean Experiment* (London: Routledge, 1988) has considered the prose poem as narrative, in perfect but minimal form, as deterritorialized and, therefore, newly empowered.

doubt that choice of genre *means*. The choice of prose poetry is subversive, strictly formally, in literary-political and in socio-ideological terms. It transgresses an established boundary, by permitting the prosaic into the world of poetry and this is compounded by adding the generically descriptive subtitle to a generically non-descriptive, thematic title. Since these prose poems are often short narratives, and narratives for the most part which themselves transgress boundaries, the labelling seems deliberately misleading (or as arbitrary and cynical as Baudelaire's dedicatory practice).

Baudelaire's aesthetic doctrine of surprise, 'après le plaisir d'être étonné, il n'en est pas de plus grand que de causer une surprise' (*OC* i. 323) might thus translate into unexpected discursive and paradigmatic shifts. Baudelaire patterns the identity of the *Petits Poèmes en prose* by moving in and out of conventional structures which trigger reader response to genres, just as he moves in and out of the conventions of the dedication. What programmes reader response to these texts is precisely the peritext (the dedicatory letter, the title of the work), as well as the title of each piece (the *intertitres*) and the mode of discourse chosen to open each autonomous part. The register not only defines the identity of the piece, it tends to define the relationship with the audience and, therefore, to establish the rhetoric. To transgress the boundaries by introducing a different sort of discourse, literary or extraliterary, not only offends, or, at very least, unsettles the audience, it also challenges the literary because it introduces extra-generic possibilities into the confines of a specific generic space. By playing upon the conventions of any form or practice, and such conventions translate into reader expectation, limits can be both abolished and respected, bringing into question the boundaries of different forms, the way in which these can identify a content, and the seriousness of the intent.[46]

By launching the concerns of the text with duplicitous rhetorical strategies allowing different value systems to coexist, Baudelaire signals what he will do with the prose poem as genre. 'L'Étranger' and 'Le Miroir', in staging exchanges which are 'sans

---

[46] The *dédicace* is quite explicit in this regard, referring to Baudelaire's hope (and, therefore, stated intention) that these prose poems might please and amuse. The earlier letter to Houssaye of 25 Dec. 1861, parts of which have already been cited, make this point, too: 'Je me suis résigné à être moi-même. Pourvu que je sois amusant, vous serez content, n'est-ce pas?' (*C* ii. 208).

queue ni tête' offer no resolution and sustain this discursive strategy. The texts are a continuum of different views, of conflicting perspectives, as mobile and as unstable as the clouds. The social interaction figured here is not properly identified (as it must at least appear to be in the *dédicace*), but is constituted only in the differential discursive positions which, because communication is dysfunctional, leave the poems as moments of enunciation, brief encounters of the unintelligible kind.

By contrast, certain poems which figure similar exchange mechanisms and which express similar confrontations and paradoxes seem almost too clear in their meaning. 'Le Chien et le flacon', for example, is a closed form, *lisible*, as opposed to *scriptible*, and can, like the *dédicace* and 'Le Miroir' be read as an allegory of reception. Henri Lemaître sees this poem as characteristic of the 'poème-boutade': 'une sorte de genre littéraire auquel il semble, d'après certains passages des *Journaux intimes*, Baudelaire ait aimé s'exercer [. . .] où tout un monde de désillusion et de rancœur se ramasse dans une incisive brièveté.'[47] There is indeed a fragment from *Mon cœur mis à nu* in the context of which this closed prosaic allegory might best be read:

Le Français est un animal de basse-cour, si bien domestiqué qu'il n'ose franchir aucune palissade. Voir ses goûts en art et en littérature. C'est un animal de race latine; l'ordure ne lui déplaît pas dans son domicile et en littérature, il est scatophage. Il raffole des excréments.   (*OC* i. 698)

This diary entry might be said to function in a similar way to the *lettre-dédicace* in that it provides an interface between text and reading tactic, with self-referential resonances which emphasize the nature of the creative (and generic) limits, as well as the limitations of reader response. 'Le Chien et le flacon' is a laboured allegory, an overdetermined text which, given its point, might be seen as a parody of just what the implied reader might achieve. This poem can, however, be read as more than a mere allegory of a certain kind of reader's limited reception, and, as the diary entry suggests, as an attempt to go beyond defined limits, beyond the *palissades* of the literary *basse-cour* (with all the limits implied by *cour* and limitations of *basse*). There is, furthermore, a playful Rabelaisian intertext which activates such a reading:

---

[47] See his edition of the *Petits Poèmes en prose* (Paris: Garnier, 1962), 185.

Mais vesites vous oncques chien rencontrant quelque os medulare? C'est, comme dict Platon [. . .] la beste du monde plus philosophe [. . .]. A l'exemple d'icelluy vous convient d'être saiges, pour fleurer, sentir et estimer ces beaulx livres de haulte gresse, légiers au prochaz et hardiz à la rencontre; puis par curieuse leçon et meditation frequente, rompre l'os et sugcer la sustantificque mouelle [. . .] avecques espoir certain d'être faictz escors et preux à ladicte lecture; car en icelle bien aultre goust trouverez et doctrine plus absconce, laquelle vous revelera de très haultz sacremens.[48]

The generic playfulness embedded in the text is here the substantial marrow in the bone. Baudelaire's poem plays upon Rabelais's own intertextual game in a complex system of allegorical signification in which the dog and bone, though not a stock allegory, can be activated to suggest the same topos of textual surface and depth and, by being juxtaposed with other stock allegories, appears to belong in the same way. The intertextual reference brings to the surface the allegorized substance of the relationship of reader to text but, whereas Plato's dog responds to the master he knows, Baudelaire's is an *indigne compagnon* who does not like what he does not know, who barks and wags his tail en *manière de reproche*.

'Le Chien et le flacon' constitutes a different kind of threshold in the text in that it appears to represent the lowest limit of poetry, no longer suggestive but heavy-handedly explicated, while all the time emphasizing the implied reader's threshold of understanding and consciously straining the limits of genre to explode textual stability and the categorization within which it simultaneously and self-consciously remains.

In making available different meanings and in staging oppositional discursive relationships in a genre which is itself dependent on contrasting formal modes, the *Petits Poèmes en prose* constitutes a textual encounter representative of the dysfunctional social and linguistic encounters it stages. The *lettre-dédicace* constitutes a tactic which enables the social release of these figural instabilities and discursive incompatibilities. And one prose poem in particular exemplifies how the discursive system of the *Petits Poèmes en prose*

---

[48] *Gargantua* (Paris: Gallimard, 1969), 58–9. This passage comes, significantly, from the prologue.

replicates the relations between the formal, the social, and the ideological.[49]

'La Fausse Monnaie' consists of various modes of dissimulation embedded in the structure of the narrative text. If we effect the same *triage* of these as the donor does of his coins, it is clear that each irony in the text is presented as a unity with its own mechanisms. In the first instance, the text presents a dramatized irony. The narrator introduces a situation to the reader which he explicitly encourages us to interpret as ironic. The explicitness of this encouragement to read in a particular way is directly related to the act of narration, for although the narrator recounts the events with the conventions of retrospect, his discourse moulds a dramatic present in the past. This is helped along by some incorporation of direct speech and includes suspense dependent upon the misinterpretation of gesture, the gradual rise to awareness and the double dupe of the narrator and (possibly) the beggar.

The complicating action, and the ironic situation, is that a beggar is given an apparently generous donation of a two-franc coin. This is established as an ironic sequence only by the structure of the narrative which begins with a description of a careful sorting of coins, one of which is *particulièrement examinée* before being placed in the right-hand pocket. There is no certainty that the coin is counterfeit, but the title and the insistence upon the details of separation activate our suspicions. The narrator's apparent unawareness of the motives for this sorting of coins is itself set apart from the text of the poem in flagrant isolation: '*Singulière et minutieuse répartition!' me dis-je en moi-même* (*OC* i. 323). This, one might insist, is a sentence ironic only when invested with the powers of retrospect. Indeed, it is a structural mechanism which comes into play only when the coin is confirmed as false, but which, nevertheless, contributes subconsciously to the reader's suspicions.

This contribution can be assigned to its position within the narrative (raising questions which are not yet to be resolved) or to linguistic elements which trigger negative responses in the receiver, indicating how discursive 'noise' interferes with the structure of

---

[49] Although his focus is not the same as mine, Jacques Derrida has considered these two poems in conjunction in *Donner le temps, 1: La Fausse Monnaie* (Paris: Galilée, 1991), chs. 3 and 4.

narrative. The division of coins is *singulière*, suggesting, on a straightforward level, something which, *de bonne ou mauvaise part*, elicits a reaction of surprise, but it has the additional meanings of separateness, of something which is different (from the Latin 'singularis' meaning unique), and, more familiarly, it carries the meaning of *peu convenable*. The ambiguities of the word reflect, therefore, the central debate of the poem which questions conventional morality. *Minutieuse* should also not go unnoticed since, while it suggests an attention to detail, these details—or 'minuties'—are normally 'choses de peu de conséquence'.

Both the structure of the tale and the terms of its telling suggest that what is morally at stake is not potentially endangering an unsuspecting beggar, or taking advantage of someone when the appearance is that of charity, but rather the motives for behaving in a conventionally immoral manner. The impact of the initial irony—a beggar receiving a counterfeit coin in good faith from an apparently generous benefactor—points to the beggar as the ironic victim, whereas the suspended focus of evaluation in this poem highlights the ironic victim as the conceited and foolish donor, since 'le plus irréparable des vices est de faire le mal par bêtise' (*OC* i. 324). Between the two, however, is situated the feigned gullibility of the narrator, who credits the donor with the generosity of the socially sensitive man and compounds that by bestowing upon him the faculties of great philosophy, soon tainted by the light of his blatant dishonesty and cheap morality.

The narrative of beggar duped by false coin reveals itself as something of a decoy (and one, moreover, which is left unresolved since we never learn the outcome of the coin or the beggar), yielding ironic supremacy to the fatuous bourgeois who, unlike the man who can *read* a situation in the eyes of a beggar, is not only blind to the *reproches*, but is also insensitive to the narrator's interpretation of his gesture.

This can be seen by comparing the direct speech of the narrator with the echoed version of the donor which comes later in the poem:

'Vous avez raison; après le plaisir d'être étonné, il n'en est pas de plus grand que celui de causer une surprise.'

'Oui, vous avez raison; il n'est pas de plaisir plus doux que de surprendre un homme en lui donnant plus qu'il n'espère.'   (*OC* i. 323–4)

The subtle shift in sentence pattern lays bare the transposition of perspective, the monistic outlook of the donor, compared with the pluralistic vision of the narrator. The friend's purblindness to what the narrator is suggesting is, therefore, emphasized by his linguistic patterning of the sentence and by the structural echo it establishes. In the self-satisfied donation of a valueless coin, the friend in 'La Fausse Monnaie' is confident that he is doing the beggar a favour and getting charity on the cheap. On every level, his gesture is counterfeit, but he himself is blind to the hypocrisy, if not to the fake coin.

What is established in 'La Fausse Monnaie' is a complex structure of moral incongruities in which a narrator offers not just a narrative but a range of interpretations of that narrative:

Mais dans mon misérable cerveau, toujours occupé à chercher midi à quatorze heures (de quelle fatigante faculté la nature m'a fait cadeau!), entra soudainement cette idée qu'une pareille conduite, de la part de mon ami, n'était excusable que par le désir de créer un événement dans la vie de ce pauvre diable, peut-être même de connaître les conséquences diverses, funestes ou autres, que peut engendrer une pièce fausse dans la main d'un mendiant. Ne pouvait-elle pas se multiplier en pièces vraies? Ne pouvait-elle pas aussi le conduire en prison? Un cabaretier, un boulanger, par exemple, allait peut-être le faire arrêter comme faux-monnayeur. Tout aussi bien la pièce fausse serait peut-être, pour un pauvre petit spéculateur, le germe d'une richesse de quelques jours. Et ainsi ma fantaisie allait son train, prêtant des ailes à l'esprit de mon ami et tirant toutes les déductions possibles de toutes les hypothèses possibles. (*OC* i. 324)

The coin, like the fictions spun by this narrator, will have an unpredictable future and the donation releases a wealth of possibilities. All of these possibilities are conceived of within a given social and ideological structure, a structure which binds the outcomes of the fiction. If the counterfeit coin operates as genuine within that system, it is an uncontrollable and potentially subversive force. As Nathaniel Wing has shown in relation to this passage, the coin is a figure for writing, for all writing which does not simply accept and repeat the language and figures of ideology:

this poem problematizes the opposition between 'serious' symbolization, here figured by gold and silver coins, and the 'non-serious', or counterfeit. The issue concerns less the 'inherent' value of one discourse or token than the precarious relativity of value in any discursive system and the capacity of fictions to lay bare the conventional relations which maintain equilibrium in discursive systems.[50]

In exactly the same way, the counterfeit gesture/discourse of the *lettre-dédicace* launches the prose poetry into a context where circulation of meanings is uncontrolled and unpredictable, or where encounters with the other might not be propitious. The economy of exchange elaborated is, in fact, also that of 'A une heure du matin' where the list of the day's activities is centred upon contact and contacts. On the one hand, the poet-narrator takes to the streets with the intention of placing his writing (for some return); on the other, he expends time and energy on meaningless encounters where others beg him for favours. A close analysis of the 'recapitulation' of the day's events is revealing.

He starts out in what we might think good company, that of *plusieurs hommes de lettres*, but these men (and their collective worth) are summarily dismissed by the rejection of one man's question. The pretension of the implied question is equalled only by its idiocy and ignorance; its heavy irony is determined by the poet-narrator's association of educated interlocutor and the asking of a stupid question (Russia as island). This distances the narrator from his interlocutor and establishes a contract with the reader through the veiled apostrophe (the parenthesis and the 'sans doute' insisting upon the joke, but excluding the butt of it). He then goes to kill time (suggesting at least some entertainment) and ends up wasting it with an illiterate *sauteuse* whose mispronunciation comes to characterize her (as *rustre*).

These encounters are compounded by an argument with another (more powerful) figure from the literary world whose retort to each and every objection, '*C'est ici le partie des honnêtes gens*', brings into question not only the honesty of his colleagues, but also his own candour and intelligence. The inclusion of direct speech here, as with the mispronunciation of *Vénus*, introduces another voice and also a different idiom, and here it expresses a view in a way which is patently at odds with that of our narrator. This dispute draws upon the same techniques of opposition as the earlier exchange, with *honnêtes gens—coquins* introducing a hierarchy of superiorities. This episode of rejection has been attrib-

---

[50] 'Poets, Mimes and Counterfeit Coins: On Power and Discourse in Baudelaire's Prose Poetry', *Paragraph*, 13 (1990), 14.

uted to a biographical detail from Asselineau's *Baudelairiana* which recounts that, upon returning a rejected manuscript, a certain M. Amail (described as a *saint-simonien* and *républicain vertueux*) said to Baudelaire: '*Nous n'imprimons pas de ces fantaisies-là, nous autres*'.[51] By drawing out through opposition and linguistic implication the attitudes inherent in such a statement, the poet-narrator can play upon this notion of *honnêtes gens* (as equivalent to *nous autres*) as heavily ironic.[52] His superiority is revealed by a dismissive attitude disclosed by the choice and position of the adverb *généreusement*, which draws attention to itself by breaking the rhythm of the sentence, slowing it down to insist upon the quality of the narrator's contribution and upon the derisive mocking of his interlocutor. The range of potential meanings calls into question the narrator's stance. Does *généreusement* here mean nobly, or at length, or does it mean without sympathy or prejudice for the interlocutor's position?[53] Retrospectively, the generosity of the narrator's spirit attracts all subsequent magnanimous acts (handshakes, letters of recommendation) and shows each such act to be counterfeit.

This same dynamic can also be seen to operate in the exchange with the theatre director, to whom the poet-narrator pays court in the hope that such an investment will pay off. The return is less than he bargains for, as he is dismissed ('congédier' having the somewhat ambiguous undertones both of the courteous 'to be given leave' and the rather more discourteous 'to be sent packing') with advice which amounts to selling his soul (to Z . . .—the initial indicating greater universality than a name—a man who is living proof that merit has no currency). There is no situation more prosaic than the need to keep body and soul together, and this list of the day's activities becomes a balance sheet on which all transactions are recorded and where outlay and profit are examined. The rejection (by *directeurs*—*de revue et de théâtre*) harnesses the stupidity of the successful to that of the press (for it is here that

---

[51] See *Petits Poèmes en prose*, ed. Lemaître.

[52] This is a commonplace which Baudelaire enjoys exploiting; cf. *Fusées*, XI: 'Ceux qui m'ont aimé étaient des gens méprisés, je dirais même méprisables, si je tenais à flatter *les honnêtes gens*' (*OC* i. 660).

[53] The Dictionnaire E. Littré defines *généreusement* in the following terms: 'D'une manière généreuse, avec un grand cœur; d'une main libérale; courageusement; se montrer magnanime; d'un naturel noble' (Paris, 1885).

reputations are made),[54] and emphasizes how little purchasing power the true artist really has.

What is worse, however, is that the exchange mechanisms of the poet-narrator do not succeed in maintaining face value either, for he brags of actions not accomplished and denies successes; he refuses simple favours to friends and writes recommendations for those for whom he has no respect or time. In other words, he is as corrupted by the transactional system as the next man. He waves to people he does not know and exchanges handshakes hypocritically (the gloves are the vestimentary equivalent of the locked door which is the threshold separating him from these exchanges),[55] ever fearful of contracting some form of contagion which is as much spiritual as physical. Each and every exchange into which he enters is, in other words, as meaningless and dishonest as the next, whether it is a question of giving or receiving. The currency is counterfeit, the power-holders corrupt, and all exchange dysfunctional. There is a progressive devaluation of mood and language, as the clamour of the day overwhelms the space reserved for poetic expansion and as it becomes apparent that the darkness of this particular night will not bring the *repos* required to compose the *beaux vers* so badly needed. The devaluation of art and of self which occurs in the day's transactions, the question of artistic merit, and the attendant frustrations and disappointments all come together in the climactic prayer. Even here, there is question of a return on earlier investment, almost as if the poet-narrator in addressing the intercessors ('Âmes de ceux que j'ai aimés, âmes de ceux que j'ai chantés') is recalling a debt. The capital once regained can be put back to work with the purpose of redemption (significantly *bought* in the French *se racheter*).

The ending of the poem is highly significant, for it returns to the desires of the opening paragraphs to frame the central vicissitudes which militate against the fulfilment of these desires. The prayer

---

[54] This is reminiscent of 'Les Tentations' where the third temptress, Fame, represents some kind of gain for favours. Here the courtesan which is the Press arrives blowing the trumpet of worldly renown, and is resisted by the poet only because the seductive virago is recognized as a woman who keeps the company of men with whom he would not wish to be associated. The poet overcomes the temptation here, but with the same form of twisted morality and worship as is present in the litany of 'A une heure du matin'.

[55] This is a reprise of a locution in Baudelaire's own *Journaux intimes* in a section where there is a high concentration of ideas occurring in the prose poems in note form: 'Beaucoup d'amis, beaucoup de gants,—de peur de la gale' (*Fusées*, XI, *OC* i. 660).

of the final paragraph is itself framed by a statement of the poet's discontent ('mécontent de tous et mécontent de moi' balancing with 'que je ne suis pas le dernier des hommes, que je ne suis pas inférieur à ceux que je méprise!'), a formulation which echoes the apparently self-deprecating conclusion of the *dédicace* and the poet's situation of his own work in relation to others, as well as the *motivation* of the gesture.

The threshold of the text, that 'zone non seulement de transition mais de *transaction*', figures the exchange economy into which the prose poems are launched. Through an analysis of the paratext, we are able to better understand not only the context of the text's production, but also the way in which the 'discours d'escorte' strives to define the project it accompanies. Moreover, in its duplicitous discursive strategies, it sets up a dysfunctional circuit of communication which prefigures the conflicting discursive and ideological discourses of the poems themselves. The text's threshold, which elaborates the problem of boundaries between the genres, suggests ways in which we might read the generic thresholds within texts. In order fully to understand the way in which this functions, we need to look more closely at the way in which prose and poetry are conjoined.

2

Lyricism and its Others

Duality ←

Toujours double, action et intention, rêve et réalité; l'un nuisant l'autre, l'un usurpant la part de l'autre.

(OC ii. 87)

Moi se fait de tout. Une flexion dans une phrase, est-ce un autre moi qui tente d'apparaître?

Henri Michaux

ALL duality exists only in terms of relationship. Doubleness is only conceivable as a pair, as opposites, as two entities existing in relation to each other. This is the dynamic defined by the prose poem, although *poème en prose* does not seem to split the atom so much as describe its particular nature. The potentially ambiguous status in English of *prose* as both noun and adjective, though here admittedly more adjective than noun, seems to bind the two elements in a more indissoluble relationship. In discussing the prose poem as genre, many critics have turned to the notion of doubleness, of the 'opus duplex', meaning both the examination of prose poetry as a genre composed of binary oppositions and an exploration of the *Petits Poèmes en prose* in relation to the verse *doublets* in *Les Fleurs du mal*.[1] Even the two complementary titles of Baudelaire's prose poetry (thematic and rhematic) provide an opportunity to examine the way in which these define the particular mechanisms of a genre born of duality.[2]

---

[1] Barbara Johnson, *Défigurations du langage poétique* (Paris: Flammarion, 1979), 14–16. Johnson uses the idea of 'le texte et son double' predominantly to explore the relationship between the prose poetry and *Les Fleurs du mal*.

[2] This is Tzvetan Todorov's starting point. He claims that Baudelaire's prose poems are

This notion is, of course, explicit not only in the title of the work, but also in the contrasting juxtapositions of many of the *intertitres*, of the titles of individual poems: 'Le Fou et la Vénus', 'Le Chien et le flacon', 'La Femme sauvage et la petite maîtresse', 'La Soupe et les nuages', 'Le Tir et le cimetière'. It is explicit, too, in those poems which present duality in its concrete embodiment: 'Le Crépuscule du soir' and 'Le Port', 'Le Miroir', 'Laquelle est la vraie?', and 'La Chambre double'.[3] It is also explicitly present in 'Un hémisphère dans une chevelure'. This hemisphere is the opposite of Parisian spleen, a tropical paradise reached by following the contours of a head and the undulations of its hair, but where the poet restores the *hemi* of a sphere not entirely sublimated by the poetic.[4] The range of dualities also incorporates sentences oscillating between two opposing terms and symmetry in the structure of the prose poems. All these are supposedly held together by the rhematic title of the work.

Léon Cellier has claimed that the poet of *Les Fleurs du mal* is 'celui qui en usant de l'antithèse et de l'oxymoron, passe d'un univers tragique à un paradis, de la dualité à l'unité'.[5] There is clearly no such attempt to achieve formal unity in the prose poems. Rather, the generic title and the enterprise it designates are figures of a duality which declares itself present and which, it will be argued, demands a reading strategy which goes beyond that more or less evident doubleness to uncover alterity, generic hybridity, and *une duplicité constitutive*.[6] This duality is present in even the most lyrical of poems, as we shall see, and it is in the doubleness of the lyrical space that figurations of the poet's self as *dédoublé* become most apparent.

'texts which in their very conception are based on the meeting of opposites'. See 'Poetry without Verse' in Mary Ann Caws and Hermine Riffaterre (eds.), *The Prose Poem in France: Theory and Practice* (New York: Columbia University Press, 1983), 64. Essay first printed in Genres du discours (Paris: Seuil, 1978).

[3] Todorov gives this list, 'Poetry without Verse', p. 66.

[4] For a detailed comparison of the verse and prose versions of this poem, see Johnson, *Défigurations*, especially ch. 2, 'La Chevelure et son double', pp. 31–55.

[5] 'D'une rhétorique profonde: Baudelaire et l'oxymoron', in *Parcours initiatiques* (Neuchâtel: La Baconnière, 1977), 194.

[6] See Ross Chambers *Mélancolie et opposition: Les Débuts du modernisme en France* (Paris: Corti, 1987), 228–9, where he explains that the 1850s is a critical moment in terms of such discourse and its reception: 'Par cette duplicité, le texte livre le sort de son identité à une instance de lecture que le contexte de production, tel qu'il est évoqué dans le texte (société répressive, hypocrite, bête) semble peu apte à fournir. La responsabilité du lecteur serait de

We should begin by examining more closely the way in which the duality of the work declares itself from within lyricism. 'La Chambre double', for example, plays upon alternations and pairs. The room is *rosâtre* and *bleuâtre*, *regret* and *désir* (past and future), *clarté* and *obscurité*, silence and voices (*OC* i. 280). More striking still is the way in which the dream in this poem is set up only to be overturned by the world beyond it. The space the text defines is double in every sense. The role of the title is accentuated by the fact that the poem begins with a paragraph acting as definition, an incomplete sentence which can only refer us back to the *chambre double* of the title: 'Une chambre qui ressemble à une rêverie, une chambre véritablement *spirituelle*, où l'atmosphère stagnante est légèrement teintée de rose et de bleu' (*OC* i. 280). The room itself is compared to a dream, it is not just the space to dream, but the experience itself, *spirituelle*. Blue and pink are projected as the colours of dream, suggestive of the twilight or the supernatural colours of an eclipse. This is the space of lyricism, an expression of what Baudelaire describes in *Fusées* as the *surnaturel*:

Le surnaturel comprend la couleur générale et l'accent, c'est à dire, intensité, sonorité, limpidité, vibrativité, profondeur et retentissement dans l'espace et dans le temps. Il y a des moments de l'existence où le temps et l'étendue sont plus profonds, et le sentiment de l'existence immensément augmenté. (*OC* i. 658)

There is an intensification of all sensory experience, *limpidité* or clarity of vision, *sonorité* or depth of sound impression and the fusion of sound with tactile sensation. Time stands still, making it possible to hold together both regret and desire, taking control of the sun and eclipsing it to provide the *rafraîchissantes ténèbres* so longed for elsewhere and here transposed into a *bain de paresse* and a *vie suprême*. Shadows are cast from furniture as elongated adjectives and become as dreamy as the poet himself; the soft furnishings 'parlent une langue muette, comme les fleurs, comme les ciels,

---

pénétrer la duplicité textuelle pour saisir la demande de lecture qui s'y véhicule; mais le texte doit se charger de réaliser, par cette duplicité, une forme de lisibilité particulière, celle qui fera le tri entre lecteurs courants — ceux qui relèvent du contexte de production — et le "bon" lecteur, qui aura la perspicacité de pénétrer la duplicité et de déceler la "vérité" du texte. Vérité qui doit établir l'identité de celui-ci par opposition aux discours de la société mais qui est, par définition, de l'ordre du non-dit et du non-dicible. Cette vérité du text, c'est clair, ne peut ni se formuler ni se définir, sinon par opposition à ce qu'elle n'est pas (le discours social), c'est-à-dire relationellement.'

comme les soleils couchants', participating in that *volupté* described in 'Elévation' and effacing 'les ennuis et les vastes chagrins' of 'la vie brumeuse' (*OC* i. 10).

This is the decor of the imagination, an attempt to create in physical objects a purely emotional state or a space where no external intrusion can obstruct the expansiveness of the inner existence. This is, initially at least, truly a poem, as Valéry defines it: 'une sorte de machine à produire l'état poétique au moyen des mots'.[7] Even the most positive aspects of the outer world, the products of other imaginations, are banned in this quest for purity of imaginative experience: 'Sur les murs nulle abomination artistique. Relativement au rêve pur, à l'impression non-analysée, l'art défini, l'art positif est un blasphème. Ici, tout a la suffisante clarté et la délicieuse obscurité de l'harmonie.' Lyricism is here presented as a divinity, a religious faith, bringing the peace and beatitude of spiritual well-being, as opposed to the plastic fixity of the finished painting, but the dialogue which is set up between this prose poem and 'Élévation', between the world of the lyrical imagination and the plastic arts (and Baudelaire's own theories of *le beau* and *l'imaginaire* in the context of his art criticism) suggests an awareness of genre. The duality of the formulation 'suffisante clarté et délicieuse obscurité' spells it out. Here we are confronted directly with the prose/poetry dialectic, as Baudelaire writes in relation to Banville 'la lyre fuit volontiers tous les détails dont le roman se régale. L'âme lyrique fait des enjambées vastes comme des synthèses; l'esprit du romancier se délecte dans l'analyse' (*OC* ii. 165). Synthesis is harmony and harmony is lyricism. Contrasts are contradictions. In evoking in 'La Chambre double' both the analytical engagement of art criticism and the 'libre essor' of 'Élévation', Baudelaire brings into focus the dynamic of this prose poem and of others, since poetry is caught in a dialogue with itself and with other forms of expression. The 'suffisante clarté et la délicieuse obscurité de l'harmonie' is a formula which can be and is reversed with too much clarity. Analysis requires otherness. It is prosaism and difference.[8]

---

[7] Paul Valéry, 'Poésie et pensée abstraite', in *Œuvres* (Paris, Gallimard, Bibliothèque de la Pléiade, 1957), i. 1337.

[8] Sartre argues that 'Si le poète raconte, explique ou enseigne, la poésie devient prosaïque, il a perdu la partie', *Qu'est-ce que la littérature?* (Paris: Gallimard, 1947), 48.

The transition in the poem is made by the appearance of the *Idole*, a sovereign installed on the throne of dream and *volupté*. A light breaks across the darkness, a light projected from the eyes, 'subtiles et terribles *mirettes*'. From a poetry of banal objects where furniture can dream and net curtains cascade like waterfalls, we are brought up short, aggressed by the contempory slang which characterizes the companion as other than poetic and presages the interruption to follow. This is for the reader, in other words, what the 'coup terrible, lourd à la porte' is to the lyrical subject, what nightmare is to dream. This reaction is expressed as a physical sensation, a 'coup de pioche dans l'estomac', the poet's tool no longer used to uncover 'maint joyau', as in 'Le Guignon', but rather turned against him. The turning point is, in fact, brought about by the *mirettes*, both in the prosaism of the slang which describes them and in the way that they invite the poet into analysis: 'Je les ai souvent étudiés, ces étoiles noires qui commandent la curiosité et l'admiration' (*OC* i. 280). The studiousness of the poet, both in contemplating these eyes and in seeking out the jewel of verse 'qui dort enseveli | Dans les ténèbres et l'oubli, | Bien loin des pioches et des sondes' (*OC* i. 17) also evokes contemporary slang (*piocheur*, meaning *travailleur assidu*) and leads us directly to the failure of lyricism: 'les manuscrits, raturés ou incomplets; l'almanach ou le crayon a marqué les dates sinistres!' (*OC* i. 281). At the same time, as has been persuasively argued in relation to other poems, the eye, 'the organ relating the reader to the poetry,' evokes the failure of communication with the Other, a failure in the reading process which is here, as elsewhere, problematized.[9]

All that was the 'chambre paradisiaque' is now horror: 'Oui! ce taudis, ce séjour de l'éternel ennui est bien le mien. Voici les meubles sots, poudreux, écornés; la cheminée sans flamme et sans braise, souillée de crachats; les tristes fenêtres où la pluie a tracé des sillons dans la poussière'. The 'senteur infinitésimale du choix le plus exquis à laquelle se mêle une très légère humidité' has become 'une fétide odeur de tabac mêlée à je ne sais quelle nauséabonde moisissure'. Desire and *volupté* have become 'le ranci de la désolation'. The *souveraine des rêves* is dethroned and now Time reigns again as brutal dictator. Doubly dethroned, since time

[9] See Margery Evans, *Baudelaire and Intertextuality: Poetry at the Crossroads* (Cambridge: Cambridge University Press, 1993), 47–58.

ousts both the dream and the Romantic lyricism here attributed, not without a little irony, to Chateaubriand's *Sylphide*. The outside world is heralded by the language it speaks and comes to define the realities of the room as the language of dream recedes. This text bears witness to a *dédoublement*: to being in two places at the same time or rather to making one place double; to a splitting of the lyric subject and voice; and, in a rarer sense, of bringing together two halves and making them one.[10] The symmetry of the text confirms this, as Todorov has shown, the nineteen paragraphs being divided in two halves—nine of dream, nine of reality—bridged by the paragraph beginning 'Mais' and bringing the knock at the door.[11] It is, in the most simplified terms, prose knocking at the door of poetry, a threshold crossed and yet contained within a single, yet double, room.

That threshold is not, however, simply and straightforwardly a prose/poetry divide, despite the symmetry and the knock from the other side of the lyrical space. Despite the lyrical voice's exploration of an inner life of thought and emotion (dream), the interruptions from beyond the boundaries of the poetic both invite the world outside (and its discourses) into lyrical space and expose as an empty fiction such lyricism and the generic territory it occupies. 'La Chambre double' may be said, then, to map a generic *dédoublement*, and to go beyond the enclosure of the single binary text by describing a more combative and dynamic role for itself in its transactions with convention, that is to say, with its predecessors and contemporaries. It does this by invoking Chateaubriand, recruiting established lyrical power. Just as in the *lettre-dédicace*, however, there is an ambivalence in the reference (reverence): 'la souveraine des rêves, la *Syphide*, comme disait le grand René'. The *grand* is as disingenuous as the *Petits* of *Petits Poèmes en prose*, and the enlistment of the model from the past (the verb is in the imperfect) is dismissive, escaping and undermining the 'authority' of such Romantic chimera.[12] More than just dismissive, it is self-mocking and encodes, to some degree, the other self-reflexive and self-referential aspects of this poem. The reference to 'Le

---

[10] See the first sense of *Dédoubler* in the *Petit Robert 1*: 'Défaire (ce qui est double) en ramenant à l'unité'.   [11] 'Poetry without Verse', 67.
[12] See Harold Bloom with reference to the English Romantic poets in *The Anxiety of Influence: A Theory of Poetry* (New York: Oxford University Press, 1973).

Guignon', though perhaps only allusive, a mere echo, also incorporates other voices, Gray and Longfellow in particular, from whom lines are borrowed.[13] In evoking other texts, both from *Les Fleurs du mal* and the *Petits Poèmes en prose*, Baudelaire engages in a dialogue with the self, showing the prose poem to be a vehicle capable of containing other texts and discourses, or what has been called 'the complex network of literary (though not only literary) seepages, interferences, convergences and collisions'.[14] It is a questioning of lyric form, an exploration of other poems designed to reflect the central dialectic of this one: an ironic interrogation of literariness. This is staged, in fact, by the way in which the poet gazes into those *mirettes* (from the verb *mirer*, like *miroir*) and is *devoured* by them. Framed in the gaze is the image of the poet, reflected in the *mirettes* of the opium dream and of the prosaic. This is reminiscent of the *dahlia bleu* of 'L'Invitation au voyage', where the verb *mirer* also occurs, and where there is multiplication of resemblances:

> Fleur incomparable, tulipe retrouvée, allégorique dahlia, c'est là, n'est-ce pas, dans ce beau pays si calme et si rêveur, qu'il faudrait aller vivre et fleurir? Ne serais-tu pas encadrée dans ton analogie, et ne pourrais-tu pas te mirer, pour parler comme les mystiques, dans ta propre *correspondance*? (*OC* i. 303)

Here the frame resembles the portrait, the country, the woman, and the portrait is of the woman (it is her image); the only thing missing is a direct resemblance between the frame and the country.[15] By framing 'La Chambre double' in this way, we can say that, if the eyes are in the image of the term which designates them and that these *mirettes* frame the poet, then the poem stages a self-questioning mirroring of the lyric persona. It frames the analogy and lays bare the *correspondances* of this particular text.

Of all the prose poems, it is 'Le Thyrse' which has repeatedly been seen as such an analogy, representing continuity between the thematic and formal planes. To 'Qu'est-ce qu'un thyrse?' it has become a critical commonplace to respond 'c'est (plus ou moins)

---

[13] See Graham Chesters, 'A Political Reading of Baudelaire's "L'Artiste inconnu"', *Modern Language Review*, 79 (1984), 64–76.

[14] Christopher Prendergast (ed.), *Nineteenth-Century French Poetry: Introductions to Close Reading* (Cambridge: Cambridge University Press, 1990), 22.

[15] Todorov, 'Poetry without Verse', 67.

un poème en prose'.[16] The analogy is tempting if one extracts the passages which could indeed be read in this way:

Et une gloire étonnante jaillit de cette complexité de lignes et de couleurs, tendres ou éclatantes. Ne dirait-on pas que la ligne courbe et la spirale font leur cour à la ligne droite et dansent autour dans une muette adoration?
Le thyrse est le représentant de votre étonnante dualité

Ligne droite et ligne arabesque, intention et expression, roideur de la volonté, sinuosité du verbe, unité du but, variété des moyens, amalgame tout-puissant et indivisible du génie, quel analyste aura le détestable courage de vous diviser, de vous séparer?   (*OC* i. 335–6)

There are, in these lines, elements which echo the prose-poetry project as defined in the *lettre-dédicace*, particularly 'le rêve d'une prose poétique, musicale sans rythme et sans rime, assez souple et assez heurtée pour s'adapter aux mouvements lyriques de l'âme, aux ondulations de la rêverie, aux soubresauts de la conscience' (*OC* i. 275–6). There is here, too, a concentration of dualistic opposites. There are twisting, curving lines, as opposed to ramrod straightness; aromas associated with colourfulness. There is 'le sens moral et poétique'—if not opposites certainly not the same thing despite the singular—as well as 'le sens physique', the material reality of the object here allegorized. The amalgam of the moral and poetic senses is, indeed, significant, for here there is a suggestion of a prose poetry cross, since *moral*, in Baudelairean terms, at least, implies something more readily associated with the forms of prose. This suggests, perhaps, an equivalent to the opposition *rêve pur*—*analyse* in 'La Chambre double', since Liszt's work, too, evokes the spiritual and defies analysis. And yet, there is something troubling in that opposition which is not quite conflictual, which is more a confluence of difference, a 'couple renversé', an '*amalgame* tout-puissant et indivisible du génie'. Liszt is duality, held in tension by this text, linked to his interpreter by a rhyme

---

[16] See, for example, Henri Lemaître, who describes this poem as 'l'image mythologique qui figure exactement son art' *Petits Poèmes en prose* (Paris: Garnier, 1962), p. xlviii; and Todorov, 'Poetry without Verse', 68–70, who also sees the 'thyrse' as a symbol of the prose poem itself. Georges Blin sees in the poem 'une métaphore particulièrement applicable à son recueil dans son entier', *Le Sadisme de Baudelaire* (Paris: Corti, 1948), 168. Johnson argues, however, that the text operates rather as 'une mise en abyme infinie de son propre incapacité à servir de modèle', *Défigurations*, 62–5.

(*Liszt/analyste*) and by the homophonic presence of his name in the analyst which seeks to desconstruct his unity. The rhetorical question plays upon a similar binding opposition, the oxymoronic 'détestable courage' both offering a challenge to and condemning the reader who might seek to undo the amalgam.[17]

The poem also opposes, or rather unifies in their difference 'fleurs et pampres' which together shape the complexity around the stick which supports them. The question which follows this duality is particularly significant: 'Et quel est, cependant, le mortel imprudent[18] qui osera décider si les fleurs et les pampres ont été faits pour le bâton, ou si le bâton n'est que prétexte pour montrer la beauté des pampres et des fleurs?' So that not only is the poet invoking the relationship between 'fleurs et pampres', but also that between these and the structure which supports them. There is a clear echo in this of Nerval's 'El Desdichado', particularly its second quatrain:

> Dans la nuit du tombeau, toi qui m'a consolé,
> Rends-moi le Pausilippe et la mer d'Italie,
> La fleur qui plaisait tant à mon cœur désolé,
> Et la treille où le pampre à la rose s'allie.[19]

In the same way as 'Le Thyrse', Nerval's poem elaborates a set of dualities and dualities centred upon objects which, despite their material reality, belong also in the realm of poetic symbols. Here, too, there are oppositional pairs: 'toi' and 'moi', 'le Pausilippe' and 'la mer d'Italie', 'la fleur' and 'mon cœur' and 'le pampre' and 'la rose' (clearly echoed by 'fleurs and pampres' of 'Le Thyrse'). Nerval's poem, like Baudelaire's, joins masculine and feminine. Nerval does this by creating an alliance of masculine and feminine elements; Baudelaire refers more specifically to 'l'élément féminin exécutant autour du mâle ses préstigieuses pirouettes'. Like 'Le Thyrse', this quatrain of Nerval's 'El Desdichado' proposes a model for alternation and intertwining ('modulant tour à tour') and

---

[17] See Gérard Gasarian, *De loin tendrement: Étude sur Baudelaire* (Paris: Champion, 1996), 84–5, who develops these observations into a theory of Baudelaire's 'style hystérique', seeing in the word *thyrse* an anagram of *hyster* (uterus).

[18] It should be noted that in the term 'mortel imprudent' there is also a duality, since both words can act as noun and adjective, creating a shifting pattern of meaning, but one in which the differences are maintained as imprecision.

[19] *Les Chimères*, in *Œuvres* (Paris, 1974), i. 160.

for joining. And what is more, it does so around a man-made construction: 'la treille'.[20]

Like the thyrsus, then, the trellis is the material object which holds such alternations in place, which enables a relatively unstable unity composed of different elements: 'un mystique fandango autour du bâton hiératique'. Such an arabesque performed around the thyrsus is evocative both of imaginative and sexual freedoms, as well as a form of mastery of these freedoms. Margery Evans sees in this image an echoing of Sterne, Diderot, and Balzac, which offers 'a variant of the parallelism of capricious sexual pursuit and spontaneous imaginative vagary'.[21] Nerval's sonnet, the most constrained and unified of forms, is an attempt to contain infinite expansion and multiple and fragmented selves (and rhythms). It is, in Baudelaire's terms 'un chant de délectation ou d'ineffable douleur' and Nerval, like Liszt, is a 'Chantre de la Volupté et de l'Angoisse éternelles'. These references to song also evoke Nerval because of the poet's interest in folk-song and his lyrical pieces set to or imitative of music.[22]

Most importantly, the crucial object at the centre of 'El Desdichado' is the musical 'lyre', the lyre of which Orpheus is master, and which can express both 'les soupirs de la sainte et les cris de la fée'. In 'Le Thyrse' Bacchus and 'la nymphe' come together to create this 'amalgame tout-puissant et indivisible du génie'; in Nerval's poem, it is Orpheus and 'la fée', the latter contained within the former (*Orphée/fée*). The 'fée' is also 'la syrène' (sy-rène rhyming with and reproducing Reine), reminiscent of that lyrical dream of 'La Chambre double', the Romantic *Sylphide* who is also 'la souveraine'. Using the constraints of the sonnet, Nerval contains the differences, the 'expansion de choses infinies' and, in the figure of Orpheus, reaches a state of unity which is represented by the lyre and, in more material terms, by the trellis (of the text). There is no mention of the lyre in 'Le Thyrse', but that is hardly surprising. The use of the term in Baudelaire's work is almost always ironic, used against the tendencies of Romanticism to emphasize the artifice of outworn modes used in all sincerity. In *L'École païenne* (1852), for example, Baudelaire writes:

---

[20] See Rae Beth Gordon's close reading of 'El Desdichado', 'The Lyric Persona: Nerval's "El Desdichado"', in Christopher Prendergast (ed.), *Nineteenth-Century French Poetry*, 86–102.   [21] *Baudelaire and Intertextuality*, 43.
[22] Rae Beth Gordon, 'The Lyric Persona', 97–8.

Pastiche! pastiche! Vous avez sans doute perdu votre âme quelque part, dans quelque mauvais endroit, pour que vous couriez ainsi à travers le passé comme des corps vides pour en ramasser une de rencontre dans les détritus anciens? Qu'attendez-vous du ciel, ou de la sottise du public? Une fortune suffisante pour élever dans vos mansardes des autels à Priape et à Bacchus? Les plus logiques d'entre vous seront les plus cyniques. Ils en éleveront au dieu Crépitus.

Est-ce le Dieu Crépitus qui vous fera de la tisane le lendemain de vos stupides cérémonies? Est-ce Vénus Aphrodite ou Vénus Mercenaire qui soulagera les maux qu'elle vous aura causés? Toutes ces statues de marbre seront-elles des femmes dévouées au jour de l'agonie, au jour du remords, au jour de l'impuissance? Buvez-vous des bouillons d'ambroisie? mangez-vous des côtelettes de Paros? Combien prête-t-on sur une lyre au Mont-de-Piété? (*OC* ii. 47)

The attitude to the rarefied terms of Romantic lyricism is here expounded in the kind of images adopted by prose poetry. These, for Baudelaire, are the clichés of Romantic lyricism. He objects to Sainte-Beuve in 1866 that, in *Joseph Delorme*, he finds 'un peu trop de *luths*, de *lyres*, de *harpes* et de *Jéhovahs*. Cela fait tâche dans des poèmes parisiens. D'ailleurs, vous étiez venu pour détruire tout cela' (*C* ii. 585); and in both *Les Fleurs du mal* and the *Petits Poèmes en prose* there is opposition to just such clichés. 'L'Examen de minuit', for example, a poem first published in 1863, like 'Le Thyrse', plays upon this, evoking mythological figures in the service of the lyre. But this poem is deeply ironic and the quasi-divine lyre brings only Bacchanalian delirium:

> Enfin, nous avons pour noyer
> Le vertige dans le délire,
> Nous, prêtre orgueilleux de la Lyre,
> Dont la gloire est de déployer
> L'ivresse des choses funèbres,
> Bu sans soif et mangé sans faim!. . .   (*OC* i. 144)

The exclamation mark and *points de suspension* are marks of an irony to be found still more embedded in rhyme since the coupling of *délire/Lyre* denotes, as Graham Robb has shown, a *lieu commun* evocative of early Romanticism. Here the rhyme is used oppositionally, both in terms of an outmoded (and worn out) form of lyricism and in terms of thematic inconsistencies.[23]

---

[23] *La Poésie de Baudelaire et la poésie française 1838–1852* (Paris: Aubier, 1993), 301.

But the thyrsus is not the lyre. It is, however, a symbol, 'un emblème sacerdotal dans la main des prêtres ou des prêtresses célébrant la divinité dont ils sont les interprètes et les serviteurs', and could thus be equated with the symbol of the lyre for the poet-priest. Significantly, though, the prose poem does not allow us to escape its material reality, 'ce n'est qu'un bâton, un pur baton, perche à houblon, tuteur de vigne, sec, dur et droit'.[24] It is a prop for the food and drink which are the sustenance evoked in the passage from L'École païenne; the *double* of the divinity celebrated at communion and the prosaic doubling of poetic bacchanals.

For Baudelaire, the thyrsus represents not only Liszt's 'étonnante dualité', but also De Quincey's, 'un esprit méditatif et enclin à la rêverie', for the symbol belongs, first and foremost, to the author of the *Suspiria*, whose mind spirals under the influence of opium.[25] De Quincey's thyrsus, 'dont il a si plaisamment parlé, avec la candeur d'un vagabond qui se connaît bien' (*OC* i. 515), is an object brought into question by this ambiguous qualification on the part of Baudelaire.[26] The implication is that De Quincey knows how his own thoughts digress and, in a tone of gentle self-mockery, invokes the thyrsus to describe himself. The question, then, is whether, in dedicating a borrowed symbol to a third party (Liszt), Baudelaire in any way undermines that act of dedication. Baudelaire, we know, admired Liszt, and sent him a copy — 'avec envoi' — of the *Paradis artificiels*.[27] The symbol was, therefore, in no sense secretly reused in the dedication to 'Le Thyrse', but rather publicly reinscribed, thereby linking Liszt with De Quincey. This notion is further reinforced by an entry in *Mon cœur mis à nu* in which Baudelaire reuses the term *vagabond*, first applied to De Quincey, but this time used in relation to Liszt as well: 'Glorifier le

---

[24] Cf. *Un Mangeur d'opium*: 'Le sujet (i.e. le thyrse) n'a d'autre valeur que celle d'un bâton sec et nu; mais les rubans, les pampres et les fleurs peuvent être, par leurs entrelacement fôlatres, une richesse précieuse pour les yeux' (*OC* i. 515).

[25] Both references to the thyrsus in *Un Mangeur d'opium* are to De Quincey's way of thinking. *OC* i. 444 and 515.

[26] A variant reads: 'dont il a déjà parlé plaisamment et avec la candeur d'un digression-iste qui se connaît bien'. See *OC* i. 1401.

[27] See Claude Pichois's notes to the correspondence (*C* ii. 728). Edward K. Kaplan also affirms this admiration, *Baudelaire's Prose Poems: The Esthetic, the Ethical and the Religious in the Parisian Prowler* (Athens, Ga., London: University of Georgia Press, 1990), 13. Baudelaire's correspondence does indeed seem clear on this point. In the letter addressed to Liszt in May 1861, Baudelaire talks of 'la sympathie que m'inspirent votre caractère et votre talent' (*C* ii. 162).

vagabondage et ce qu'on peut appeler le Bohémianisme, culte de la
sensation multipliée, s'exprimant par la musique. En référer à
Liszt' (*OC* i. 701). Implied in this is also a notion of exchange,
since Liszt had sent Baudelaire a copy of *Des Bohémiens et de leur
musique en Hongrie*—also 'avec envoi'. Here the circulation of
ideas is made evident by the reproduction of a certain vocabulary.
There is, in other words, a reasonable case, here, for reading the
'dédicace' as an artistic announcement since 'elle affiche une relation, intellectuelle ou privée, réelle ou symbolique'.[28] If we build
into this circulation the dedicated *exemplaire* of the *Paradis artificiels*, we build in, too, another intellectual and artistic dimension
to the Baudelaire–Liszt exchange. The dedication of the poem
is public and part of the paratext; the reference to De Quincey
private, forming a part only of the epitext. If 'Le Thyrse' does owe
any debt at all to Nerval's 'El Desdichado', there is a further
dimension to the intellectual programme here established and one
which, because tacit, emphasizes the essential ambiguity of the act
of dedication, which addresses both a determined reader and an
unknown one invited to bear witness to the public (and private)
act(s) of recognition.[29] And, as Genette has indicated, 'cette affiche
est toujours au service de l'œuvre, comme argument de valorisation
ou thème de commentaire'.[30]

As such, 'Le Thyrse' is a remarkable poem for the way in which
it figures an artistic programme. It is, necessarily, an exploration of
the relationship between poetry and prose, but it goes far beyond
this in its attempts to bring together creativity and sexuality, artifi-
cial stimulus, music, the lyric persona, and the mythological. It is a
manifestation of the Wagnerian notion of *Gesamtkunstwerk*, 'la
réunion, la coïncidence de plusieurs arts, comme l'art par excellence' (*OC* ii. 782). Quoting Liszt, Baudelaire, in his essay on
Wagner, refers to the 'idéale mysticité' which brings about his state
of *rêverie* and which, in turn, he links to the responses of other
artists, seeking to demonstrate that 'la véritable musique suggère
des idées analogues dans des cerveaux différents' (*OC* ii. 783–4).
The experience is that of 'Correspondances', self-referentially

---

[28] Genette, *Seuils*, 126.

[29] See ibid.: 'il y a toujours une ambiguïté dans la destination d'une dédicace d'œuvre,
qui vise toujours au moins deux déstinataires: le dédicataire, bien sûr, mais aussi le
lecteur, puisqu'il s'agit d'un acte public dont le lecteur est en quelque sorte pris à témoin',
p. 126.   [30] Ibid. 126.

cited, but without attribution, in the midst of Baudelaire's critical elaboration, the 'analogie réciproque' being not just a relationship existing between things, but translated across minds and works to create an intellectual world which is as much of a 'complexe et indivisible totalité' as creation itself (*OC* ii. 784). 'Le Thyrse', then, is the manifestation of this artistic principle; it is a translation of a particular kind of artistic enterprise which is the confluence of all forms, not just of poetry and prose. It is materiality and spirituality, self and other, and the literal and figurative.[31] 'Le Thyrse' is a rare example in the *Petits Poèmes en prose* of harmonious balance, the equivalent of Liszt's appreciation of Wagner as an equation; the passage is cited by Baudelaire: 'le chant religieux et le chant voluptueux [. . .] "sont ici posés comme deux termes, et qui, dans le finale, trouvent leur équation"' (*OC* ii. 794). In this case, the divinity celebrated is a creative muse (with intellectual/ intertextual intercessors) which is coupled with a sexual dynamic duplicitously parodying the models it evokes. The apparent equation dissipates only to reveal that lyricism's others are foils for literary duplicity, or, as Evans argues:

the 'tutelage' traditionally implicit in all author/reader relationships is drawn attention to in *Le Spleen de Paris* and problematized by a series of bantering references which transpose into the sexual arena the prosyletising of the disciple by the moral authority. In this respect, as in others, *Le Spleen de Paris* offers a striking display of poetry provocatively abandoning earlier codes of seemliness and courtly preciosity and delighting in the most indelicate of metaphors.[32]

If this prose poem is addressed to Liszt, as the dedication would imply, it is an address which invokes others who would share the artistic ideals of the *dédicateur* and *dédicataire*, whether they be De Quincey, Wagner and Nerval, Sterne, Diderot and Balzac, or the reader, to whom the poem is necessarily also addressed. In this

---

[31] Johnson has argued this latter point quite forcefully, concluding that the infinite relationship between the literal and the figurative ends in the failure of the model: 'le thyrse est une figure du rapport entre le littéral et le figuré, mais de sorte que l'expression même de ce rapport, étant elle-même une figure qui se réfère indéfiniment à d'autres figures, fait éclater la possibilité d'isoler et de distinguer entre le figuré et le littéral, entre le "poétique" et le prosaïque, pour donner un sens "propre" à leurs rapports. Au lieu de fixer la structure d'un rapport entre poésie et prose, ce modèle des *Petits Poèmes en prose* est une mise en abyme infinie de sa propre incapacité de servir de modèle'. *Défigurations*, 65.

[32] *Baudelaire and Intertextuality*, 44.

respect, the way in which the reader engages with the public dedication is a representation of the nature of the reading processes at
work elsewhere in the text. Here it is a particularly acute staging of
the process, since the dedicated poem sets up a relationship which
excludes the reader, while requiring him to be witness to the act of
dedication. This act, in other words, sets up a narrator–narratee
relationship, and one which is further emphasized by the apostrophes of the poem, while all the time insisting on the text–reader
relationship as well. As in all apostrophes, there is an implied exclusion zone. The reader can witness the address, but not participate
in it. Except that this is a text, an act of narration with an intended
narratee. Either the reader must seek to identify with the narratee,
to substitute the named dedicatee for himself and see the text as
directly addressed to him, or he must accept that he operates in the
exclusion zone, at which point he becomes a spectator of the staged
relationship.

In this respect, 'Le Thyrse' does offer a model for the reading of
the *Petits Poèmes en prose*, not as a simple prose-poetry cross, but as
the representation of a reading strategy. This is not dissimilar to
Chambers's notion of the 'narrative function' and the 'textual
function', where reading entails a shift between two addressee positions and two constructions of subjectivity: identification with the
narratee and interpretative or reading subject.[33] In this sense, the
discursive strategies of 'Le Thyrse' are very similar to those identified in the threshold *lettre-dédicace*, where Houssaye was seen to
be a *déstinataire-relais*. Through reference to Liszt, or through dialogues with others (as in 'L'Étranger', 'Le Miroir', and 'Le Chien
et le flacon'), the reader experiences 'aucune peine à démêler et
recevoir ce qui, de toute évidence, à travers un tiers ou par-dessus
son épaule, lui revient en propre'.[34] In the case of this poem, this
refers not just to the extra-dedicatory communication, but to what
is communicated through a range of different references within
and beyond the text itself. The essential dualities of 'Le Thyrse',
in conjunction with other duplicities suggested by covert references in the poem, split the lyric persona and the textual identity
to engender an 'interprétabilité sans fin',[35] making the text

---

[33] See Ross Chambers, *Room for Maneuver: Reading (the) Oppositional (in) Narrative*
(Chicago and London: Chicago University Press, 1991), 32–5.
[34] Genette, *Seuils*, 181.   [35] Chambers, *Mélancolie et opposition*, 234.

endlessly readable and analytically irreducible as a play of difference. If 'Le Thyrse' does engage with Nerval's 'El Desdichado', as
with other texts and other voices, it is to leave undone the dualities,
the alliances which would be concentrated and distilled in the lyric
persona, woven into the trellis and definitively coupled, in order to
expose the lyrical self as irreconcilably other, as 'hors de soi'.[36]

'Les Foules' is an exploration of this phenomenon: a transposition of the intratextual–intertextual opposition, an account of the
relationship between the lyric persona and the crowd. This prose
poem, quite apart from the Parisian crowd it evokes, also represents intertextual others, like those we can see operating in 'Le
Thyrse'. 'Les Foules' owes a debt to Poe's *Homme des foules*,
Baudelaire describing the way in which Poe's convalescent 'se
mêle, par la pensée à toutes les pensées qui s'agitent autour de lui'.
The elements borrowed from Poe (as well as other elements cast in
this prose poem) are similarly to be found evoking Guys in *Le
Peintre de la vie moderne* (*OC* ii. 687–94). And if 'Le Thyrse' has
been seen as the ultimate statement of the prose-poetry enterprise,
there is no reason why one could not make the same claim for 'Les
Foules', containing as it does the essence of the thematic-poetic
claims of the *lettre-dédicace* ('c'est surtout de la fréquentation des
grandes villes, c'est du croisement de leurs innombrables rapports,
que naît cet idéal obsédant') and one of the proposed titles for the
collection of the prose poems (*Le Promeneur solitaire*). What is
most interesting and significant here, however, is the way in which
the lyric subject is represented.

In the essay on Guys, Baudelaire refers to the artist's capacity to
enter the crowd and remain himself, to take from the crowd that
which can be used in the creative enterprise. The significant passage reads as follows:

La foule est son domaine, comme l'air est celui de l'oiseau, comme l'eau
celui du poisson. Sa passion et sa profession, c'est d'épouser la foule.

[36] This notion is the basis of Michel Collot's essay on Rimbaud and Ponge, and is defined
as follows: 'Etre hors de soi, c'est avoir perdu le contrôle de ses mouvements intérieurs, et
de ce fait même, s'être projeté vers l'extérieur. Ces deux sens de l'expression me semblent
constitutifs de l'émotion lyrique, ce transport et ce déport qui porte le sujet à la rencontre
de ce qui le déborde du dedans comme au-dehors', 'Le Sujet lyrique hors de soi', in
Dominique Rabaté (ed.), *Figures du sujet lyrique* (Paris: Presses universitaires de France,
1996), 114.

Pour le parfait flâneur, pour l'observateur passionné, c'est une immense jouissance que d'élire domicile dans le nombre, dans l'ondoyant, dans le mouvement, dans le fugitif et l'infini. Être hors de chez soi, et pourtant se sentir partout chez soi; voir le monde, être au centre du monde et rester caché au monde, tels sont quelques-uns des moindres plaisirs de ces esprits indépendants, passionnés, impartiaux, que la langue ne peut que maladroitement définir. L'observateur est un *prince* qui jouit partout de son incognito. [. . .] Ainsi l'amoureux de la vie universelle entre dans la foule comme dans un immense réservoir d'électricité. On peut aussi le comparer, lui, à un miroir aussi immense que cette foule; à un kaléido-scope doué de conscience, qui, à chacun de ses mouvements, représente la vie multiple et la grâce mouvante de tous les éléments de la vie. C'est un *moi* insatiable du *non-moi*, qui, à chaque instant, le rend et l'exprime en images plus vivantes que la vie elle-même, toujours instable et fugitive. (*OC* ii. 691–2)

In describing Guys, Baudelaire generalizes in terms commonly interpreted to be self-inclusive. What we notice most of all are the terms used to describe the man of the crowds, all of which are unspecific. There is, for example, no mention of the painter or indeed the artist, here. Rather, the description is, as one might expect, in the third person and impersonal, culminating in that crucial expression of otherness, 'C'est un *moi* insatiable du *non-moi*'. Partly, this is an indication of a borrowed idea, since Baudelaire is here describing Poe's notion of this figure as much as he is describing Guys's art. We have, in other words, moved into the domaine of criticism, the analytical account of process which is unindividuated (and, in any case, shared).

In the prose poem, the process is applied strictly to the poet, but the same sort of critical distance is maintained by the impersonal third-person narrator. The poet is here specifically mentioned, but in impersonal terms, or rather, in general terms which distance the narrator from his subject, despite his evident familiarity with it. 'Les Foules' reads as a general lesson in poetic interaction with the crowd, brimming as it is with sententiousness,[37] and corresponds closely to the form of the essay quoted above. Like 'Le Thyrse', 'Les Foules' is a poem which suggests dualities:

---

[37] e.g. 'Il n'est pas donné à chacun de prendre un bain de multitude'; 'Jouir de la foule est un art'; 'Qui ne sait pas peupler sa solitude, ne sait pas non plus être seul dans une foule affairée'; 'Il est bon d'apprendre quelquefois aux heureux de ce monde [. . .] qu'il est des bonheurs supérieurs au leur' (*OC* i. 291–2).

individuation as opposed to multitude, accumulation of binary descriptions, opposites (self and other, openness and closedness, the known and unknown, multitude and solitude). Like 'Le Thyrse', too, there is a play between the male and the female, between conventionally active and passive roles, from which emerges a neuter which destabilizes polarization and enables the multiplication of difference.[38] So that what, in the end, emerges from this poem is a sense of mastery of the other and replication of self in the other.

Collot has shown, with reference to Merleau-Ponty, that the lyric subject is usually projected on to another (an ideal other) which is translated by the intersubjectivity of language: 'le sujet ne peut s'-exprimer qu'à travers cette chair subtile qu'est le langage, qui donne corps à sa pensée, mais qui demeure un corps étranger'.[39] The passage from *Le Peintre de la vie moderne* and the prose poem 'Les Foules' explore the way in which this other can be made flesh in artistic terms, but which are highly problematic for the lyric subject, bringing together as they do the material reality of the world and the material reality of language, the inner and outer worlds of the poet, and thereby provoking a sort of subjective identity crisis which is expressed in generic terms. In *L'Art philosophique*, an essay which can be linked to the prose-poetry project in a number of ways,[40] Baudelaire expresses this idea in his definition of modern art: 'Qu'est-ce que l'art pur suivant la conception moderne? C'est créer une magie suggestive contenant à la fois l'objet et le sujet, le monde extérieur à l'artiste et l'artiste lui-même' (*OC* ii. 598). The object of such exploration is to complete the self, since reflection and introspection are inadequate. The poet's exposure to the outside world creates in him 'un étrange "en-dedans-en-dehors"' which can only be accommodated by reflection and introspection:

C'est hors de soi qu'il peut la trouver. L'é-motion lyrique ne fait peut-être que prolonger ou rejouer ce mouvement qui constamment porte et déporte le sujet vers son dehors, et à travers lequel seul il peut ek-sister et s'ex-primer. C'est seulement en sortant de soi, qu'il coïncide avec lui-même, non sur le mode de l'identité, mais sur celui de l'ipséité,

---

[38] See Nathaniel Wing, 'On Certain Relations: Figures of Sexuality in Baudelaire', in *The Limits of Narrative: Essays on Baudelaire, Flaubert, Rimbaud and Mallarmé* (Cambridge: Cambridge University Press, 1986), 38–40, who sees in this poem 'a mobile and exhilarating network of differences'.   [39] 'Le sujet lyrique', 115.

[40] *The Notes diverses sur 'L'Art philosophique'* reveal several references to the *Petits Poèmes en prose* project, see esp. *OC* ii. 607.

mais qui n'exclut pas mais au contraire inclut l'altérité [. . .]. Non pour se contempler dans le narcissisme du moi, mais pour *s'accomplir soi-même comme un autre.*[41]

Lyricism, 'la forme accomplie du poème', gives shape to such an identity and the poet *is* that verbal accomplishment of matter and emotion.[42] What is increasingly questioned by poetry after 1850 is not so much lyricism itself, but the forms of that lyricism and, most significantly, the way in which the lyrical subject is figured in the text. The intertexuality we saw in play in 'Le Thyrse' is clearly one manifestation of the lyrical subject's openness to others, an openness which one might characterize by Nerval's statement 'Je suis l'autre', but where the Romantic identity crisis has become positive expansion of the self or multiplication of potential fictive selves. The openness of the lyrical subject means abandonment to the possibilities of chance encounter in the material world, whether that be in terms of subject matter or language itself. Usually it is both. We can see this process clearly in 'Le *Confiteor* de l'artiste' where the poet opens himself to the natural world and its expansiveness (space and language) and where that world then becomes the inner soul of the poet, assuming his identity and playing him like an instrument:

Grand délice que celui de noyer son regard dans l'immensité du ciel et de la mer! Solitude, silence, incomparable chasteté de l'azur! une petite voile frissonnante à l'horizon, et qui par sa petitesse et son isolement imite mon irrémédiable existence, mélodie monotone de la houle, toutes ces choses pensent par moi, ou je pense par elles (car dans la grandeur de la rêverie, le *moi* se perd vite!); elles pensent, dis-je, mais musicalement et pittor-esquement, sans arguties, sans syllogismes, sans déductions.

Toutefois, ces pensées, qu'elles sortent de moi ou s'élancent des choses, deviennent bientôt trop intenses. L'énergie dans la volupté crée un malaise et une souffrance positive. Mes nerfs trop tendus ne donnent plus que des vibrations criardes et douloureuses.   (*OC* i. 278)

This poem elaborates the relationship between the lyrical sub-ject, the outer world, and expression. In its subject matter, it is

---

[41]   Collot, 'Le Sujet lyrique', 115–16.
[42]   René Char says in *Moulin premier*: 'Audace d'être un instant soi-même la forme accomplie du poème. Bien-être d'avoir entrevu scintiller la matière-émotion instantanément reine'. *Le Marteau sans maître*, suivi de *Moulin premier* (Paris: Corti, 1970) 124. Cited by Collot, 'Le Sujet lyrique', 116.

stereotypically lyrical in that it engages with the world and the poet's powers to express it. What is remarkable here, however, is the oscillation between a lyrical 'je'—the poet will here address the reader as himself rather than as a fictive Other—and a universal and impersonal 'énonciateur' which means that the subjective identity (that of 'l'artiste') can be assumed by another. The ritualized form of the confession confirms this, as indeed do the impersonal constructions ('il est de certaines sensations', 'Grand délice que celui de noyer') and the impersonal possessive ('*son* regard').[43] The self is soon lost both because of the lyrical openness, the 'expansion des choses infinies', but also because it is generalizable, assailed by the Other (whoever or whatever it may be). The self is also lost, however, because the lyrical *moi* is but a temporary state, a single aspect of a multiple persona here concentrated on lyricism. The duality of this poem, like that of 'La Chambre double' is, first, to be found in the return to anxiety from a state of sublime lyricism, a return seen as characteristic of the Baudelairean temperament, a sort of 'spleen et idéal'.[44] What occurs in 'Le Confiteor', however, is an oscillation between a generalized lyrical subject, first identified as the *Je* of the poet, and a second, less generalized, first person who appears—separated in time from the first (by *bientôt* and *maintenant*)[45]—only to reject the lyrical established in the first part of the poem.

Et maintenant la profondeur du ciel me consterne; sa limpidité m'exaspère. L'insensibilité de la mer, l'immuabilité du spectacle, me révoltent... Ah! faut-il éternellement souffrir, ou fuir éternellement le beau? Nature, enchanteresse sans pitié, rivale toujours victorieuse, laisse moi! Cesse de tenter mes désirs et mon orgueil! L'étude du beau est un duel où l'artiste crie de frayeur avant d'être vaincu.' (*OC* i. 278–9)

Rather than a manifestation of the bipolar *moi*, this can be read as an opposition of the different personae the lyrical subject projects. In other words, we should see operating, even within the more

---

[43] I am indebted to Laurent Jenny's essay 'Fictions et figurations du moi', in Dominique Rabaté (ed.), *Figures du sujet lyrique*, 99-111, which informed my thinking on 'Le *Confiteor*'.

[44] See for an example of this sort of argument, J. A. Hiddleston, *Baudelaire and Le Spleen de Paris* (Oxford: Clarendon Press, 1987), 92. Hiddleston sees this as the defeat of art and, perhaps, an expression of Baudelaire's ambivalence to the status of prose poetry.

[45] Jenny notes that these deictics themselves represent different timescales, one generic, the other present. 'Fictions et figurations du moi', 101.

lyrical poems, figurations and fictions of the self which are an interplay of the *moi* and the *non-moi*. This is all the more apparent since the shift in the voice of the poem also indicates a shift in *destinataire*, with Nature apostrophized, both as tormenter and confessor, before a return to sententiousness which seems to move the text once again beyond the confines of the confessional. The coda is significant in a number of ways. First, it represents a return to the *destinataire* of the opening paragraphs of the poem and to the generalized *Je*. Secondly, it generalizes the conflict, extending the possibilities of rivality beyond that of artist versus nature to a *duel* which might be said to embrace the different enunciating personae (the Artist and an Other), as well as the witnesses, in the form of shifting *destinataires*. In this struggle, where the death of lyricism is figured as a repeated act, new aesthetic possibilities are born of the defeat. This means that in figuring and fictionalizing other selves, the artist is able to maintain a hold on 'l'étude du beau', even in the face of lyrical defeat.

The same sort of duel is explored in 'Le Fou et la Vénus', a poem which might be said to repeat the patterns of 'Le *Confiteor*'. It opens in much the same way with a lyrical exclamation: 'Quelle admirable journée!' and develops, in the first three paragraphs, a similar mood in which the natural world is musical harmony (*correspondances*) and expressive desire:

L'extase universelle des choses ne s'exprime par aucun bruit; les eaux elles-mêmes sont comme endormies. Bien différente des fêtes humaines, c'est ici une orgie silencieuse.

On dirait qu'une lumière toujours croissante fait de plus en plus étinceler les objets; que les fleurs excitées brûlent du désir de rivaliser avec l'azur du ciel par l'énergie de leurs couleurs, et que la chaleur, rendant visibles les parfums, les fait monter vers l'astre comme des fumées. (*OC* i. 283)

Here, too, we see a duel, this time within Nature, as colours become the figure of expression. In both poems, the moment is intense, and short-lived, since the mood is broken, in 'Le Fou et la Vénus, by the *Cependant* of the fourth paragraph and, in 'Le *Confiteor*' by the *Toutefois* opening the third. Where one might see the poems diverging is in the introduction of a character in 'Le Fou et la Vénus' and, therefore, of a third-person narrator. The *être affligé* introduced by the narrator is clearly a figure for the artist, as a number of critics have shown.[46] However, the manner in which he is introduced indicates the same sort of separation between the enunciating *Je* and the artist as we saw in 'Le *Confiteor*'. This separation is here carried one stage further by a generalized figure (a metonymic commonplace) and a narrative instance which clearly represents a different person, grammatically speaking, from the mountebank.

In 'Le Vieux Saltimbanque', a poem which takes up a similar theme, such a separation is made clearer still by the way in which the first-person narrator explains the metonymy:

Et, m'en retournant, obsédé par cette vision, je cherchai à analyser ma soudaine douleur, et je me dis: Je viens de voir l'image du vieil homme de lettres qui a survécu à la génération dont il fut le brillant amuseur; du vieux poète sans amis, sans famille, sans enfants, dégradé par sa misère et par l'ingratitude publique, et dans la baraque de qui le monde oublieux ne veut plus entrer! (*OC* i. 297)

There is here, then, a clear distinction between the enunciating *Je* which is the narrative instance and the figure of the artist, despite the empathy made manifest by the poet-narrator's hysteria, by his obsession and *soudaine douleur*. This empathy, the explicated metonymy, makes clear the similarity whilst retaining the distinction. It is an image of a generalized poet, a reflection of the *vieil homme de lettres*. It is, then, not so much an image of the self, but a projection of what it might become in the future. It is, indeed, more than just a fear of artistic failure. The mountebank represents the passing of a cultural moment; he is the detritus of literary evolution. One might argue that this is a stereotypical image of lyricism: the artist must suffer and, in his suffering, he proclaims his isolation and, aggressively or humorously, his difference from society and the forms of expression it generates. In the case of the mountebank, however, the difference is expressed not in creatively expressive terms, but in isolation. It is an isolation and separation upon which the poet-narrator insists:

Au bout, à l'extrême bout de la rangée de baraques, comme si, honteux, il s'était exilé lui-même de toutes ces splendeurs, je vis un pauvre saltimbanque.

---

[46] See, for example, Enid Welsford, *The Fool: His Social and Literary History* (London: Faber, 1935); Jean Starobinski, *Portrait de l'artiste en saltimbanque* (Geneva: Skira, 1970) and 'Sur quelques répondants allégoriques du poète', *Revue d'histoire littéraire de la France*, 67 (Apr.–June 1967), 402–12; and Louisa E. Jones, *Sad Clowns and Pale Pierrots: Literature and the Popular Comic Arts in Nineteenth-Century France* (Lexington, Ky.: French Forum, 1984).

Partout la joie, le gain, la débauche; partout la certitude du pain pour les lendemains; partout l'explosion frénétique de la vitalité. Ici la misère absolue, la misère affublée, pour comble d'horreur, de haillons comiques, où la nécessité bien plus que l'art, avait introduit le contraste. Il ne riait pas, le misérable! Il ne pleurait pas, il ne dansait pas, il ne gesticulait pas, il ne criait pas; il ne chantait aucune chanson, ni gaie ni lamentable, il n'implorait pas. Il était muet et immobile. Il avait renoncé, il avait abdiqué. Sa destinée était faite.   (*OC* i. 296)

The isolation is self-imposed exile from the frenetic and *explosive* fête of the fairground; the mountebank, unlike all the other adults including the poet-narrator, is unmoved by the *jubilé populaire*. He is the archetype of the morose lyrical subject, absorbed here, though, in a narcissistic anti-lyricism ('il ne chantait aucune chanson'). To see this figure as the poet is to see the prose poetry as defeat, as indeed a number of critics have done. Hiddleston, for example, sees this particular poem as 'a direct criticism of the essence of art itself', an art that is 'a mere diversion in which the poet himself no longer believes and whose sole function is to "faire épanouir la rate du vulgaire"'.[47] Marie Maclean, on the other hand, does suggest that the modernism of this poem is in the fragmentation of the self 'whereby the poet becomes both the fairground *flâneur* and the poor clown he spies upon, both the observing I and the I observed'.[48] This notion of fragmentation comes closer to the duality and separations explored in this chapter, but still does not take full account of the complex relationship the narrator has with the observed figure in 'Le Vieux Saltimbanque'.

The narrator in this poem is distinct from both 'le peuple' and the old acrobat. He is intoxicated by the crowd and the atmosphere, but moved by the poverty and decrepitude of the isolated figure he observes. This ambivalence is played out in the penultimate paragraph of the poem:

Que faire? À quoi bon demander à l'infortuné quelle curiosité, quelle merveille il avait à montrer dans ces ténèbres puantes, derrière son rideau déchiqueté? En vérité, je n'osais; et dût la raison de ma timidité vous faire rire, j'avouerai que je craignais de l'humilier. Enfin, je venais de me résoudre à déposer en passant quelque argent sur une de ces planches, espérant qu'il devinerait mon intention, quand un grand reflux de peuple, causé par je ne sais quel trouble, m'entraîna loin de lui.   (*OC* i. 296)

[47] *Baudelaire and Le Spleen de Paris*, 14.   [48] *Narrative as Performance*, 58.

The narrator is moved to do something, but does not know what to do. His response is not one that suggests identification with the *saltimbanque*, marked as it is by a combination of pity and embarassment. And even as he decides upon a course of action, he is swept away in the crowd. One might conjecture that the narrator's act of charity is at best half-hearted and that, in the end, he moves with the crowd (it, too, driven to act by some 'trouble'). His ambivalence, in other words, is overcome only by external forces (the 'grand reflux'). Whatever talent the *saltimbanque* may have, it lies behind outmoded and impoverished drapes. The narrator recognizes it (and perhaps some small part of himself in it), but he is not the *saltimbanque* and his art is not that of defeatism, lyrical isolation, and self-pity. The poet-narrator does not enter into an exchange with the *saltimbanque*. He thinks of doing so, and says he intended to, but his gesture is that of the crowd (financial tokenism) and it is significant that it is the crowd which, in the end, obstructs the gesture. In other words, no exchange takes place here. The narrator's art is to be found in the energy of the crowd, in the expansiveness of the exuberance. The separation of the narrator from this figure is, then, the differentiation of the modern poet from an outmoded form of lyricism, but one to which the narrator nevertheless feels he owes some debt.

This reading of the poem is supported by Baudelaire's discussion of lyricism in his essay on Banville, an essay which appeared only three months before 'Le Vieux Saltimbanque' in the *Revue fantaisiste*.[49] Here, too, he distinguishes between forms of lyricism, between the 'moyens anciens d'expression poétique' and 'la poésie moderne' in its 'état mixte' (*OC* ii. 167–8). The modern lyricism expounded here is, significantly, *carnavalesque*:

Mais enfin, direz-vous, si lyrique que soit le poète, peut-il donc ne jamais descendre des régions éthéréennes, ne jamais sentir le courant de la vie ambiante, ne jamais voir le spectacle de la vie, la grotesquerie per-pétuelle de la bête humaine, la nauséabonde niaiserie de la femme etc?... Mais si vraiment! le poète sait descendre dans la vie; mais croyez que s'il y consent, ce n'est pas sans but, et qu'il saura tirer profit de son voyage. De la laideur et de la sottise il fera naître un nou-veau genre d'enchantements. Mais ici encore sa bouffonnerie conservera

---

[49] Both were first published in 1861. The essay on Banville on 1 Aug.; the prose poem on 1 Nov.

quelque chose d'hyperbolique; l'excès en détruira l'amertume, et la satire, par un miracle résultant de la nature même du poète, se déchargera de toute sa haine dans une explosion de gaieté, innocente à force d'être carnavalesque. (*OC* ii. 166–7)

Rather than advocating the lyricism of the 'régions éthéréennes' or bemoaning its loss as might be represented by the *vieux saltimbanque*, this passage seems to be promoting a new poetry, 'un nouveau genre d'enchantements'. It is a poetry born of productive interaction with the crowd, a sort of exploitation of that crowd without compromising the self. Indeed, the way in which such *descent* is described here equates with the third paragraph of 'Les Foules'. The purpose is not the same kind of *élévation* afforded by lyrical expansion in those *régions éthéréennes*, but rather an explosive gaiety, hyperbole, excess without rancour, satire without hatred, a childlike delight in the grotesqueness of the everyday. The separation between the poet-narrator and the *vieux saltimbanque* is a matter of genre. It is a matter of form and innovation opposing stasis and degeneration. It is, indeed, one of the most positive expressions of the popular in the prose poems. By distancing itself from the figure of the *saltimbanque*—by denying, in other words, identification of observer and observed—the lyric persona becomes narrator only. His differentiation from the *saltimbanque* is, then, not only a matter of form (in every sense), but a figure for the way in which the 'nouveau genre d'enchantements' which is the prose poem will function.

In 'Les Foules' there is something of the same dynamic that we have seen operating in other poems, and particularly in 'Le Vieux Saltimbanque'. There is no denial of the self in the *universelle communion*, but rather a doubling of the self, since the poet-narrator retains his identity as such, as well as adopting a series of roles through observation. It is a talent not simply of observation, but also of appropriation. The observer passes into the subjects of his gaze, precisely because of his innate 'goût du travestissement et du masque'. How better could one describe the appropriation of fictional narrators than to adopt the poet's description, in that third paragraph of the poem, of simultaneous self-effacement and self-expansion through assimilation with the crowd?

Le poète jouit de cet incomparable privilège qu'il peut à sa guise être lui-même *et* autrui. Comme ces âmes errantes qui cherchent un corps, il entre, quand il veut, dans le *personnage* de chacun. Pour lui seul, tout est vacant; et si de certaines places paraissent lui être fermées, c'est qu'à ses yeux *elles ne valent pas la peine d'être visitées.*   (*OC* i. 291, emphasis mine)

Entering into the character of each individual, as if the crowd constitutes the *dramatis personae* of imaginary and street scenarios, the poet adopts as his own all roles, 'toutes les professions, toutes les joies, toutes les misères que la circonstance lui présente' (*OC* i. 291).[50] Baudelaire's use of the word *personnage* is significant here, denoting not only distinct dramatic roles but also suggesting, at its etymological root in the Latin *persona*, the importance of mask, of transformation and concealment on the theatrical stage. Not only does this involve an assumed image (a change in external appearance), but an adoption of psychological, emotional, and behavioural attributes belonging to that individual. The Latin *persona* can, therefore, be seen to contribute both the concepts of person and personality, the latter being what is characteristic of the person or, in Kantian terms, man's moral essence.[51] Emphasizing the importance of the mask as *persona* in certain cultures, one critic points to anthropological evidence which suggests that 'to don the mask in the appropriate ceremonial circumstances and settings is not to enact a role, to make believe, but temporarily to incarnate cosmic reality [. . .]: instead of the mask as a bogus front, hiding the real person behind it, the mask mediates the highest reality of all'.[52] This would seem to be a notion borne out by Baudelaire in that the poet of 'Les Foules' has a clear choice to make in his adoption of masks, rejecting those which he deems worthless. And Fancioulle, the poet's artistic double, is a *parfaite idéalisation* of his role in 'Une mort héroïque' becoming the self that began only as a role. On the other hand, certain roles may be the antithesis of the identity attributed to the poet-narrator. They might, indeed, be chosen for this reason, the mask then becoming a vehicle of parody. From this, then, we can assume that the *personnages* selected for visitation are significant either as an embodiment of an aspect of interest or as a source of conflict.

---

[50] This is a particular characteristic of the popular Deburau. See Ch. 4 below.

[51] Immanuel Kant, 'Foundations of the Metaphysics of Morals', in *Critique of Practical Reason and Other Writings in Moral Philosophy*, trans. and ed. Lewis White Beck (Chicago: University of Chicago Press, 1949), 86–7.

[52] Robert C. Elliott, *The Literary Persona* (London: University of Chicago Press, 1982), 21.

This communion with others, as Nathaniel Wing has shown, is described in highly sexual terms.[53] At the very beginning of 'Les Foules', the poet states that 'jouir de la foule est un art', suggesting unambiguously that this interplay excites him. As Leo Bersani would have it: 'psychic penetrability is fantasized as sexual penetrability'.[54] By the fifth paragraph of the poem, the comparison has found a more concrete expression:

Ce que les hommes nomment amour est bien petit, bien restreint et bien faible, comparé à cette ineffable orgie, à cette sainte prostitution de l'âme qui se donne tout entière, poésie et charité, à l'imprévu qui se montre, à l'inconnu qui passe. (*OC* i. 291)

The interplay of sexual enjoyment, penetration of another, and artistic activity is 'described throughout the text as disruptions of the polarities between subject and object in a constant exchange and affirmation of differences, without loss or gain of presence'.[55] The poet both assaults and is assaulted in this relationship between self and other, whether it be active engagement of the imagination or passive submission to a reading public.[56] Sexually, as we might expect from a writer with a professed interest in being both *bourreau* and *victime*, the poet accomplishes the dual role and emerges, from this experience at least, intact and with the self-righteous message that sexual intercourse cannot rival imaginative intercourse nor the ecstasies of communing with the crowd:

Les fondateurs de colonies, les pasteurs de peuples, les prêtres missionnaires exilés au bout du monde, connaissent sans doute quelque chose de ces mystérieuses ivresses; et, au sein de la vaste famille que leur génie s'est faite, ils doivent rire quelquefois de ceux qui les plaignent pour leur fortune si agitée et pour leur vie si chaste. (*OC* i. 292)

What is significant in this passage is not simply the return to a stabilizing neuter, or a neuter of mocking superiority, but the implication of extreme (discursive) power over weaker individuals,

---

[53] 'On Certain Relations: Figures of Sexuality in Baudelaire', in *The Limits of Narrative*, 39–40.

[54] *Baudelaire and Freud* (Berkeley and Los Angeles: University of California Press, 1977), 12. [55] See Wing, 'On Certain Relations', 39.

[56] Wing goes a step further to suggest that the roles played fulfil fixed positions, from the conventionally masculine (active) and feminine (passive) roles, to the neuter, the celibate male whose fecundity is other than sexual. 'On Certain Relations', 38 and 40.

whether sexually, pastorally, or politically. In narrative terms, this clearly echoes the realist convention of penetrating external reality, Balzac's notion of 'l'avide scalpel du Dix-Neuvième', which is exploited by Baudelaire in a number of poems and most obviously in 'Les Veuves':

C'est surtout vers ces lieux [les jardins publics] que le poète et le philosophe aiment diriger leurs avides conjectures. [. . .]
   Un œil expérimenté ne s'y trompe jamais. Dans ces traits rigides ou abattus, dans ces yeux caves et ternes, ou brillants des derniers éclairs de la lutte, dans ces rides profondes et nombreuses, dans ces démarches si lentes ou si saccadées, il déchiffre tout de suite les innombrables légendes de l'amour trompé, du dévouement méconnu, des efforts non récompensés, de la faim et du froid humblement, silencieusement supportés. (*OC* i. 292)

It has been argued that this model is invoked with parodic intention, and it is true that the 'pompous certainty' of the narrator-observer does suggest such a parody, especially when contrasted with 'the celebration of the poet's own independent and exclusive "rêverie" in the counterpart verse poem "Les Petites Vieilles"'.[57] Significantly, 'Les Foules' seems both to celebrate the imaginative possibilities of the crowd and to betray the the same pompous certainty (expressed in the same impersonal terms) as 'Les Veuves'. Nowhere is this more evident than in the last paragraph of the poem: 'Il est bon d'apprendre quelquefois aux heureux de ce monde, ne fût-ce que pour humilier un instant leur sot orgueil, qu'il est des bonheurs supérieurs au leur, plus vastes et plus raffinés' (*OC* i. 291). The power of the artist is here unequivocally stated and yet, in destabilizing the self-satisfaction of the other, there is also the implicit destabilization of the ironist's position.[58] What is evident, then, is that, despite the multiplication of the self

---

[57] Margery Evans, *Baudelaire and Intertextuality*, 56–8.

[58] Wayne Booth makes this point clearly in his analysis of the way irony functions: 'the process is in some respects more like a leap or a climb to a higher level than like scratching a surface or plunging deeper. The movement is always toward an obscured point that is intended as wiser, wittier, more compassionate, subtler, truer, more moral, or at least less obviously vulnerable to further irony. [. . .] Successful reconstruction obviously does not require that the reader finally accept without question the superior edifice. He may conclude that the choices should be drawn differently, with perhaps a third edifice, even higher, for whose inhabitants the author of the original irony is himself an ironic victim.' *A Rhetoric of Irony* (Chicago and London: University of Chicago Press, 1974), 36–7.

advocated in this poem, the voice of a unitary narrator remains powerful and does so because of the duplicity it manifests.

The externalization of self in helping the flock or the colony then mirrors the exploration of self through the crowd and the giving of oneself (the holy prostitution) in art. In other words, both in the creation of roles and of art, the poet plays God, hence the suggestion that 'this schema has a certain basis in power and ideology',[59] but equally, he is subject to the dominant ideology of society (as is Fancioulle in 'Une mort héroïque') which may or may not value the goods on offer. The *sainte prostitution* of 'Les Foules' finds numerous parallels in the *Journaux intimes*, where art, love, and God are also defined as prostitution. In *Fusées*, Baudelaire writes 'Qu'est-ce que l'art? Prostitution' (*OC* i. 649); in *Mon cœur mis à nu*, he formulates the same question, this time with respect to love:

> Qu'est ce que l'amour?
> Le besoin de sortir de soi.
> L'homme est un animal adorateur.
> Adorer, c'est se sacrifier et se prostituer.
> Aussi tout amour est-il prostitution.   (*OC* i. 692)

The artist finds himself in a curious relationship: chaste because 'foutre, c'est aspirer à entrer dans un autre, et l'artiste ne sort jamais de lui-même' (*OC* i. 702); prostituted, because he gives himself up to an assaulting reading public (largely for economic reasons). Unlike God, however, 'l'ami suprême de chaque individu, le réservoir commun, inépuisable de l'amour' (*OC* i. 692), the poet refuses the dissipation of such whole-hearted giving and determinedly retains a sense of the private through the cultivation of his artistic difference:

> Plus l'homme cultive les arts, moins il bande.
> Il se fait un divorce de plus en plus sensible entre l'esprit et la brute.
> La brute seule bande bien, et la fouterie est le lyrisme du peuple.
> (*OC* i. 702)

Although he is bound by the economic requirements of publication, and subject to rape by the critical public, like every good prostitute, he can feign a *persona* to which the client is dupe. In this way, the prostitute retains a sense of privacy and dignity (the sacrifice and

---

[59] Wing, 'On Certain Relations', 40.

pleasure being only performance) and the poet retains his spiritual integrity. Prostitution is not only, then, as has been suggested, *sacred* (because God is the most prostituted being),[60] but retains something of the divine without the utter self-sacrifice.

Etymologically, *prostituer* means to set forth (*statuere*) in public (*pro*). Charles Bernheimer has suggested that Baudelaire may have had this etymology in mind in stating that art (the exposure of one's creativity), as well as the multiplication of the self in exploring the other, is prostitution. He has also persuasively argued that 'as an emblem for [. . .] artistic practice, [prostitution] represented creative artifice, surface illusion, seductive falsity, even a kind of inspiring void'.[61] Each of these elements might be said to have its equivalent in the rhetoric of 'Les Foules'. The prostitute is a figure for social exclusion, she is the other of the other (woman) and the modern conception of the prostitute is posited on identity (sameness) and otherness (difference).[62] Baudelaire gives his relationship to the prostituted *persona* an unequivocal formulation when he writes in *Mon cœur mis à nu* that 'la gloire, c'est rester *un*, et se prostituer d'une manière particulière' (*OC* i. 700, emphasis mine). The relation of the phallocentric *I* to the prostitute's self-exposure is one of presumed control and mastery. Baudelaire's formulation is posited on control. His prostitute discourse expresses not only the complexity of gender relations in the period and in his work, discussion of which falls beyond the scope of this study,[63] but also, and more significantly from a formal perspective, artistic exclusions. These exclusions exist only in relation to the dominant discourse which constructs identity (by sameness), and the act of exclusion is itself constitutive of identity. All exclusions are, in

---

[60] Ibid. 21.

[61] Charles Bernheimer, *Figures of Ill Repute. Representing Prostitution in Nineteenth-Century France* (Cambridge, Mass., and London: Harvard University Press, 1989), 1. See also pp. 71–4 for a discussion of the references to prostitution in Baudelaire's *Journaux intimes.*

[62] See Alexandre Parent-Duchâtelet, *De la prostitution dans la Ville de Paris* (Paris: Baillière, 1836) and William Acton, *Prostitution Considered in its Moral, Social and Sanitary Aspects in London and Other Large Cities and Garrison Towns* (London: Frank Cass, 1870 [1857]). See also Shannon Bell, *Reading, Writing and Rewriting the Prostitute Body* (Bloomington and Indianapolis: Indiana University Press, 1994), 40–72.

[63] For discussion of such gender issues in 19th-cent. France, see Bernheimer, *Figures of Ill Repute*. He briefly discusses Baudelaire's treatment of gender in 'Les Foules' on p. 74. For a fuller and more detailed study of Baudelaire's androgyny, see Gasarian, *De loin tendrement*, 19–96.

other words, the *non-moi* of such an identity. Art as prostitution is self-exclusion from the conventional, but Baudelaire's formulation suggests mastery of a sort which, although it operates on the margins, defies codification and regulation by the (bourgeois) other. The same process is at work in the blasphemous association of God and prostitution.

In his formulation, Baudelaire specifically opposes the notion of unity (unitariness) to that of prostitution which is associated with multiple appropriation of the body or the appropriation of multiple bodies. Defined by difference from the other, poetic and narrative identity can be expressed only in terms of difference (le *non-moi*). In the *Petits Poèmes en prose*, this finds its articulation in generic difference, in the lyric *dédoublements* explored above, and in the multiple figurations and fictions of the self in narrative form. For difference to be perceived, however, the *moi* has to be present in the *manière particulière*.

In mapping the way in which the lyric *I* mutates within the more poetic of the prose poems and then separates from other actants as it becomes a narrator, it can be seen how voice fragments and multiplies in the *Petits Poèmes en prose*. This has led many critics to see the work as lacking in any unity, and especially lacking a unitary narrator of the sort which provides a foil for difference. Barbara Johnson's outstanding study of Baudelaire's prose poems makes reference to the head-and-tail conundrum of the *lettre-dédicace* to express very forcefully the view that this is a work without a *maître*, to use her term:

> Ce qui est visé, dans cette première phrase de la *Dédicace* comme dans la dernière, c'est la hiérarchie, la suprématie de la *tête*. La maîtrise de la volonté créatrice, comme l'identité de la chose faite, sont éclatées par une *différence* qui replace la puissance du travail toujours ailleurs. Ces 'petites babioles' ont une volonté à elles; ici, il n'y a pas de maître, il n'y a qu'un serpent coupé et recollé, découpable et recollable à l'infini. Ce qui vient en tête de l'ouvrage, c'est l'absence de tête; œuvre décapitée dont la tête n'est jamais là où on la cherche. Œuvre décapitée, mais qui se situe précisément dans la 'capitale', la grande ville où le 'croisement innombrable de rapports' tient lieu de centre, où la linéarité, toute serpentine qu'elle soit, se retourne et se recoupe pour aller nulle part, pour n'avoir pas de sens.[64]

---

[64] *Défigurations*, 27–8.

Baudelaire's snake metaphor refers specifically to the order of the poems. There is no beginning or end in a conventional (linear) sense, but both are nevertheless present.[65] We can enter and leave the text anywhere and the truncations of our individual reading will nevertheless be joined together. What is being required of us is a revision of our reading strategy in respect of narratives: a strategy which would take account of the texts as dynamic, embedded, and superimposed, embracing an ever greater number of possibilities or transpositions. Indeed, the autonomous fragments would not recreate the snake or behave kaleidoscopically without resonances which broadened the scope of each individual fragment. Such resonances are generally made available through the signs of a common ideology, an informing world-view—a retrievable creative identity.

What is troubling in the 'headless' view of the prose poems is, then, that no *maître* is identified, and this despite the presence of a recurring lyric subject and a preponderance of first-person narratives, many of which identify the enunciating *I* as a poet or artist. The question, in a sense, comes down to focalization and to voice. More than twenty of the prose poems are written in the first person, and although one should not confuse focalization and voice with grammatical person, it is a first person one might readily acknowledge as enunciating Baudelairean preoccupations. What is more, many of the poems which are not first-person enunciations sustain the tone, ideological position, and artistic aspirations of the predominant enunciating *Je* of the collection.

The real key to the problem of who speaks in the prose poems must be defined by the reading contract, since, as Lejeune has noted, 'c'est ce contrat qui définira le genre (avec les attitudes de lecture qu'il implique) et qui établira, éventuellement, les relations d'identité qui commandent le déchiffrement de pronoms personnels et celui de l'énonciation'.[66] And here is the problem. We have already seen how the prose poem defies simple classification and, indeed, how, even within the lyrical prose poems the enunciating *Je* is double. The reading contract established by the *lettre-dédicace* assures only duality (prose and poetry), multiplicity ('le croisement

---

[65] In asking that his verse poems be approached not as a *pur album*, but as a linear experience with beginning and end, Baudelaire requests for poetry what he denies his narratives. This is a significant reversal of convention.

[66] *Je est un autre: L'Autobiographie, de la littérature aux médias* (Paris: Seuil, 1980), 33.

de leurs innombrables rapports'), and duplicity (an unreliable enunciating *Je*). The reading contract established by the prose poems themselves is no less complex, constantly shifting between what appears to be the *Je* of a conventional lyric persona, that of a homodiegetic (and sometimes autodiegetic) narrator, and the third-person of apparently heterodiegetic narration.[67]

Since the relationship between prose and poetry comes down to a relationship between the lyrical *Je* (associated with the emotions of the poet) and fictions and figures of both the lyrical and narrative persona, one might argue that any reading contract can be based only upon the autonomous fragment, the individual poem. But because there is a unifying identity behind the different voices, something akin to Lejeune's notion of the *pédale sourde*,[68] we are more inclined to read the *Je* and its fictions as the voice of the poet, despite the preponderance of narrative texts. This is, first, because only a small proportion of the texts are heterodiegetic.[69] Secondly and perhaps most significantly in terms of tipping the balance, those which are homodiegetic often stage a poet-narrator as *témoin* of the action.[70] And finally, one third of the collection, including many of those poems which are lyrical, can be said to be autodiegetic.[71]

The *Je* who speaks, however, often determinedly maintains a stance of impersonality. Many of the poems have lengthy and generalized introductions, descriptions, or hypotheses, depending for

---

[67] The terms are Genette's. The heterodiegetic narrator is absent from the story told; the homodiegetic narrator is present as a character in that story; and where he or she is the leading character in the story, the narration is said to be autodiegetic. *Figures III* (Paris: Seuil, 1972), 251–3.

[68] This would imply that the different narrators are all aspects of the poet, figures rather than fictions. The third person is, then, a *figure d'énonciation* 'dans un texte qu'on continue à lire comme discours à la première personne. L'auteur parle de lui-même *comme si* c'était un autre qui en parlait, ou comme s'il parlait d'un autre.' He goes on to see this form of writing as a 'une sorte de décapage et de transposition du discours personnel' where the silencing of the self is applied with the *pédale sourde*. On release of the pedal 'les vibrations se rétablissent'. *Je est un autre*, 33–4.

[69] e.g. 'Les Dons des fées', 'Les Projets', 'La Belle Dorothée', 'Portraits de maîtresses', 'Le Galant Tireur', and 'Le Tir et le cimetière'.

[70] Such as 'Chacun sa chimère', 'Le Fou et la Vénus', 'Le Vieux Saltimbanque', Le Gâteau', 'La Fausse Monnaie', and 'Le Miroir' to name but a few.

[71] Poems in which the poet is the principal protagonist as well as the enunciating *Je* would include, by way of example, 'Le *Confiteor* de l'artiste', 'Le Mauvais Vitrier', 'La Chambre double', 'Assommons les pauvres!', and, particularly interesting in its je/tu interplay, 'Anywhere out of the world'.

the most part on impersonal grammatical constructions, before eventually introducing the enunciating subject. Certain poems maintain this impersonality throughout, presenting themselves as philosophical *exposés*. This is the case in 'Les Foules' and, to a lesser extent, 'Les Veuves', where the protagonist is referred to in the third person as *le poète, le promeneur solitaire*, and *le philosophe*. The fact that our narrator is so able to identify what marks the artist out as different identifies him as belonging to that group himself and there is, in any case, slippage towards a *Je* caused by the lyrical enthusiasms which 'Les Foules' articulates and by the punctual reappearance of the personal pronoun throughout 'Les Veuves', especially (and emphatically) at the point where two narratives meet.[72] Indeed, even before the *Je* appears in 'Les Veuves', there is, as we have seen, something of the *maître* about this poem, something in the reference to *pâture*; and then, after an explicit reference to the insinuations of the first person, something still more suggestive of mastery in the reference to the *œil experimenté* and to the focalized *flâneur*'s deciphering of *les innombrables légendes*. These terms all recur elsewhere, in the *Salon de 1859*, in 'Le Joujou du pauvre' (albeit slightly modified), and in 'Les Fenêtres' respectively. They might be said to be key terms, since they reflect Baudelaire's conception of the representation of modern life. In other words, despite a distance between the narrator and the artist-protagonists of these two poems, and despite narrative and grammatical strategies which distinguish the lyric-narrative *I* from the *il*, an authorial voice breaks through, undermining that impersonality with the imposition of what can justifiably be called authorial discourse.[73]

It has been argued that 'in terms of content, the narrator remains the same throughout'.[74] Although one can point to shifts in narrative, or indeed lyrical, instance, there can be no question that there is a unifying discourse, that which proclaims its otherness, and a common set of preoccupations which create a sense of

---

[72] See Christopher Prendergast, *Paris and the Nineteenth Century* (Oxford: Blackwell, 1992), 180 for a discussion of the narrative split.

[73] Margery Evans's thesis, discussed earlier in this chapter, requires the terms to be Balzacian. It is, however, precisely such meshing of different voices which is at issue here and, for the parody to function, the voice of the ironist must be discernible.

[74] Edward K. Kaplan, 'Solipsism and Dialogue in Baudelaire's Prose Poems', in Barbara T. Cooper and Mary Donaldson (eds.), *Modernity and Revolution in Late Nineteenth-Century France* (Newark: University of Delaware Press, 1992), 88.

unity in the collection. Those preoccupations are central to the reading contract and to genre, since they not only explore the alternating locations and dislocations of the lyrical subject in the social context determined by the poems, they also generate a sceptical reader. In other words, the splitting of the lyric *I* within even the lyrical poems is a way of questioning a particular aesthetic. By going a step further and telling that *I* as an *il* (or occasionally even as an *elle*), more complex separations, figures, and narratives of the self are possible.[75] The self-critical nature of the narrator-*flâneur* already sets up a separation and invites the *destinataire* to respond to the different postures adopted by the *Je*. Once elaborated into more complex narrative sequences, this same technique allows for a range of ironic strategies which further entrench duplicity in the fabric of the text.

This is particularly evident in 'Le Mauvais Vitrier', where the narrator sets himself apart from the figures whose acts of folly he describes, despite the fact that these acts are illustrative of a state of mind to which he himself soon testifies, both in word and deed. The poem starts out as an exploration of human behaviour with a list of these 'natures purement contemplatives', each one introduced by the impersonal formula of exemplarity 'tel qui'.[76] As the poem progresses, however, the narrator moves closer and closer to a personal testimony by introducing accounts of the exploits of friends, affirming his own narrative role, and, finally, by slipping into autodiegesis before returning, with the coda, to the impersonality of a philosophical *exposé*. The narrator neither judges nor approves those who commit acts of folly and recounts the events with a deadpan seriousness:

Un de mes amis, le plus inoffensif rêveur qui ait jamais exister, a mis une fois le feu à une forêt pour voir, disait-il, si le feu prenait avec autant de facilité qu'on l'affirme généralement. Dix fois de suite, l'expérience manqua; mais, à la onzième, elle réussit beaucoup trop bien.   (*OC* i. 285)

---

[75] Béatrice Didier has discussed the telling of the self in different grammatical persons in her study of the diary. See *Le Journal intime* (Paris: Presses universitaires de France, 1976), 147–58.

[76] What appear here as clear separations have been read by some critics, especially Charles Mauron, as 'un moi éclaté', expressions of internal psychological conflict; this is a reading he has also applied to 'Le Vieux Saltimbanque'. See *Le Dernier Baudelaire* (Paris: Corti, 1966), 116–17.

Narrative distance is established by the attribution of the action —and indeed of the telling ('disait-il')—to a nameless friend, as well as by the impersonal affirmation of what usually happens in such circumstances. What starts out as trivial conversation about how easily forests catch fire soon becomes a grotesque drama. The introduction to the actant of this event prepares us for a moment of foolish abandon whilst at the same time offering a reference to the good character of the friend. He is, after all, *le plus* inoffensif *rêveur* (emphasis mine). The *vitrier*, on the other hand, as the title states unequivocally, is *mauvais*. This mitigates our judgement of the friend and prepares us to excuse the incursion later perpetrated by the narrator.

There is comic tension in the stylized philosophical exposition and the contrasting flatly delivered example from which this emerges. The long parenthesis draws attention to itself as a pompous (and portentous) aside:

(Observez, je vous prie, que l'esprit de mystification qui, chez quelques personnes, n'est pas le résultat d'un travail ou d'une combinaison fortu-ite, participe beaucoup, ne fût-ce que par l'ardeur du désir, de cette humeur, hystérique selon les médecins, satanique selon ceux qui pensent un peu mieux que les médecins, qui nous pousse vers une foule d'actions dangereuses ou inconvenantes.)   (*OC* i. 286)

The elevated tone of the apostrophe, with its pondered expression and inverted imperfect subjunctive, is in direct contrast to the more familiar tone of the narrative, so that not only do we find the same process of identification and distancing between narrator and actant, we also find generic alterity created by a mismatch between discourse and situation. The comic effect is compounded by the contrast between the actions committed and the men described as so ill-suited to adventure. The choice of exploits is also purposefully comic, not least because in each case the outcome is itself predict-ably comic in a slapstick sort of way. Comic, too, is the tenacity of the friend in testing the forest-fire theory. The ten failures of his enterprise are a relief; the eleventh trial a scandal.The brisk statement of these facts almost reproduces the flat repetition of each abortive attempt and understates the final blaze of success. The positioning of the words *beaucoup trop bien*, indeed the very presence of the superfluous qualifiers, are semantic and stylistic indices of duplicity in the narration, of ironic discourse. In the same way, the parenthesis discussed above reveals itself as ironic when the narrator picks up a reference to the mockingly alliterative *moralistes et médecins qui prétendent tout savoir*, made earlier in the poem, and elaborates it into the diagnosis of *hysterical*. We should be alerted to this satire by the tempo and the tone, but are seduced into agreement with such a diagnosis before the narrator ironically corrects it by suggesting that those who think it satanic are altogether better informed. In this way, he achieves a critique of the medical profession and of those who would take a similar cut-and-dried view of human behaviour; in addition, he parodies the claimed superiority of the medical diagnosis by speaking in a deliberately elevated manner in this consciously formulated *exposé* of human behavioural patterns.

The same pseudo-scientific discourse is used to suggest the narrator's mathematical calculation of his gesture. This is first evident in his assessment of the glazier's difficulties in climbing the stairs: 'l'homme devait éprouver quelque peine à opérer son ascension et accrocher en maint endroit les angles de sa fragile marchandise'; and, then, in his aiming of the flower pot:

Je m'approchai du balcon et je me saisis d'un petit pot de fleurs, et quand l'homme reparut au débouché de la porte, je laissai tomber perpendiculairement mon engin de guerre sur le rebord postérieur de ses crochets; et le choc le renversant, il acheva de briser sous son dos toute sa pauvre fortune ambulatoire qui rendit le bruit éclatant d'un palais de cristal crevé par la foudre.   (*OC* i. 287)

The signs are charged with irony, the *perpendicular* dropping of the pot being an exaggeratedly calculated and almost farcical gesture reminiscent of a clown's foolery. The 'pot de fleurs' itself is linguistically and actually transposed into an *engin de guerre*, the general term for weaponry before the invention of the cannon, evoking both primitive forms of attack from a strategic height and a pun on Baudelaire's own creative armoury (Poe/ *Fleurs du mal*).[77] Such puns are themselves indicative of an otherness in the discursive mode and, like other forms of ironic discourse, require reconstruction. Like other intertextual references we have examined, this pun covertly supplies connections, and connections

---

[77] Jonathan Culler draws attention to this pun in an excellent article which examines Baudelaire's use of 'le calembour en action' in 'Baudelaire and Poe', *Zeitschrift für französische Sprache und Literatur*, 50 (1990), 69–70.

which are at the very heart of the text's functioning, since here Poe's 'imp of the perverse' finds the instrument of execution in a namesake. The punning in this poem also reveals a relationship of cause and effect which operates at a narrative level in this text, since there is a semantic connection between 'action d'éclat', the narrator's immediate movement towards the 'fenêtre' and his sighting of the 'vitrier'.[78] A retroactive retrieval of *une action d'éclat* is compounded by the *bruit éclatant* the glazier makes as he falls on his own wares. This self-destruction is, in itself, a cruel irony. The pot does not smash the glass directly, but forces the glazier down to ruin himself with the weight of his own body; a cruelty comparable with that of the donor in 'La Fausse Monnaie', albeit committed in all consciousness on this occasion. Further semantic indicators suggest ironic discourse. The mathematical *postérieur* as a positional epithet is almost superfluous, but since the glazier falls backwards, has the added connotation of the ridiculous and humiliating *tomber sur son postérieur*. The use of these terms removes the situation from an acceptable linguistic context, or style. The divergence in fact from the stylistic level appropriate to the subject or to ostensible meaning indicates not only the sort of generic shift we have seen elsewhere, but also an ironical manner, or what has been called 'Impersonal Irony'.[79] There is also the question of tempo in the narration. Delaying tactics, such as the accumulation of examples and digressive asides, serve to increase the suspense and the impact of the early pun.

In mixing discourses in this way, the narrative instance creates a tension between competing registers. These find their distillation in the final images of the poem, since the discursive edifice built by the prose poem is a modern (scientific) construction *par excellence*, a *palais de cristal*[80] destroyed by a bolt from the blue. It is definitively

---

[78] This point is made by Steve Murphy in '"Le Mauvais Vitrier" ou la crise du verre', *Romanic Review*, 82 3 (1990), 348.

[79] D. C. Muecke defines this as 'falling just short of the covert' and 'characterized by a recognizable ironical style or manner, the chief feature of which is a ponderously or excessively latinate vocabulary and a hackneyed urbanity'. *The Compass of Irony* (London: Methuen, 1980 [1969]), 76.

[80] Steve Murphy has linked this reference to the construction of the Crystal Palace for the London Exhibition of 1851 and sees it as an attack on bourgeois utilitarianism and material progress, '"Le Mauvais Vitrier" ou la crise du verre', 346. Dolf Oehler also makes this connection, and reads the 'palais de cristal' as a symbol for the Haussmannization of Paris in *Ein Hollensturz der Alten Welt. Zur Selbsterforschung der Moderne nach dem Juni 1848* (Frankfurt am Main: Suhrkamp, 1988), 296.

brought down to earth by the narrator's cries for 'la vie en beau', a vulgarization of the figurative 'la vie en rose', the first colour mentioned in the request for coloured panes. The competing discourses are Parisian sites as real as the topographical ones evoked in the poem—*palais de cristal* versus *quartiers pauvres*—and the *Je* in the poem clearly situates himself in the zone of social exclusion. In adopting and parodying the discourse of the other, however, he undermines the power of such scientific discourse and proposes the puns, shattering colloquialisms and *clichés filés* as a counter-discourse.[81]

The ultimate power of the pun is, however, present in the title of this poem, as we have already suggested. But that pun is not restricted only to the epithet *mauvais*, since there are also at least three *vitriers* implicated: the glazier (an ambiguous figure in the period),[82] the narrator as perpetrator of the crime against him (a window breaker),[83] and Arsène Houssaye (by association with his poem of the same title). In the detailed analysis of *lettre-dédicace*, the withering reference to Houssaye's model was noted as ironic and oppositional.[84] Baudelaire's duplicitous discourse with respect to Houssaye was well practised,[85] and it was accompanied by other

[81]   The term is here used in the sense given to it by Richard Terdiman as a discourse by which 'writers sought to project an alternative, liberating newness against the absorptive capacity of [. . .] established discourses'. *Discourse/Counter-Discourse*, 13. These notions of ideological subversiveness and the politics of discursive and generic experimentation will be explored in greater detail in the next chapter.

[82]   See Richard D. E. Burton's 'physiognomie du vitrier' in 'Destruction as Creation: "Le Mauvais Vitrier" and the Poetics and Politics of Violence', *Romanic Review*, 83 1 (Jan. 1992), 299–306.

[83]   In 19th-cent. French slang, the term *vitrier* applies to the *chasseurs de Vincennes*, the regiment which played a central role in the suppression of the 1848 insurrection and in that of 1851. The derivation of this slang term is uncertain. According to Alfred Delvau, it arose as a result of the resemblance between the soldiers' packs and the *sellette* of the *vitrier*. *Dictionnaire de la langue verte* (Paris: Dentu, 1867), 501. Since Delvau was a friend of Baudelaire's, he may well have known this definition and this might have influenced the insistence on the 'crochets' of the *vitrier*'s pack in the poem. Another derivation is offered by Hector France which refers particularly to the soldier's conduct in June 1848: 'au lieu de tirer sur les insurgés en fuite, ils s'amusèrent à casser à coups de fusil les carreaux des fenêtres', a conduct said to have inspired a popular song. *Dictionnaire de la langue verte: Archaïsmes, néologismes, locutions étrangères, patois* (Paris: Librairie du Progrès, 1907), 475. Both derivations are cited and discussed at some length by Steve Murphy, '"Le Mauvais Vitrier" ou la crise du verre', 342–6 and by Richard Burton, 'Destruction as Creation', 297–8.

[84]   See *OC* i. 1309-11. Claude Pichois has drawn attention to the irony of Baudelaire's reference to this as a model for his own prose poem, in particular to the verb *tenter* and to the ambiguity of the chosen adjective *désolantes*.

[85]   Cf. letter of Christmas 1861: 'Mon cher Houssaye, Vous, qui avez l'air inoccupé, savez

appropriate acts of giving in material rather than just ritualized forms.[86] Houssaye was a powerful figure, in literary and Second Empire politics. In so successfully dissimulating its criticism, Baudelaire's *double discours* takes issue not only with an individual, but with a literature and an ideology against which his own creativity is pitted. In this context, Baudelaire's conception of art as prostitution can be understood as a close encounter with the other which would jeopardize the creative integrity of the poet were it not for the fact that the nature of this encounter is marked by ironic separation. The examples cited of similar behaviour are set out as other, and each of the *vitriers* is other in relation to the next. In the *manière* adopted, separation from the engagement is assured. But it is a separation, a rupture indeed, which reveals a unitary identity which is *maître* both of the literary strategy (or at the head of the text) and of the discursive exchange system.

Seen in this context, the coda of 'Le Mauvais Vitrier' is revealing:

Ces plaisanteries nerveuses ne sont pas sans péril, et on peut souvent les payer cher. Mais qu'importe l'éternité de la damnation à qui a trouvé dans une seconde l'infini de la jouissance? (*OC* i. 287)

This *finale* operates a shift from the narrative to the moral plane whilst retaining the opposition at the core of each: an opposition between prank (pleasure) and retribution. In the first sentence, we remain firmly rooted in the real, not least because the outcome of this particular *plaisanterie nerveuse* points semiotically to the likely form that the retribution will take. The *gratuity* of the act is, therefore, called into question. The verb *payer* activates the implicit proverb 'qui casse les verres les paie'. By the same token, the perilous attack on the precursory 'model' has potential political (in the literary sense) and therefore financial implications for

si bien remplir une journée, trouvez quelques instants pour parcourir ce spécimen de poèmes en prose que je vous envoie. [. . .] Vous serez indulgent; car vous avez fait aussi quelques tentatives de ce genre, et vous savez combien c'est difficile' *C* ii. 207; and the letter of May 15 1862: 'J'ai encore le souvenir du ton général de mon article: je parlais du caractère pénétrant de vos poésies, des premières sensations que j'avais éprouvé en les lisant; j'insistais sur leur caractère mélodique et sur la sincérité absolue du ton. [. . .] Il me revient même que j'ai osé dire de vos poésies, ce que je pense, en somme, des poésies de quelques autres et des miennes surtout, à savoir, que tout en plaisant et en charmant, elles donnaient envie de les refaire—ce qui est à la fois éloge et critique.' *C* ii. 245.

[86] See Baudelaire's letter to Poulet-Malassis, *circa* 17 Jan. 1861, which includes a 'liste de distribution' for the 1861 edition of 'Les Fleurs du mal': 'Arsène Houssaye (directeur de La Presse) (très important) (avec *L'Artiste*, cela ferait un double).' *C* ii. 125.

Baudelaire. A further resonance of this proverbial retribution might be said to emerge by association with window-breaking and the punning on *vitrier*. Between 1848 and 1851, it is almost certain that some glaziers participated in the rioting. Window makers, in other words, might well have become window breakers. One writer of the period claims that they have

> une raison particulière pour se mêler aux émeutes, le proverbe '*qui casse les verres les paie*' n'étant pas toujours vrai. L'on assure que, réunis aux Vitriers ambulants, il se trouvent toujours au milieu des attroupements. Leurs armes favorites sont, dit-on, les pierres, et celles qu'ils dirigent contre les municipaux vont frapper les carreaux des maisons voisines... Heureuse maladresse![87]

By their dissimulation as other than simple glaziers, such window breakers were able to ply their trade very successfully without penalty. This aspect of the first half of the coda makes clear a shift from the temporal to the eternal. The higher moral discourse of the second sentence raises the question of final retribution (who sees?). By simultaneously evoking moral (religious) damnation and the notion of posterity or literary damnation, Baudelaire brings into question value systems of completely different orders, levels them in ironic rejection of both, and offers this prose poem as the ultimate in the framing, or window-making, of *jouissance*. In the duplicitous strategies employed here, Baudelaire emphasizes the energies of an irony which closely resembles *la blague*: 'l'indif-férenciation même, une posture d'indifférence qui mélangent les langages, les cibles, les sources, les références, les valeurs, qui neutralisent les différences elles-mêmes'.[88]

The examples examined in this chapter underline a systematic *dédoublement*—of the lyric persona, of the narrative instance, of semantic and generic categories—by means of which Baudelaire creates discursive and generic otherness. This other-ness challenges stable categories and, in the forms of opposition that it stages, makes apparent a unitary ideological identity albeit one that is sometimes in conflict with itself.[89] The patterns of con-

---

[87] Émile de la Bedollière, 'Le Vitrier ambulant', in *Les Industriels: Métiers et professions en France* (Paris: A. Pigoreau, 1842), 86–96.

[88] Philippe Hamon, *L'Ironie littéraire: Essai sur les formes de l'écriture oblique* (Paris: Hachette, 1996), 145.

[89] The lyrical poems are often those which stage such conflicts most dramatically, although Richard Burton has argued that 'Le Mauvais Vitrier' and 'Assommons les pau-

flict and antinomy, which have here been shown to be primarily literary (or *l'exigence esthétique*),[90] necessarily evoke the inflections of
equivalent socio-political opposition, not only because of the
explicitly social contradictions they explore, but also because of the
social situatedness of the discursive systems available. What
remains to be seen is the extent to which the discursive strategies
that we have seen in operation in the prose poems are explicitly
political in the way that some critics have claimed, as well as the
extent to which the dehierarchization of value systems and the
destructuring of principles of coherence by means of ironic discourse make it possible to speak of Baudelaire's prose poems as a
politics of form.

vres!' can be read as a political-ideological struggle taking place simultaneously within
Baudelaire and between him and certain orthodoxies or myths of both the Second Republic
and the Second Empire.' 'Destruction as Creation', 311–17. See also his analysis of
Baudelaire's shifting political positions in *Baudelaire and the Second Republic: Writing and
Revolution* (Oxford: Clarendon Press, 1991), 94–184.

[90] The term is from Julia Kristeva, *La Révolution du langage poétique: L'Avant-Garde à la
fin du dix-neuvième siècle* (Paris: Seuil, 1974), 617. This *exigence* is here specifically associated with Baudelaire and set in opposition to forms of social intervention.

3

The Politics of Form

L'homme d'esprit, celui qui ne s'accordera jamais avec personne, doit s'appliquer à aimer la conversation des imbéciles
et la lecture des mauvais livres. Il en tirera des jouissances
amères qui compenseront largement sa fatigue.

(*OC* i. 704)

THE window-breaking of 'Le Mauvais Vitrier' is emblematic of the
difficulties posed by the prose poem. In its elaborate punning, with
intra and intertextual resonances, this prose poem foregrounds discursive duplicity and holds in a tension textual and contextual referents. In reconstructing meanings from the discursive duplicities,
the reader is able to juxtapose, or superimpose, potential networks
of signification without the text apparently privileging one or other
of these. This means that the violent extravagance of the poet-
narrator can be read as an explosion of gratuitous and satanic
laughter,[1] as a politically motivated attack,[2] and as a textual assault
on the model(s) it contains and subverts.[3] This notion of the prose
poem as a form of textual assault can clearly be seen to embrace the

---

[1] The forms that such laughter might take are explored in Baudelaire's essays on the
comic, essays which will be explored in more detail in the next chapter. Several critics have
noted the black humour and satanic laughter of this particular poem. See, for example, J. A.
Hiddleston, *Baudelaire and Le Spleen de Paris*, 95–7; Margery Evans, *Baudelaire and
Intertextuality*, 92–3; and Richard Burton 'Destruction as Creation', 317–22.

[2] See Steve Murphy, '"Le Mauvais Vitrier" ou la crise du verre', 348–9, and Richard
Burton, 'Destruction as Creation', 297–322.

[3] Both of the previous interpretations necessarily contain some element of the aesthetic.
See Edward K. Kaplan, who sees this poem as 'a parable of *esthetic* experience' and as a
counter-model to Houssaye's 'bad writing, superficial sociology and trivial ethics',
Baudelaire's Prose Poems, 47–8.

two other meanings of the poem, not least because all three read-ings emerge from a figurality which the form of the prose poem then comes to embody. Punning on the word *vitrier* can be seen as a play on the instability of its meanings. In exactly the same way, the prose poem challenges relatively stable generic categories which depend on the reader's presupposition of a set of more or less established conventions. And, because of the social situated-ness of language and literature, the way these inflect moral and social conventions necessarily also comes into play, particularly in the nineteenth century.[4]

The word *play* is used advisedly for, as Ross Chambers has so persuasively argued, it is 'in the space of 'play' or 'leeway' that oppositionality arises'.[5] In discursive terms, this means that the speaker works with the linguistic (or literary) conventions and makes use of these for *other* purposes. Language invites play within the system: the speaker 'reçoit de la communauté qui l'intègre un 'système de langage' avec un 'mode d'emploi', mais aussi un mode de 'contre-emploi', qui permet en même temps d'affirmer la maîtrise du mode d'emploi'.[6] This notion of play, and of a system, can be applied to genre as well as discourse, and by working with and within the discourses of power, as we have already seen in rela-tion to Baudelaire's dedicatory and intertextual practices, the speaker is able to assert that mastery and, significantly and simul-taneously, to 'tap the strength of power to neutralize it'.[7]

Such play within the system (social and generic) can be seen to inscribe political and social comment, so that what Jameson refers to as 'the symbolic enactment of the social within the formal and aes-thetic'[8] opens the way for varied political and politicized readings. A great deal of critical energy has been deployed in mapping Baudelaire's political interests, and such studies have tended to

---

[4] See Richard Terdiman, who argues: 'The opposition between 'poetry' and 'prose' might have remained abstract, purely descriptive, and theoretically reversible in some imag-inary conjecture. But in the nineteenth century it carried a highly charged and irreducibly *normative* signification. It was implicated in a structure of power which was anything but abstract for those who experienced its determinations.' *Discourse/Counter-Discourse*, 274.

[5] *Room for Maneuver*, p. xiii. In connection with such *play* in punning, see also Walter Redfern, *Puns* (Oxford: Blackwell, 1984), 22–3.

[6] Marina Yaguello, *Alice au pays du langage* (Paris: Seuil, 1981), 141.

[7] See Jean-François Lyotard, 'On the Strength of the Weak', *Sémiotexte*, 3/2 (1978), 207.

[8] Fredric Jameson, *The Political Unconscious* (Ithaca, NY, and London: Cornell University Press, 1981) 76–7.

concentrate on the broadly socio-political themes of the prose poetry, and on various forms of life writing (elliptical entries in the *Journaux intimes*, or what we can learn of his activities from the testimonies of those who worked closely with the poet on journalistic projects or who were personal associates), all of which are carefully plotted against the poet's collaboration on political newspapers, his correspondence, and his critical and creative work. Illuminating though this can be, it takes us away from the crucial notion that the prose poem genre is itself 'visibly antagonistic',[9] independently of (and concomitantly with) any socio-political content (whether manifest or repressed) and any biographically documented activity.

The central question is one of influence. This influence can be read as political, and specifically socialist (Blanquist, Fourierist, Proudhonian, etc.),[10] or it can be read, as indeed Richard Terdiman reads it, as the influence of the dominant discourse on the artist:

> What haunts their [all the writers whose works compose the cultural canon of this period] efforts at expression is the fear that the dominant discursive apparatuses, the increasingly pervasive and powerful languages of everyday life which confront them, will block and swallow *all* efforts to differentiate. The fear is that distinction, even signified in the consecrated and previously protected medium of the esthetic object, may *already* have become impossible.[11]

More significantly still, however, it can be read as a desire to influence, to construct an 'influencing text',[12] so that *reading* the oppositional in texts becomes the production of the oppositional and may—in some projected future or in some unconscious way—bring about change in the system. This is especially true of the prose poetry genre and of duplicitous literary discourse, since both have a constitutively split identity which implies an appeal to be read otherwise. Genre, like irony, is, as we have seen, the production through reading of a meaning that is not said. This, it is true, offers sufficient play or leeway for political readings, but the dynamic of such readings is contextualization rather than textualization. It is the self-reflexivity, the self-referentiality of the prose

---

[9] Fredric Jameson, *The Political Unconscious*, 95.
[10] This is what Richard D. E. Burton traces in his account of Baudelaire's political life, *Baudelaire and the Second Republic*.   [11] *Discourse/Counter-Discourse*, 277.
[12] The term is Ross Chambers's, who defines influence as 'the effect of a (mediated) misreading that itself mediates a deflection of desire', *Room for Maneuver*, 236.

poem and its discursive strategies which is most powerfully oppo-sitional, since these engage the reader in the perception of other-ness without overt social confrontation.

Baudelaire's response to Houssaye's *Chanson du vitrier* in fact speaks volumes about his ironic strategy. Quite apart from the mention of this text in the *lettre-dédicace* and the implicit criticism of it in the title of Baudelaire's own poem, 'Le Mauvais Vitrier' reworks elements of Houssaye's text in a way which, to use Pichois's words, can only be 'accablante pour Houssaye' (*OC* i. 1311). Houssaye's *chanson*, a genre charged with populist intentions,[13] recounts an encounter between the first-person narra-tor and a glazier. The narrator is keen to underscore how isolated his gesture of charity is ('moi seul au milieu de tous ces passants') and promotes himself as an acute observer and listener, seeing and hearing the pitiful tone in the glazier's cry and immediately under-standing (for there is no direct exchange) that the man is hungry. Instead of offering him food, however, he offers *un verre*. The ground for a catastrophic outcome to this charitable gesture has already been prepared, for the glazier is, even before he takes a drink, 'appuyé sur le mur comme un homme ivre'. The effects of the offering are almost immediate: 'Je trinquai avec lui. Mais ses dents claquèrent sur le verre, et il s'évanouit—oui, madame, il s'é-vanouit;—ce qui lui causa un dégât de trois francs dix sous, la moitié de son capital! car je ne pus empêcher ses carreaux de casser' (*OC* i. 1310).

Rather than benevolence, what is offered is still greater wretchedness, since the loss of half the glazier's capital worsens his material situation. What is worse, the narrator pays for the glazier's drink—and is, therefore, responsible for his undoing—but is unable to take his charity further ('je n'osais plus rien offrir'). Were there a trace of irony, or black humour, in Houssaye's writing, we might read this as an elaborate 'morale de l'assommoir' and Baudelaire might have approved the escape into 'ivresse', however ephemeral it might prove to be. But Houssaye's poem, like his nar-rator's gesture, is offered in all seriousness—and worthlessness. Baudelaire's objections to this *chanson* are not overtly formulated, either in the *lettre-dédicace* or in the prose poem. But two statements

---

[13] See Richard D. E. Burton on the *chansonniers* of the period, in *Baudelaire and the Second Republic*, 185–219.

by Baudelaire elsewhere shed further light on his ironic reworking of the motif. The first is in *La Morale du joujou* where, in describing parents who do not like to give toys to their children, he makes a connection between poetry and charity:

Ce sont des personnes graves, excessivement graves, qui n'ont pas étudié la nature, et qui rendent généralement malheureux tous les gens qui les entourent. Je ne sais pourquoi je me figure qu'elles puent le protestantisme. Elles ne connaissent pas et ne permettent pas les moyens poétiques de passer le temps. Ce sont les mêmes gens qui donneraient volontiers un franc à un pauvre, à condition qu'il s'étouffât avec du pain, et lui refuseront toujours deux sous pour se désaltérer au cabaret. Quand je pense à une certaine classe de personnes ultra-raisonnables et antipoétiques par qui j'ai tant souffert, je sens toujours la haine pincer et agiter mes nerfs.   (*OC* i. 586)

The link between the child and the poet is consistently made by Baudelaire, and here this is elaborated into a link between poetry, wine, and charity. The connections with Houssaye, echoed in the *lettre-dédicace*, will be clear, as will the tokenism of his offered *verre/vers*. The relationship between power and poetry implicates Houssaye in a set of relationships—all triangular—involving Baudelaire and the glazier figure which, in their turn, evoke the power relations of contemporary social and literary politics.

The narrative of Houssaye's *chanson* maps unironically on to his gift of the text and, rather like the *moralité* of 'La Fausse Monnaie', emphasizes the importance of self-awareness. This, indeed, is the second Baudelairean statement about charity evoked by Houssaye's poem and Baudelaire's reworking of it in 'Le Mauvais Vitrier': 'On n'est jamais excusable d'être méchant, mais il y a quelque mérite à savoir qu'on l'est; et le plus irréparable des vices est de faire le mal par bêtise' (*OC* i. 324). This coda, in its stylistic and rhetorical patterning, could be said to be equivalent to the equally sententious one that concludes 'Le Mauvais Vitrier'. It is a coda appropriate to the narrative and to the fact that Houssaye (and his narrator) are 'excessivement graves' in their execution of it. In Baudelaire's prose poem, in an ironic inversion, it may be the narrator who is 'ivre', but at least he offers his 'pot' with 'la conscience dans le mal'.

The false fraternity of Houssaye's *chanson* is, then, played out as a lack of fraternity in Baudelaire's prose poem, as a deliberate act of violence against the glazier. This act can be seen as mere *folie* ('the imp of the perverse'). It has been read, too, as anger with the *peuple*'s lack of resistance to the coup of 1851 and with their lack of idealism (*vitres magiques*).[14] And it has been read as violence against the self (the poet, too, is the *vitrier*), the ultimate gesture of self-destruction arising out of powerlessness.[15] The play or leeway in the text allows for all of these interpretations of the attack on the glazier, but always at the forefront and most compelling as the 'raison d'être' of the violence is the attack on Houssaye's *vitrier*. The figure is, in other words, little more than a title (twice over); a figure activated by the titling (as, indeed, the title designates Houssaye himself), and one which is more active and meaningful as title, designating as it does an attack on power, poor literary quality, false charity, and pseudo-humanitarian rhetoric. In using the title of another, and in engaging parodically with the text it designates, Baudelaire is able to place the politics of this prose poem centre-stage.

That politics is textualized, first and foremost, in its relations with the intertext (what Terdiman terms 'corrosive intertextuality'),[16] but this does not preclude, indeed it includes, a contextualized struggle of a similar nature. Baudelaire's relationship with Arsène Houssaye has already been documented, but certain aspects of that relationship are worth recalling here.[17] Houssaye was an extremely powerful figure in cultural politics,[18] but he was also a laughing stock among more serious artists of the period, including Baudelaire.[19] He had political aspirations, and had clashed publicly with Baudelaire in this context in 1848.[20] In many ways, then, Houssaye represented all that genuine artists found to despise about the political-ideological order of the Second Empire. He was, in short, the embodiment of cultural power and of the 'faux

---

[14] This is Burton's view in 'Destruction as Creation', 318–19.

[15] This is Jérôme Thélot's reading of the poem in *Baudelaire: Violence et Poésie*, 100–11.

[16] This is the title of the second part of his study. *Discourse/Counter-Discourse*, 147 ff.

[17] See Richard D. E. Burton, 'Destruction as Creation', 306–11.

[18] He was, for example, editor of a number of publications including *L'Artiste* and *La Presse* and chief administrator/director of the Comédie Française 1849–56.

[19] He was the brunt of literary jokes and spoofs such as the 'Parodie de Sapho' which appeared in *le Corsaire Satan* on 24 Nov. 1845 (*OC* ii. 4–5). He was also despised by writers such as Flaubert, Zola, and the Goncourts. See Burton for examples of such literary testimonials, 'Destruction as Creation', 308–11.

[20] For an account of this, see Claude Pichois and Jean Ziegler, *Baudelaire* (Paris: Julliard, 1987), 262.

artiste',[21] influential, important and feared, flattered and despised throughout the period of Baudelaire's career. Steve Murphy has suggested that Houssaye is the archetypal bourgeois and that 'Le Mauvais Vitrier', as an attack on this group, indicates Baudelaire's belief that:

après la monarchie bourgeoise de Louis-Philippe, après la deuxième République non moins bourgeoise, le second Empire, tout aussi indéfectiblement bourgeois, ne proposera pas non plus de solution aux problèmes du pauvre. Houssaye, en tant que Bourgeois, choisira toujours l'ordre, puisque quel que soit le nom de l'ordre politique qui gouverne, ce sera un ordre bourgeois. Baudelaire, dégoûté encore davantage par les rêves trompeurs des faux progressistes que par la répression ouverte, trouvait dans l'hypocrite prose de Houssaye une formidable incitation à la violence textuelle.[22]

There can be no doubt that Baudelaire was, in relation to Houssaye, in the same situation of powerlessness and intellectual superiority he felt himself in with respect to the bourgeois. Indeed, the premiss of 'Aux Bourgeois', the dedicatory opening of the *Salon de 1846*, is precisely the incontrovertible fact of bourgeois power and influence with respect to the arts. The debate still rages as to the extent of the duplicities of this text, despite general agreement on the presence of some irony,[23] but in those much-cited opening lines, 'vous êtes la majorité — nombre et intelligence; — donc vous êtes la force, — qui est la justice' (*OC* ii. 415), there seems to be exactly the same approach and tone as we have observed in Baudelaire's overtures to Houssaye. There is, in fact, a great deal of Baudelaire's notion of *la lettre d'un fat* in both texts: 'mélange d'emphase sincère et d'emphase ironique' (*OC* i. 372). If such a

---

[21] See Jules et Edmond de Goncourt, *Journal*, ed. Robert Ricatte (Paris: Fasquelle & Flammarion, 1956) for examples of this: e.g. Houssaye is described there as 'fourré dans toutes les antichambres du pouvoir et chantant, de huit jours en huit jours, les réceptions de la princesse Mathilde et de Nieuwerkerke' (i. 934, 12 June 1861) and as having, in art and in literature 'le goût du faux' (iv. 982, 14 May 1896). Both are cited by Burton, 'Destruction as Creation', 308.

[22] Murphy, '"Le Mauvais Vitrier" ou la crise du verre', 348–9.

[23] For a range of views, see *Le Salon de 1846*, ed. David Kelley (Oxford: Clarendon Press, 1975); Dolf Oehler, *Pariser Bilder I (1830–1848): Antibourgeoise Ästhetik bei Baudelaire, Daumier und Heine* (Frankfurt am Main: Suhrkamp, 1979), 56–71; Annie Becq, 'Baudelaire et "l'amour de l'art": La Dédicace "aux bourgeois" du *Salon de 1846*', *Romantisme*, 17–18 (1977); Ross Chambers, 'Baudelaire's Dedicatory Practice', 16; Gretchen Van Slyke, 'Les Épiciers au musée: Baudelaire et l'artiste bourgeois', *Romantisme*, 55 (1987), 55–66; and Richard D. E. Burton, *Baudelaire and the Second Republic*, 32–40.

'mélange d'emphase' does not entirely oppose the artist to the bourgeois, and indeed counters that cliché, what does emerge from the duplicitous discursive modes of the *Salon* is a clear attack on the *artiste-bourgeois*. Baudelaire makes this clear in *Le Musée du Bazar Bonne Nouvelle*:

Nous avons entendu maintes fois de jeunes artistes se plaindre du bourgeois, et le représenter comme l'ennemi de toute chose grande et belle. — Il y a là une idée fausse qu'il est temps de relever. Il est une chose mille fois plus dangereuse que le bourgeois, c'est l'artiste-bourgeois, qui a été créé pour s'interposer entre le public et le génie; il les cache l'un à l'autre. Le bourgeois qui a peu de notions scientifiques va où le pousse la grande voix de l'artiste-bourgeois. — Si on supprimait celui-ci, l'épicier porterait E. Delacroix en triomphe.   (*OC* ii. 414)

From the commonplace of an opposition between the bourgeois and the artist, Baudelaire passes to the commonplace in art. Such commonplace art and artists are supported by the the Académie and the State and, in their turn, accommodate (à la Horace Vernet) *poncifs* and platitudes. These are the 'tableaux de salle à manger' (*OC* ii. 396), the works which are 'd'une universalité désespérante' (*OC* ii. 488). It was in this close relationship between *bourgeois-artiste* and *bourgeois-consommateur* that Baudelaire saw a threatening sterility and, worse, a lack of distinction (including the notion implicit therein of differentiation). In interposing himself between the public and what Baudelaire terms *le génie*, the *artiste-bourgeois* 'facilite par trop l'initiation culturelle de la bourgeoisie en lui offrant de l'art adapté aux capacités du grand public'.[24]

Such works in the plastic arts are the equivalent of those produced by Houssaye in the literary realm, described by the Goncourts as 'ces bonheurs-du-jour en bois de rose, de la confection des ouvriers du faubourg Saint-Antoine, avec des plaques de Sèvres peintes par des enlumineuses de gravures de parfumerie'.[25] What is more, they represent the sort of art which might very well have constituted Houssaye's own collection, itself described, again

---

[24] Gretchen Van Slyke, 'Les Épiciers au musée', 62.

[25] Goncourt, *Journal*, i. 699 (2 Feb. 1860). Cf. Baudelaire, 'Pourquoi la sculpture est ennuyeuse', *Salon de 1846*: 'Du reste, il ne faut pas croire que ces gens-là manquent de science. Ils sont érudits comme des vaudevillistes et des académiciens; ils mettent à contribution toutes les époques et tous les genres; ils ont approfondi toutes les écoles. Ils transformeraient volontiers les tombeaux de Saint-Denis en boîtes à cigares ou à cachemires, et tous les bronzes florentins en pièces de deux sous.' (*OC* ii. 488–9).

by the Goncourts, as 'peut-être unique comme ne contenant pas un seul tableau vrai'.[26] The antagonisms present in the textual violence directed against the bourgeois artist and Houssaye are identical. Indeed, Baudelaire himself makes it clear that this antagonism has a basis in literature as well as in art when, in writing of Vernet, he states:

Je hais cet homme parce que ses tableaux ne sont point de la peinture, mais une masturbation agile et fréquente, une irritation de l'épiderme français;—comme je hais tel autre grand homme dont l'austère hypocrisie a rêvé le consulat et qui n'a récompensé le peuple de son amour que par de mauvais vers,—des vers qui ne sont pas de la poésie, des vers bistournés et mal construits, pleins de barbarismes et de solécismes, mais aussi de civisme et de patriotisme.   (*OC* ii. 470)

Baudelaire here compares Vernet to the poet Béranger, but there is in the expression 'tel autre grand homme' a more generalizing impulse which communicates the proliferation of the phenomenon. But these are (relatively) weak targets and duplicitous discursive tactics are in proportion to the power and influence of their subject/object. This accounts for the ambiguities of 'Aux Bourgeois' and the *lettre-dédicace* compared with the straightforwardness of the attack on the *artiste-bourgeois* and a poet such as Béranger.

As we have already noted with respect to the *lettre-dédicace* to Houssaye, dedications textualize certain elements relating to the context of production and 'make available the contextual *meaningfulness* the text may claim as a social and historical entity'.[27] In entitling the opening section of the *Salon de 1846* 'Aux Bourgeois', Baudelaire simultaneously designates a dedicatee and a subjectmatter. Most significantly, however, the nature of that designation determines the 'aux Bourgeois' text as an object of reading rather than an address.[28] This reproduces the same discursive *dédoublement* that we have noted in the *lettre-dédicace*. Reading brings into play the textualized otherness which is, in fact, realized by the otherness of the reading instance.[29] The otherness of the critical voice

[26]   Goncourt *Journal*, iv. 982 (14 May 1896).
[27]   Ross Chambers, 'Baudelaire's Dedicatory Practice', 6.   [28]   Ibid. 11–12.
[29]   Cf. Ross Chambers: 'Through the mediation of reading (as its "other"), the *text* is produced as ironic, duplicitous, split—as endlessly other than itself': *Room for Maneuver*, 173. The otherness produced by the reading is located in the recognition and recuperation of

is located in the negation of the artist–bourgeois polarization,[30] in apparent self-contradiction and in textual irony. Critical posture makes separation from the groups and individuals evoked possible and serves to generate, through discursive separation, a sense of artistic isolation.

The ambiguities of this aesthetic ideology elaborated in this way by Baudelaire raise important questions about his tactics in the *Petits Poèmes en prose*. In fact, with respect to both Houssaye and the *artiste-bourgeois*, Baudelaire is opposing a particular form of bourgeois consumerism. He is setting out his artistic stall as fundamentally *other* and appealing, both ironically (parodically/counter-discursively) and unironically (from within the dominant discourse), for distinction to be recognized. Whereas in 1846 there may have been some idealism on his part which would allow for a more open appeal (an attempt at dialogue with the bourgeois), by the 1860s, indeed long before that, the opposition was more covert and more intense.

The discussion of contextualized opposition in the prose poems has so far centred on Baudelaire's relationship with Houssaye but, as the encounters of 'A une heure du matin' so unequivocally suggest (*OC* i. 288), relationships such as this are a daily socio-economic ritual for the artist and the Pharisaic prayer, itself a form of oppositional discourse, is a genuine *cri de cœur* for distinction: 'Seigneur mon Dieu! accordez-moi la grâce de produire quelques beaux vers qui me prouvent à moi-même que je ne suis pas le dernier des hommes, que je ne suis pas inférieur à ceux que je méprise!' Once the work is produced, it has to be *placed*. Baudelaire's scorn for other artists and literary directors of all kinds is clear in this prose poem which is an attack on the 'vilaines canailles' (*OC* i. 742).[31] In 1848 and in the 1860s, Baudelaire is

---

these disjunctions, in which case difference is in distance from the text's object (ideological or historical) and a form of complicity.

[30] See the *Salon de 1845*: 'à propos de cette impertinente appelation, le *bourgeois*, nous déclarons que nous ne partageons nullement les préjugés de nos grands confrères artistiques qui se sont évertués depuis plusieurs années à jeter l'anathème sur cet être inoffensif' (*OC* ii. 351).

[31] See alo entry XXVIII of *Mon cœur mis à nu*: 'Les directeurs de journaux, François, Buloz, Houssaye, Rouy, Girardin, Texier, de Calonne, Solar, Turgan, Dalloz. — Liste de canailles. Solar en tête' (*OC* i. 694). With respect to other artists, see entry XXXII: 'Les autres hommes de lettres sont, pour la plupart, de vils piocheurs très ignorants' (*OC* i. 697).

consistent in his scorn for the *directeur de journal*.[32] In 1848, in the *Salut public*, for example, he attacks Girardin with a stinging irony:

Il faut rendre justice à qui de droit, maintenant que nous avons le temps.

Le citoyen Girardin se conduit admirablement. Au milieu du trouble, du désordre qui envahissent momentanément toutes choses publiques et particulières, le journal du citoyen Girardin est mieux fait que jamais. Cette habileté connue, cette aptitude rapide et universelle, cette énergie excessive, tout cela tourne au profit de la République.

Tous les jours les questions importantes et actuelles sont mâchées dans La Presse.

Le citoyen Girardin prend pour devise: UNE IDÉE PAR JOUR!

Son journal, jusqu'à présent, dit ce que tout le monde pense.

(*OC* ii. 1037)

It is a form of attack which is not reserved exclusively for *La Presse*, since in the *Salon de 1859* Baudelaire is moved to write in not dissimilar terms of *Le Siècle*, describing the newspaper as a 'vaste monument de la niaiserie' which is 'penché vers l'avenir comme la tour de Pise': 'Il y a un brave journal où chacun sait tout et parle de tout, où chaque rédacteur, universel et encyclopédique comme les citoyens de la vieille Rome, peut enseigner tour à tour politique, religion, économie, beaux-arts, philosophie, littérature' (*OC* ii. 653).

Both of these cited examples underscore the universalizing nature of the publications, a universalization which eroded political *partiality* and, with the newspaper's new bias towards advertising and commercialism, turned readers into consumers.[33] It was Girardin's *La Presse* which initiated these changes, with the result that

the discourse of political *opinion* which had been a primary content of the traditional paper tended to be replaced by a flattened 'objective' discourse of *information*. For the first time, a newspaper began to conceive its audience not exclusively but *inclusively*, to project its mode of intervention in

---

[32] The *Journaux intimes* offer a number of instances of such sniping. Baudelaire's attitude to Girardin does not, for example, change. See entry II of *Mon cœur mis à nu*: 'Les sottises de Girardin' (*OC* i. 676–7), and with respect to *Le Siècle*, the 'Canevas des "Lettres d'un atrabilaire"' (*OC* ii. 781–2).

[33] In the sense both of consuming the press and the products it advertised. The relationship between the two has been persuasively argued by Richard Terdiman. See *Discourse/Counter-Discourse*, ch. 2, 'Newspaper Culture: Institutions of Discourse; Discourse of Institutions', esp. pp. 117–35.

the broader social text not as confrontation and challenge but as *co-optation*. With *La Presse* the valuation of conscious social and political difference was radically inverted.[34]

In addition to this, as Terdiman has shown, the drive towards commercialism actually shaped the newspaper, due to the economics governing the disposition of space. In this way the newspaper would become the equivalent of the department store, deliberately unorganized in order to expose the consumer to a range of unrelated articles and advertisements, since 'in both cases the manipulations of space and time oblige the person who would navigate within them to submit to a logic which is incomprehensible in terms of anything the subject can know or feel'.[35]

This raises important questions about the place of the literary in the institutionalized dominant discourse of such daily newspapers. Baudelaire's *lettre-dédicace*, as we have seen, foregrounds the seductive strategies necessary to bring the placement of the prose poems about. Alongside the ironic flattery of Houssaye, then literary editor at *La Presse*, we find Baudelaire voicing the pragmatic concerns of the newspaper editor. The text can be cut anywhere, thus playing to the supreme logic of the newspaper layout. This, Baudelaire says, represents 'admirables commodités' for all concerned, deliberately echoing through this choice of words the other sorts of commodities which the newspaper routinely promotes. In explicitly rejecting the 'fil interminable d'une intrigue superflue', Baudelaire challenges something on which the success (the circulation) of *La Presse* was increased, the *roman-feuilleton*, whilst indicating a move away from such organic literary discourse (which did not appeal to less literary readers) into the realms of a literature adapted to the newspapers (and the society's) 'unorganic confusion' or 'constructed disorder'.[36]

Like the *magasin de nouveautés*, then, Baudelaire proposes something different which might catch the eye of the reader, a collection of *bagatelles* (*C* ii. 493) or *babioles* (*C* ii. 473): commodities which tempt the consumer and which, despite the lack of suspense, are

---

[34] Ibid. 131.   [35] Ibid. 137.

[36] *La Presse*, and *Le Siècle*, developed the *roman-feuilleton* as a sales strategy in 1836, but such literary serials did not appeal to the average petit-bourgeois reader as much as bloody *faits divers* or the discourse of *l'information*. See Terdiman, *Discourse/Counter-Discourse*, 134–7.

nevertheless organized to create desire. The prose poems were indeed a commodity which sold well *en journal*, at least at first.[37] Later, however, as Baudelaire explains to his mother, they were to become a discontinued line, owing to lack of (consumer) interest: 'C'est tout simplement parce que mes poèmes ennuyaient tout le monde (m'a dit le directeur du journal) qu'on les a interrompus' (*C* ii. 350).The flattery of Houssaye and Baudelaire's comparison of his own efforts with those of the literary editor of *La Presse* suggest a further reaching representation to the bourgeois consumer. In placing the poems in *La Presse*, Baudelaire was making use of an instrument which represented the interests of the dominant group (and, indeed, those of the Government), but one which was nevertheless *tolérant* and which could be persuaded to print almost anything.[38] Publication in this newspaper guaranteed a large circulation and, therefore, offered an opportunity, for Baudelaire as for advertisers, to reach a wider consuming public. But it was not just the dominance of the medium which attracted Baudelaire, it was its dominant discourse, its interests and its idiom, for these *nouvelles à la main*, these *choses vues* or *scènes* were all part of a journalisic repertoire which was ripe for parody.

'La confection de ces petites babioles' was not a task Baudelaire undertook lightly and it was one which caused him immense creative difficulty.[39] The combination of the trivial with (more covert) literary and ideological concerns required 'une grande concentration d'esprit' (*C* ii. 473), in the sense both of focusing his mind and distilling his wit. The prose poems had to be entertaining ('assez vivants pour vous plaire et vous amuser') and they therefore needed to be written with humour. For Baudelaire, this meant conjuring up a sort of feel-good spirit, an uncharacteristic self-satisfaction which modulates the tone: 'Faire cent bagatelles

---

[37] See Baudelaire's correspondence. 'Je voudrais trouver un moyen de tirer des *Poèmes en prose* la totalité approximative de leur valeur (en journal)' (*C* ii. 213); 'Les *Poèmes en prose* passeront aussi à *La Presse*. 1000 francs!' (*OC* ii. 237); 'les *Poèmes en prose* marchent' (*C* ii. 259). There is, furthermore, a letter from Hetzel to Houssaye which links the success of Baudelaire's prose poems to the singularity of the talent behind them. In this letter Hetzel praises Baudelaire as 'le prosateur le plus original' and says: 'il n'y a pas de journal qui puisse faire attendre cet étrange classique des choses qui ne sont pas classiques; publie-le donc *vite* — mais *vite* — et mets-moi à même de le lire. Les vrais singuliers sont rares!' Cited in Baudelaire, *Petits Poèmes en prose (Le Spleen de Paris)*, ed. H. Lemaître, p. III.

[38] See Goncourt, *Journal*, i. 933–4 (12 June 1861). Cited by Richard Burton, 'Destruction as Creation', 310.

[39] 'Ah! ce *Spleen*, quelles colères, et quel labeur il m'a causés!' (*C* ii. 627).

laborieuses qui exigent une bonne humeur constante (bonne humeur nécessaire même pour traiter les sujets tristes), une excitation bizarre qui a besoin de spectacles, de foules, de musique, de réverbères même, voilà ce que j'ai voulu faire' (*C* ii. 493). In striving to represent a range of journalistic subjects and to strike a tone evocative of the medium used to promote the prose poem, Baudelaire was engaged in reproducing (or re/citing)[40] the dominant discourse. In writing to Houssaye that these 'elucubrations en prose' (*C* ii. 223) remain far from his 'mystérieux et brillant modèle', Baudelaire is emphasizing, as indeed he does in the *lettre-dédicace*, the *singulière différence* from the model. The notion of the work's singularity is crucial, for it underlines the unicity of the individual creativity as well as the exceptional quality of what is being offered. Singularity and model are posited as opposites, and this is all the more true in a situation where the model is the *quotidien*, the prosaic: banality.[41] Baudelaire's conception of the singularity of this work recurs in a letter to Madame Aupick; in the same letter, indeed, where the poems are described as *petites babioles*: 'j'espère que je réussirai à produire un ouvrage singulier, plus volontaire, du moins, que *Les Fleurs du mal*, où j'associerai l'effrayant avec le bouffon, et même la tendresse avec la haine' (*C* ii. 473). Here the opposites are cast quite clearly and what emerges is a rudimentary definition of humorous oppositionality, the individual pitted against the collective: the isolation of the ironic voice in its confrontations with the collective 'nous' of the bourgeoisie. In engaging with the journalistic model in this way, Baudelaire is clearly involved in a parody of the *quotidien*,[42] so that

[40] The term is Terdiman's. For a definition, see *Discourse/Counter-Discourse*, 68–70.

[41] The antonyms of *singulier* are given, in the *Petit Robert*, as 'collectif, banal, commun, général, ordinaire, normal, fréquent, régulier. Pluriel.' It is no coincidence that the term *quotidien* refers both to everydayness and the daily newspaper, nor that the term prosaic mutates in this period, acquiring a meaning of banality and the platitudinous.

[42] See Margaret A. Rose, where parody is defined as 'first imitating and then changing either, and sometimes both, the "form" and "content", or style and subject-matter, or syntax and meaning of another work, or, most simply, its vocabulary. In addition to, and at the same time as the preceding, most successful parodies may be said to reproduce from the comic incongruity between the original and its parody some comic, amusing, or humorous effect, which, together with the changes made by the parodist to the original by the rewriting of the old text, or juxtaposition of it with the new text in which it is embedded, may act as "signals" of the parodic nature of the parody work for its reader.' *Parody: Ancient, Modern and Post-Modern* (Cambridge: Cambridge University Press, 1995), 45. See also, for theorization of the *quotidien*, Michel de Certeau, Luce Giard, and Pierre Mayol, *L'Invention du quotidien* (Paris: 10/18, 1980), 2 vols.

the duplicitous discursive strategies of the *lettre-dédicace* and the intertextual parody of 'Le Mauvais Vitrier' single Houssaye out, but amidst a universalized opposition of the same nature to the institutionalized discourse of the *quotidien*.

The singling out of Houssaye in this universalized parody reveals another important distinction; that between citation of attributed text and the textualization of a more generalized social discourse. Indeed, it is in the intersection of the two, in what one might call the corruptive influence of the bourgeois appropriation of culture, that the parody often seems to work best. Misquotation, particularly, activates this sort of parody, since the change brought about by the error results in a new text which circulates more freely than the attributed original. Baudelaire engages in this very process when, in writing of *Le Siècle* in his *Salon de 1859*, he introduces the attack (already cited) with a misquotation from Molière's *Le Misanthrope*, punning on the newspaper's title: 'Le mauvais goût du siècle en cela me fait peur' (*OC* ii. 653). Baudelaire's deliberate misquotation, which replaces *méchant* with *mauvais*, is generated by his quoting of what he takes to be an editor's note: '*comme n'étant plus du goût de ce siècle*'. This is, then, italicized as citation and effectively attributed as an unwitting pun which, when brought into contact with the ironic citation of Molière, also reveals, by mixing the discourse of cultivation, the idiocy of the editorial.

This is a tactic to which Baudelaire resorts in the prose poems, quoting and misquoting Vauvenargues in 'Les Veuves', Buffon in 'Les Bons Chiens', and La Bruyère and Pascal in 'La Solitude'.[43] 'La Solitude' presents us with a *gazetier philanthrope* who, although an atheist, cites the *paroles des Pères de l'Église*, apparently unaware ('comme tous les incrédules') of the contradiction in his argument. The narrator's attack on him and his kind is clear:

Il est certain qu'un bavard, dont le suprême plaisir consiste à parler du haut d'une chaire ou d'une tribune, risquerait fort de devenir fou furieux dans l'île de Robinson. Je n'exige pas de mon gazetier les courageuses vertus de Crusoé, mais je demande qu'il ne décrète pas d'accusation les amoureux de la solitude et du mystère. [. . .]
Je désire surtout que mon maudit gazetier me laisse m'amuser à ma

---

[43] For a discussion of these examples, see J. A. Hiddleston, 'Fusée, maxim and common-place in Baudelaire', *Modern Language Review*, 80/3 (July 1985), 565–6.

guise. 'Vous n'éprouvez donc jamais — me dit-il, avec un ton de nez très apostolique, — le besoin de partager vos jouissances?' Voyez-vous le subtil envieux! Il sait que je dédaigne les siennes et il vient s'insinuer dans les miennes, le hideux trouble-fête. (*OC* i. 313)

Here Baudelaire plays upon the synonyms *gazetier/bavard* ('personne qui aime à colporter des nouvelles') and the relationship between such circulation and isolation. The narrator has no time for the feigned wisdom of those who moralize or judge others and he differentiates his voice by directly citing the *gazetier*, whose stupidity can speak for itself, although the narrator imputes a *ton de nez*, just to be sure. He does not condemn what motivates the *gazetier* to speak, and so, apparently, he upholds the freedom to do as one pleases in an egalitarian society: 'Je ne les plains pas parce que je devine que leurs effusions oratoires leur procurent des voluptés égales à celles que d'autres tirent du silence et du recueillement; mais je les méprise' (*OC* i. 313).

The narrator's quotation of La Bruyère and Pascal in response to the citation of the Bible, counters the argument by parodically employing the same citational technique. Quotation for quotation, solitude is set in opposition to the benefits of the crowd:

'Ce grand malheur de ne' pouvoir être seul!.....' dit quelque part La Bruyère, comme pour faire honte à tous ceux qui courent s'oublier dans la foule, craignant sans doute de ne pouvoir se supporter eux-mêmes.

'Presque tous nos malheurs nous viennent de n'avoir pas su rester dans notre chambre', dit un autre sage, Pascal, je crois, rappelant ainsi dans la cellule du recueillement tous ces affolés qui cherchent le bonheur dans le mouvement et dans une prostitution que je pourrais appeler fraternitaire, si je voulais parler la belle langue de mon siècle. (*OC* i. 314)

Baudelaire is clearly playing with this idea of the citational. It has been suggested that, in misquoting one of Pascal's most often quoted thoughts, 'a commonplace recognizable by any schoolboy', Baudelaire's motive is 'to play down the wisdom of a great man and [. . .] to cast doubt upon the validity of such acknowledged truths which, before the complexities of real life, appear as glib and facile as an "idée reçue"'.[44] Not only does the narrator misquote Pascal, he casts doubt upon the authorship of the words with the attribution sandwiched as it is between the indeterminate

---

[44] Hiddleston, ibid. 565–6.

'un autre sage' and the uncertain 'je crois'. Likewise, the La Bruyère quotation is vaguely referenced as being 'dit quelque part'. These uncertainties bring into question the identity of the utterance and undermine the erudition of the narrator, while at the same time eroding the difference between the authority of the citation and the gloss which follows. Such recourse to quotation reflects the user's recognition of textual authority in a general sense, but it is the widespread peddling of acquired culture which emphasizes its status as a received idea. The more celebrated the quotation, the more common it will be in everyday exchange, and the more it is quoted, the more susceptible it will be to inexact or inappropriate reproduction by the next user. The suggestion here, it seems, is that those who rush off to lose themselves in the company of others cannot tolerate their own company and that Pascal is not so wise for wanting to invite them all into the *cellule du recueillement*, for then the very benefit of the silent retreat would be lost to noisome turbulence.

The final paragraph of this poem is, in fact, almost self-destructive in its citational dynamic. The quotation from Pascal is followed by narrative subversion of the truth it offers and by some conversational hesitation, which shifts the discourse into an entirely different register. The scorn for those who cannot be alone then comes across more clearly, with this need for others defined as prostitution, but the citational impulse continues with the italicized epithet *fraternitaire* attached to prostitution in a relationship which clearly undermines the republican ideal. The poem concludes with a clear statement of the parodic engagement with what the narrator refers to as 'la belle langue de mon siècle'. This coinage, itself pseudo-citational, sets in parodic contrast to the quotations from the seventeenth- and eighteenth-century moralists, the language spoken in the *gazettes*, and by those who read them, the language of pontification, the repetition of received ideas, be they from the Church, newspapers, or literature.

The citation of moralists of this kind, and their universal truths, allows for a generic slippage towards the unattributed truism, towards the textualizing of these forms which already constitute a generally circulating ideological discourse. These attributed maxims are, in other words, the genuine (literary) form of a discursive phenomenon which, once adopted and corrupted by generalized discursive habit, would, in this period, be compiled in a *sottisier* or

in the *Dictionnaire des idées reçues*.[45] In textualizing the phenomenon in this way, Baudelaire undoes the difference between literary
and socially prevalent forms of the moralist tradition to show the
banality of the latter as an ideological and discursive threat. At the
same time, however, in emphasizing the citational impulse by *parodically* quoting or italicizing, Baudelaire introduces an irony
which differentiates his meaning in citing from the meaning of the
discourse cited. The *singulier* thus makes itself heard, despite being
embedded in the clichéd or, as Baudelaire puts it, 'Créer un poncif,
c'est le génie. Je dois créer un poncif' (*OC* i. 662).

The parody of discursive patterns arises, if only in part, as a
result of generic parody, where the model is *la chose vue* or *le
tableau*, either an anecdote by means of which a moral can be prof-
fered (such as 'La Fausse Monnaie', 'La Corde', 'Le Joujou du
pauvre', etc.) or a narrative illustration of a proverb or moral (such
as 'chacun sa chimère', 'les auréoles changent souvent de tête', or
'la vie en beau'). There is, in other words, a clear linguistic relationship between the two. Just as Baudelaire adopts linguistic *lieux
communs*, so he adapts the generic commonplace of such newspaper and publishing items, which themselves often adopt a
clichéd discourse. It has been pointed out that Baudelaire makes
use of literary clichés, such as the banality which links old age and
infancy ('Le Désespoir de la vieille'),[46] and that he regularly makes
use of commonplaces such as the observer following a passer-by
and the *examen de conscience*.[47] Indeed, Graham Robb, has shown
that even poems like 'Un cheval de race' and 'Le Vieux
Saltimbanque', which one might think specific to Baudelaire, have
their precedents in already existing newspaper items.[48] All of this
contributes to the effect of the citational, itself often used for parodic purposes by connecting and contrasting the parodic text with
its model. The varied forms which suggest pre-existing discursive
patterns are brought into contact with other linguistic formations
which contrast with them. In this way, too, the broad range of the

---

[45] For a wider discussion of this discursive phenomenon in Flaubert and Marx, see
Terdiman, *Discourse/Counter-Discourse*, 209–26.

[46] Hiddleston, 'Fusée, maxim and commonplace in Baudelaire', 568.

[47] Graham Robb 'Les Origines journalistiques de la prose poétique de Baudelaire', *Lettres
romanes*, 44 (1990), 15–25. Robb offers a wide range of examples of the phenomenon discussed here and offers suggestive and stimulating ways of thinking about Baudelaire's prose
poems and journalistic expression.   [48] Ibid. 17.

newspapers' content is reproduced both in the structure of the prose poems and in a similar aesthetic of the unexpected and the unconnected which finds its linguistic equivalent in the clash of styles: 'le calembour, un mélange d'actualité et d'allusions classiques, de lieux communs et de maximes déformées, d'argot et de préciosité, d'expressions familières et de mots savants'.[49]

In assimilating prevalent discursive forms into his own prose, Baudelaire is able to include the cited forms as a distinct code, ironizing it, criticizing it, and effectively refunctioning it,[50] whilst all the time that prevalent discourse acts as a mask for this counter-discursive assault of naive imitation—and still more naive reception—of other texts. In *Hygiène*, which seems to be an attempt to formulate a modus operandi, Baudelaire writes 'Sois toujours poète, même en prose. Grand style (rien de plus beau que le lieu commun)' (*OC* i. 670).[51] Baudelaire clarifies his passion for such commonplaces by stating, in *Fusées*, that their interest lies in the original depths, hidden by our familiarity with their formulation: 'Profondeur immense de pensée dans les locutions vulgaires, trous creusés par des générations de fourmis' (*OC* i. 650).[52] This particular 'fusée'[53] uses the form to talk about itself, using structures reminiscent of the popular saying to present itself as both seductively accessible and highly suggestive; stressing both its fixity as a linguistic unity and its ability to reinvent itself, or be reinvented, so

---

[49] Graham Robb 'Les Origines journalistiques de la prose poétique de Baudelaire', *Lettres romanes*, 44 (1990), 22.

[50] The term is used to describe the new literary functions gained by a text in the context of the parody. See Margaret Rose, *Parody*, 29 n. 9.

[51] The prevalence of sententious forms in *Hygiène* is reinforced by the heading on the second *feuillet* 'Hygiène. Conduite. Morale' (*OC* i. 669). Dating from the same period as many of the prose poems (*c.*1862), it is possible to see in these *feuillets* an extension of the experimentation with (and parody of) citational and sententious forms and their intersection with the *quotidien*.

[52] Cf. a similar statement in the *Salon de 1859*: 'existe-t-il [. . .] quelque chose de plus charmant, de plus fertile et d'une nature plus positivement *excitante* que le lieu commun?' (*OC* ii. 608–9). The idea of the *fourmis* is also worth considering in its relation with the popular image of the city as a 'fourmilière humaine' and in the way in which it symbolizes *petitesse*.

[53] The term itself is interesting. Claude Pichois notes that, along with *Mon cœur mis à nu*, Baudelaire may have borrowed the title from Poe's *Marginalia*, where the term 'sky rocketing' is used. He also notes, however, that the term is recorded in French in the Littré and exemplified with a sentence from a letter from Voltaire, who speaks of 'des fusées volantes qui crèvent sur la tête des sots' (*OC* i. 1473). Most meanings attributed to the word arise as a result of form and the term seems appropriate for the concision and explosive impact of these sententious items.

that 'the triteness of the 'time-honoured' precept hides a capacity to astonish, to *faire rêver*'.[54] As has been shown, Baudelaire uses these forms for a range of different purposes: to introduce a clash of register, covertly to underpin an anecdote, or to figure the relationship of the poet to his art.[55] In all three respects, what is significant is the relationship of the form to its content and the way in which the form itself might be charged with (parodic) content. In his re-citation of existing commonplaces and maxims, the cliché is reworked, so that Baudelaire is able both to parody usage and to capitalize on it in order both to seduce the reader and to communicate the higher truth it can convey. The same is true of the aphoristic forms of his own making—what have been called his 'aphorismes-abîmes'[56]—which, although they do not exist as figures of generalized exchange, nevertheless reproduce and, most importantly, lay bare the structure and functioning of the figure itself. In this respect, such clichés are the linguistic equivalent of the prose poem genre. On the one hand, like poetic figures, the cliché depends on the exploitation of a rarefied *langage imagé*, on the other it represents the already said. It is concision and concentration (distillation of form and essence), but it is made commonplace by its circulation.

At one and the same time, then, Baudelaire's use of the commonplace reproduces the prosaic and expresses a distance from such prosaism; in its strangeness, it is poetically provocative; it is, to borrow Riffaterre's terms, both *usée* and *inusable*.[57] On the one hand it seems to uphold the stability of the discourse and the world in which it circulates, while on the other it undermines this stability with paradox and 'une morale désagréable'. It privileges the language of the Other only to reveal the citing subject's otherness. This phenomenon has been described by Ruth Amossy and Elisheva Rosen:

Si l'ironie est la dérision qui confirme l'impuissance, elle constitue toutefois le lieu de la prise de conscience. Similairement, l' 'esthétisation'

---

[54] Graham Robb, 'The Poetics of the Commonplace in *Les Fleurs du Mal*', *Modern Language Review*, 86/1 (Jan. 1991), 57.

[55] These are the categories proposed by J. A, Hiddleston, 'Fusée, maxim and commonplace in Baudelaire', 568. See also Hiddleston, *Baudelaire and Le Spleen de Paris*, 35–56.

[56] Hiddleston, *Baudelaire and Le Spleen de Paris*, 51.

[57] Cited in R. Amossy and E. Rosen, *Les Discours du cliché* (Paris: CDU & SEDES, 1982), 139.

— rythme, renouvellement des expressions toutes faites, effets de surprise—a pour visée, non de rétablir le triomphe du Créateur, mais —
tout au moins — de poser une prise de distance délibérée par rapport à
la parole commune (ou au vertige de la désignation) où se figent et se
désintègrent les significations.[58]

In using commonplaces to establish the otherness of art,
Baudelaire does not use the figure only for discursive subversion,
he uses it to be ideologically subversive, since any questioning of
the form necessarily implies an interrogation of its truth,[59] and
challenges from within the hegemony of such discourse.

Nowhere is this more deliberately played out than in those
poems where Baudelaire engages most directly with socio-
ideological issues, in 'Les Yeux des pauvres' and 'Assommons les
pauvres!', in 'Le Joujou du pauvre' and 'Le Gâteau'. Each of these
poems makes calculated use of citational forms, and particularly of
maxims. These are problematic texts precisely because of the
réversibilité these discursive forms allow, so that what presents itself
as potentially hegemonic text is susceptible, both in its discursive
and ideological patterns, to all sorts of inversion.

In 'Les Yeux des pauvres', Baudelaire sets up a symbolic division
between the narrator and his companion and the poor. On one side
of the symbolic barrier there is the street, on the other there is the
clean brightness and elaborate adornment of the new café:

Le café étincelait. Le gaz, lui-même, y déployait toute l'ardeur d'un
début, et éclairait de toutes ses forces les murs aveuglants de blancheur,
les nappes éblouissantes des miroirs, les ors des baguettes et des
corniches, les pages aux joues rebondies traînés par les chiens en laisse, les
dames riant au faucon perché sur leur poing, les nymphes et les déesses
portant sur leurs têtes des fruits, des pâtés et du gibier, les Hébès et les
Ganymèdes présentant à bras tendus la petite amphore à bavaroises ou
l'obélisque bicolore des glaces panachées; toute l'histoire et toute la
mythologie mises au service de la goinfrerie.   (*OC* i. 318).

The café's interior is rich in splendour and bourgeois poor taste,
glowing with bright colours, representing the figures of Classical

---

[58]   *Les Discours du cliché* (Paris: CDU & SEDES, 1982), 82.
[59]   Cf. Amossy and Rosen: 'à partir du moment où un fonctionnement discursif se trouve
désigné dans sa stéréotypie, il apparaît comme une organisation verbale figée reproduisant
une vision conventionnelle des choses. En fait, chaque langage est un système artificiel
opérant une mise en forme du réel', *Les Discours du cliché*, 114.

antiquity serving the grotesque appetites of the middle classes, well-fed and gay *convives*. The mirrors and white tablecloths are the crisp cleanliness of a world that can afford every luxury and are echoed in the crisp sterility of the relationship which occupies the centre of this sumptuous stage. The narrator and his companion do not enter the café, but decide to sit outside as part of a different (but equivalent) spectacle, that of the *boulevard neuf*. As a result, the opposition presented by the gaze of the poor is unmediated by protective barriers and occurs in the street. The narrator reads the three gazes and uses a citational technique to attribute meaning:

Les yeux du père disaient: 'Que c'est beau! que c'est beau! on dirait que tout l'or du pauvre monde est venu se porter sur ces murs.' — Les yeux du petit garçon: 'Que c'est beau! que c'est beau! mais c'est une maison où peuvent seuls entrer les gens qui ne sont pas comme nous.' — Quand aux yeux du plus petit, ils étaient trop fascinés pour exprimer autre chose qu'une joie stupide et profonde. (*OC* i. 318)

In expressing the desiring gaze as speech ('les yeux *disaient*'), there would seem to be a desire to distinguish the narrative voice, which quotes, from the sentimentality of this reading of the gaze.[60] Indeed, we see the same technique applied to the companion, whose own expression, when confronted with the family, reproduces an element of the unspoken expression of the small boy. She says: 'Ces gens-là me sont insupportables avec leurs yeux ouverts comme les portes cochères! Ne pourriez-vous pas prier le maître du café de la éloigner d'ici?' Within this citation is the popular expression for the wide-eyed gaze which symbolically anchors the discourse in a particular class and generalizes the objection, as well as evoking another door through which the poor child is unlikely to pass.

In the double-edged representation of both other parties, the narrator is isolated. He assimilates himself into the projected glance, aware simultaneously of both what he perceives and how he is perceived (indeed, how he suddenly sees himself). His glance is met with the same barrier within class as the elder child's is across the social divisions for, far from being irritated by the three on-lookers, as is his partner, the narrator claims to be moved: 'Non seulement j'étais attendri par cette famille d'yeux, mais je me

---

[60] Monroe offers a Marxist reading of this citational technique, arguing that since the poor 'cannot present themselves, they must be represented', *A Poverty of Objects*, 111.

sentais un peu honteux de nos verres et de nos carafes plus grands que notre soif' (*OC* i. 319). In this heavily ironic reworking of the familiar saying 'avoir les yeux plus grands que le ventre', there is a semblance of guilt and compassion which the narrator seeks to alleviate by sharing the troubled moment in a glance of understanding with the woman, but the half-hearted measure of it is felt in the revealing irony of '*un peu* honteux' (my emphasis). The woman's failure to understand or to respond to this situation and, in fact, her expression of the opposite pole of reception of this experience, become the central issue of the poem: the selfish enclosure of romantic love and the failure of reciprocity.

This prose poem begins with an apostrophe: 'Ah! Vous voulez savoir pourquoi je vous hais aujourd'hui' which, although it is directed at 'le plus bel exemple d'imperméabilité féminine', necessarily implicates the reader because of the delay in establishing the identity of the *vous*. In the case of the mistress, the hatred springs from her failure to meet the clichéd ideal of absolute communion which is at the centre of the poem:

Nous nous étions bien promis que toutes nos pensées nous seraient communes à l'un et à l'autre, et que nos deux âmes désormais n'en feraient plus qu'une; — un rêve *qui n'a rien d'original, après tout*, si ce n'est que, rêvé par tous les hommes, il n'a été réalisé par aucun.   (*OC* i. 318, my emphasis)

The same failure is true of *tous les hommes* with respect to benevolent social relationships. The inability to establish such a communion is meaningful in the context both of sexual and class difference, for the woman does not understand the narrator any more than she does the significance of the spectacle in which she is both participant and observer. The sexual problematic of this poem is entwined with the social one which, like a *mise en abyme*, stands within the lovers' conflict. The relationship between narrator and loved one becomes the central problem, as the former averts his gaze from the social spectacle which troubles his humanitarian sentiment to seek refuge in the eyes of his companion. This plays out another familiar locution associated with the gaze and the enclosure of love: 'n'avoir d'yeux que pour quelqu'un'. This desiring gaze fails, too, since it is not reciprocated. Instead, the sought after communion of that gaze is corrupted by the eyes that stare in from outside the relationship. As Prendergast has noted 'the poor do not protest, they disrupt by virtue of their sheer presence'.[61] By organizing the looking in the way he does, Baudelaire is able not only to parody the emptiness of all sentiment in this poem and the emptiness of all expression, he is also able to parody the bourgeois fear of the gaze, to show it as contaminating and humiliating.

The parodies of this poem are multiple, then. The café represents culture as a gaudy commodity 'au service de la goinfrerie'. The citational technique which translates the meaning of the gaze is, as has been suggested, an 'autocritique of French Romantic poetry's aestheticization of poverty, the poeticization of a prosaïc world'.[62] It is an attack on sentimentality in the representation of wretched misery, the 'tristesses des pauvres' that Baudelaire associates with Hugo (*OC* ii. 136). And it may even be a direct parody of the sort of popular form mentioned later in the poem, the *chanson*, and specifically of Pierre Dupont's *Chant des ouvriers*.[63] In his 1851 essay on Dupont, Baudelaire's praise for this *chant*, if it is to be taken at face value, demonstrates marked populist sympathies:

Quand j'entendis cet admirable cri de douleur et de mélancolie, [. . .] je fus ébloui et attendri. Il y avait tant d'années que nous attendions un peu de poésie forte et vraie! Il est impossible, à quelque parti qu'on appartienne, de quelques préjugés qu'on ait été nourri, de ne pas être touché du spectacle de cette multitude maladive respirant la poussière des ateliers, avalant du coton, s'imprégnant de céruse, de mercure et de tous les poisons nécessaires à la création des chefs-d'œuvre, dormant dans la vermine, au fond des quartiers où les vertus les plus humbles et les plus grandes nichent à côté des vices les plus endurcis et des vomissements du bagne; de cette multitude soupirante et languissante à qui *la terre doit ses merveilles*; qui sent *un sang vermeil et impétueux couler dans ses veines*, qui jette un long regard chargé de tristesse sur le soleil et l'ombre des grands parcs, et qui, pour suffisante consolation et réconfort, répète à tue-tête son refrain sauveur: *Aimons-nous!* (*OC* ii. 31)

But this prose poem, first published in 1862, reveals more complex emotions in the face of the 'spectacle' (compassion, guilt,

---

[61] *Paris and the Nineteenth Century*, 38.   [62] Ibid. 111.

[63] One stanza in particular might be said to reflect the expression attributed to the father's gaze: 'Quel fruit tirons-nous des labeurs | Qui courbent nos maigres échines? | Où vont les flots de nos sueurs? | Nous ne sommes que des machines. | Nos Babels montent jusqu'au ciel, | La terre nous doit ses merveilles; | Dès qu'ils ont fini le miel, | Le maître chasse les abeilles', *Le Chant des ouvriers* (Paris: L'Auteur, 1848).

repugnance, and fear) and, notwithstanding the influence Baudelaire's friendship with Dupont may have had on his poetry in the period of the Second Republic,[64] this prose poem seems to parody his earlier critical response to the intertext with a reworking of the refrain 'Aimons-nous!' There is, at very least, an ironizing of the narrator of 'Les Yeux des pauvres!', of his commonplace and self-indulgent expression of compassion and of his hopeless desire to find in his female companion's gaze '[s]a pensée'. The conclusion of the poem, a moral message secured by the formal attributes of the maxim, maintains the parody of truisms: 'Tant il est difficile de s'entendre, mon cher ange, et tant la pensée est incommunicable, même entre gens qui s'aiment!' But by offering here a maxim of his own creation, an 'aphorisme-abîme', Baudelaire does not clarify the moral in the distillation of moral form. Rather, he uses the form to emphasize the ambiguities.

This practice is further complicated in 'Assommons les pauvres!', another poem where the cited maxim 'Celui-là seul est l'égal d'un autre, qui le prouve, et celui-là seul est digne de liberté, qui sait la conquérir'[65] forms the ambiguous truth at the heart of the poem, and a truth which here has to be tested by praxis. The narrator feels this truth forming in his mind, and the way in which he describes it is significant: 'Il m'avait semblé que je sentais, confiné au fond de mon intellect, le germe obscure d'une idée supérieure à toutes les formules de bonne femme dont j'avais récemment parcouru le dictionnaire. Mais ce n'était que l'idée d'une idée, quelque chose d'infiniment vague' (*OC* i. 358). The context in which such truisms flourish is, then, the domain of the popular saying, the earthy wisdom of old wives, complemented by principles catalogued for easy reference, perhaps reminiscent of Flaubert's *Dictionnaire des idées reçues*.[66] The implication is surely that there is fundamentally no difference between these 'formules de bonne femme' and the 'mauvaises lectures' which are so comically described in the opening paragraph of the poem: 'des livres

---

[64] See Burton, *Baudelaire and the Second Republic*, 185–219, where he argues that Baudelaire draws upon the same matrix of theme and image as Dupont's songs.

[65] Cf. a similar maxim which occurs in the *Journaux intimes*: 'En politique, le vrai saint est celui qui fouette et tue le peuple pour le bien du peuple', *Fusées* (*OC* i. 655).

[66] Pichois notes that the manuscript shows a scoring out of the alternative *catalogue* in preference for *dictionnaire* (*OC* i. 1349). In fact, the alternatives reflect Flaubert's designations: *Dictionnaire des idées reçues* ou 'le catalogue des idées chics'.

où il est traité de l'art de rendre les peuples heureux, sages et riches en vingt-quatre heures', 'toutes les élucubrations de tous ces entre-preneurs de bonheur public, — de ceux qui conseillent à tous les pauvres de se faire esclaves, et de ceux qui leur persuadent qu'ils sont tous des rois dé trônés'. Modern theories of how to achieve social equality are undermined by their equation not only with less scientific truths, but also with other circulating discourses which are here patently challenged. Even the look on the beggar's face is interpreted in the light of such theories as 'un de ces regards inoubliables qui culbuteraient les trônes, si l'esprit remuait la matière, et l'œil du magnétiseur faisait mûrir les raisins'. In refer-ring to works which were 'à la mode dans ce temps-là', a period clearly situated in the past as 1848, the narrator insists on tempo-ral as well as philosophical distance from the cited discourses. Whether Baudelaire was convinced by such utopian theories in 1848 and afterwards has prompted a great deal of discussion and a large number of politicized readings of this poem.[67] What is cer-tain is that the poem's citational tactic addresses Proudhon, who, as is well known, was, in the early manuscripts of the poem, mentioned by name and in the form of an interrogation to respond: 'Qu'en dis-tu, Citoyen Proudhon?'

Richard Burton has cogently argued that 'Assommons les pauvres!' is 'shot through from beginning to end with concepts drawn from Proudhonian discourse' and that 'the text is at one and the same time a celebration, parody and subversion of that dis-course'.[68] Like Baudelaire's other anecdotal extrapolations of max-ims or sayings ('Le Mauvais Vitrier', for example), this poem describes an absurd playing out of the moral lesson. The narrator applies, in purely physical terms, a lesson in standing up for one-self. The beggar returns the beating, but doubles the punishment. This parody of mutualism results in the narrator's submission: 'Monsieur, *vous êtes mon égal!*' (*OC* i. 359). But here the concept, defined by Proudhon as an 'idée de mutualité, réciprocité, échange, JUSTICE, substituée à celles d'autorité, communauté ou charité',[69] is far from equal, since the narrator comes off worse (in both

---

[67] See Burton, *Baudelaire and the Second Republic*, 324–52, where he not only offers a close reading of this poem, but also an overview of critical response to it.

[68] Ibid. 329 ff.

[69] This is the Proudhonian concept singled out as being the political intertext of the poem. Cited in Burton, *Baudelaire and the Second Republic*, 346.

physical and economic terms) and still engages in what is fundamentally an act of charity. The division is upheld by the hegemony of the philosophy which prompts and concludes the beating. The authority of the narrator, which supersedes that of the utopian tracts he has read, reasserts itself after the beating he receives at the hands of the beggar. The narrator takes the credit for the moral lesson; he closes the discussion; he expects to be *obeyed* (*OC* i. 359). The equality is, in other words, a sham. Proudhon argues that only in separation from the other can such equality be attained by the 'peuple' and the narrator glimpses this in the look of hatred which he reads as a good sign for the future (using the cliché—here italicized—'*de bon augure*'). What occurs here, though, is rather the separation of the narrator, both from the model he parodies and the discourse he cites, so that the poem, like a shaggy-dog story, seems to offer an elaborate *blague* whose punchline labours the joke: 'souvenez-vous, si vous êtes réellement philanthrope, qu'il faut appliquer à tous vos confrères, quand ils vous demanderont l'aumône, la théorie que j'ai eu la *douleur* d'essayer sur votre dos' (*OC* i, 359).

This sort of italicizing is the textualization of distance and difference. It enables words to be activated according to their context. Here *douleur* refers to the philosophical anguish of having to apply the lesson, to the masochism of it, and to the injuries sustained in its application. At the same time, however, the word triggers a proverb which works against the articulation of such things: 'Les grandes douleurs sont muettes'. The revitalization of words in the prose poems is all the more marked if the italics mark a departure (or deviation) from an accepted normal usage or if they reinvest the word with meaning lost by usage. Barbara Johnson has shown how this reinvestment is achieved in 'Le Galant Tireur', where the expression 'tuer le temps' is revived, reinterpreted, reapplied, indeed even rewritten as '*tuer* le Temps'. In typographically indicating emphasis, Baudelaire 'rend à une simple figure d'usage la force de frappe que l'habitude linguistique lui avait ôtée. L'italique redonne au verbe "tuer" toute sa littéralité, accentuée par son association avec l'activité de *tirer*.'[70] This, indeed, is a technique of emphasis Baudelaire uses elsewhere. The Devil in 'Le Joueur généreux', for example, draws attention to the reclaiming of a

---

[70] Johnson, *Défigurations du langage poétique*, 84.

familiar expression, not only by italicizing it, but by pausing to draw attention to his use of it: 'Je veux que vous gardiez de moi un bon souvenir, et vous prouver que Moi, dont on dit tant de mal, je suis quelque fois *bon diable*, pour me servir d'une de vos locutions vulgaires' (*OC* i. 327). On other occasions, italics are used to pinpoint a linguistic joke, a double entendre, such as the 'expérience physiologique d'un interêt *capital*' of 'Une Mort héroïque' (*OC* i. 320) or 'tous les *lunatiques*' in 'Les Bienfaits de la lune' (*OC* i. 342). Such italicizing, as we saw in 'Assommons les pauvres!', emphasizes the double-coded nature of parodic discourse and is also capable of suggesting the citational.[71] This technique is also used to highlight politically charged terms such as *fraternitaire, gâteau*, and *égale* in 'Le Gâteau' and 'Le Joujou du pauvre', drawing attention to them and requiring that they be re-examined in the light of the prose poem's exploitation of them.

'Le Gâteau', in fact, exemplifies the oppositionality implicit in the citational and combines this with a thematized representation of conflict. The setting is pastoral, rather than urban, and this allows for a parody of the Romantic rural idyll, as well as further exploring the *multitude/solitude topos* that operates through citation in 'La Solitude'. The harmony of the landscape is reflected in the soul of the narrator, and the accumulation of details contributing to this clichéd literary model[72] eventually undermines the integrity of the meditation and makes the text's otherness readable. The style shifts with the more prosaic, 'bref', which moves the poem from citation of a literary model (which has gone on too long) to the philosophical contention which frames the poem, here attributed to a particular sort of newspaper: 'j'en étais venu à ne plus trouver si ridicules les journaux qui prétendent que l'homme est né bon' (*OC* i. 297–8). The literary–journalistic mix is further enhanced by this attribution to the press of a philosophy which also has clear literary origins, notably in Rousseau:

Les méditations y prennent je ne sais quel caractère grand et sublime, proportionné aux objets qui vous frappent, je ne sais quelle volupté tranquille qui n'a rien d'âcre et de sensuel. Il semble qu'en s'élevant

---

[71] See Antoine Compagnon, *La Seconde Main*, 9–91 and, especially with respect to this point, pp. 40–2.

[72] Hiddleston argues this case persuasively in *Baudelaire and Le Spleen de Paris*, 75–7, where he reads the opening passage as a cliché and a parody of Lamartine's 'L'Isolement' and 'Le Vallon'.

au-dessus du séjour des hommes on y laisse tous les sentiments bas et terrestres, et qu'à mesure qu'on s'approche des régions éthérées l'âme contracte quelque chose de leur inaltérable pureté.[73]

The intertextual reference to Rousseau is no less present for being unattributed, but Baudelaire creates from it an object of greater parody by associating the ideology with a certain kind of journalism.

The shift in tone becomes still more evident with the turning away from matters of the spirit to the lunch box, both of which are associated with the 'ascension'. What ensues brings about the conflict which is at the centre of the poem. He sits down to eat his lunch in the idyllic rural landscape, sharing a fragment of it with a small boy who suddenly appears. When a second boy appears, a battle ensues for the scrap of food; a battle which could have been averted with another slice of bread. The intrusion of brutality contrasts with the landscape and establishes a tension between the spiritual and social worlds already implicit in the parody of different discourses. There is a profound sense of Romantic naivety which is troubled by these ironic indicators, so that the narrator becomes the shocked instigator of a scene which he pretends neither to expect nor to understand. In this, there is an element of feigned innocence which liberates him from any political responsibility or intention, but which nevertheless reflects badly upon the Romantic aestheticization of surroundings and spirit, particularly when these are brought into direct contact with the same idealization of human nature and of the poor.

In effect, the naivety and the detached manner in which this narrative is recounted serve only to emphasize the self-irony and to arouse the suspicions of the reader. The detachment of the narrator is, then, both that of the narrator-observer and that of the parodist. The silent observation of the battle which occurs between the boys for the one slice of bread constitutes the same sort of ideological exemplification and establishes the same social barriers that are physically in place in 'Le Joujou du pauvre' and 'Les Yeux des pauvres'. In a sense, the narrator transgresses this barrier in offering the first slice of bread, but his failure to offer a

---

[73] *La Nouvelle Héloïse, Œuvres complètes* (Éditions de la Pléiade; Paris: Gallimard, 1964), ii. 78. Cited by Barbara Johnson, *Défigurations*, 78. See pp. 77–82 for her reading of this poem.

second comes from the urge to tempt and observe which is in operation with the penny playthings in 'Le Joujou'. Here the curiosity is opportunistic, rather than calculated, but the experiment is identical, as can be seen when passages from the two poems are directly compared:

Lentement il se rapprocha, ne quittant pas des yeux l'objet de sa convoitise; puis, happant le morceau avec sa main, se recula vivement, comme s'il eût craint que mon offre ne fût pas sincère ou que je m'en repentisse déjà.   ('Le Gâteau', *OC* i. 298)

Vous verrez leurs yeux s'agrandir démesurément. D'abord, ils n'oseront pas prendre; ils douteront de leur bonheur. Puis leurs mains agripperont vivement le cadeau, et ils s'enfuiront comme font les chats qui vont manger loin de vous le morceau que vous leur avez donné, ayant appris à se défier de l'homme.   ('Le Joujou du pauvre', *OC* i. 304)

The experiment and the reactions of the subject under examination are the same. The children approach the desired object with animal-like interest and caution, afraid that the hand which offers might be withdrawn in a moment of human caprice. After all, even in a moment of absolute harmony, the narrator succumbs to the temptation of putting man's essential goodness to the test. His satanic curiosity gets the better of him; he watches with no desire to put an end to the fight. It is a fight which benefits neither child. The token slice of bread is reduced to crumbs in the struggle, a material symbol of ideological differences, for as the narrator remarks: 'il n'y avait plus, à vrai dire, aucun sujet de bataille' (*OC* i. 299).

The narrator's final analysis of the scene returns us to the way in which the thematization of conflict is consonant with discursive difference.

Ce spectacle m'avait embrumé le paysage, et la joie calme où s'ébaudissait mon âme avant d'avoir vu ces petits hommes avait totalement disparu; j'en restai triste assez longtemps, me répétant sans cesse: 'Il y a donc un pays superbe où le pain s'appelle du *gâteau*, friandise si rare qu'elle suffit pour engendrer une guerre parfaitement fratricide!'   (*OC* i. 299)

Suddenly the landscape has lost its charm, just as in 'Les Yeux des pauvres' the beauty of the day spent with a loved one is lost in an instant. It is a loss of personal idealism, or worse, an egocentric desire for the troubles of the world to disappear so that tranquillity can reign. The Romantic cliché which associates childhood with purity is subverted, not least in the reference to the boys as *petits hommes*, microcosmic symbols of human evil, of all that is uncontrolled, of greedy selfishness and protection of property. The poet's reaction to the struggle is to feel *triste*, a rather weak expression of the emotions one might expect from a man so transported by his natural surroundings and spirituality. And his lost idealism is expressed with bitter irony in the narrator's citational presentation of his concluding thoughts, 'un pays superbe' evoking 'L'Invitation au voyage', although here the *cocagne* is replaced by *gâteau*, re-citing the boy's word and almost imperceptibly fusing it with his own text. Finally, the journey suggested by the opening lines 'je voyageais' establishes the land as unmistakably that of post-revolutionary France where the poor are an emblem for the bold claims of 'liberté, égalité, fraternité'. Such equality means, in 'Le Gâteau' at least, that each has the right to fight for food; and fraternity is all too quickly transmuted into a 'guerre parfaitement fratricide'.

In 'Le Joujou du pauvre', also an exploration of class distinction and fraternity, Baudelaire sets up a similar narrative situation. In this poem, however, the narrator plays a more deliberate role, engaging in an experiment which purports to be 'un divertissement innocent'. But immediately he subverts this claim with the exclamation of a platitude: 'Il y a si peu d'amusements qui ne soient pas coupables!' (*OC* i. 304). A symbolic stage set is established which is reinforced by the divisions implicit in the narrator's language; divisions separating wealthy children from the 'enfants de la médiocrité ou de la pauvreté'. On one side of the 'barreaux symboliques' is luxury, sunshine, whiteness, 'un enfant beau et frais', 'coquetterie', grass, and 'un joujou splendide'. On the other, a 'marmot-paria', filth, the 'répugnante patine de la misère', blackness ('fuligineux' being associated with 'la suie'), nettles and thistles, and a rat, a *joujou* 'tiré de la vie elle-même'. A human barrier is established in the very presentation of the poor child as some kind of *untouchable*, as transgressing the boundaries of the 'civilized' body. In contrast, the wealthy child is a familiar sight, one of 'ces enfants-là'. The 'barreaux symboliques' are simply a reinforcement of a division already established, at the narrative level as much as at the receptive one, with readers bringing their class prejudices to a text which seems, at every level, to confirm them. Every level, that is, except one: the rich child's avid interest in, and his unhesitating attraction to, the the poor one. The 'joujou splendide', with all its unplayable-with finery, lies abandoned on the grass, as the centre of interest is focused on the rat. This raises a number of questions. The lack of division, of discrimination, between the children signifies at one level the profound innocence of their relationships, since it is only socialization which erects the symbolic bars of class differ- ence. It is possible, therefore, to read the boys' communion as a positive sign that greater understanding between the classes is possible in the right conditions.

The conditions here, however, are quite unequal. The rich child is cooped up within the château walls and it is *through* the fence, across barriers determined by an elite adult world, that the poor boy, upon the *grande route*, proudly shows his living plaything, also in a 'boîte grillée', to his newfound friend, exciting the rat to enter- tain him. Jonathan Monroe sees this deliberate excitement as 'sug- gestive of the energy that might be released by the proletariat in the class struggle'.[74] But this overstates the analogies, for there is never any suggestion that the rat *will* be released, nor indeed that the wealthy child is not secure in his enclosed environment. Rather than an act of aggression against the wealthy child, what the poor boy's agitation of the imprisoned rat suggests is a reflection of the same kind of oppression as that perpetrated by the ruling class against the proletariat. Beneath the patina of misery, then, there is visible to the 'œil du connaisseur' not only the same beauty, but also the same oppressive tendencies. Class conflict is both upheld (by the very manner in which the story is recounted) and appar- ently undone (by the shared laughter): 'Et les deux enfants se riaient l'un à l'autre fraternellement, avec des dents d'une *égale* blancheur' (*OC* i. 305). But this closing line, with its italicization, is a parody of the revolutionary slogan. The final lines do not resolve, as a non-parodic reading of them would do, the divisions entrenched in the narration. Rather, they uphold them, socially and textually, by revealing facile over-simplifications of social equality for what they are. With this concluding statement, Baudelaire parodies all those texts in which, from the standpoint of inequality, a satisfactory outcome is celebrated. Houssaye's *Vitrier* is amongst these, for it is not difficult to read in the conclusion of

---

[74] Monroe, *A Poverty of Objects*, 108.

that poem—'la fraternité avait trinqué avec lui'—a model for the sort of superficial utopianism and undistinguished writing against which such parody (a far from innocent 'divertissement') is to be read. What is more, in uniting the children in the focus of their interest (and their desiring gaze), Baudelaire emphasizes not only their shared animality but also the attraction of the 'low'.

It has been suggested that the wealthy child's plaything, 'un joujou splendide, aussi frais que son maître, verni, doré, vêtu d'une robe pourpre, et couvert de plumets et de verroteries', represents the aristocratic form of classical French poetry, not least in its alliterations and its diction; a poetry like Gautier's, 'majestueuse et précieuse', 'comme les personnes de cour en grande toilette', with 'la pourpre régulière et symétrique d'une rime plus exacte' (*OC* ii. 126).[75] The counter-model to this is the prosaic, a language 'tiré de la vie elle-même', 'la médiocrité', or worse, 'la pauvreté'. The poor child's plaything, which complements his filth, characterizes moral and cultural depravity, the cultivation of the animal rather than the intellectual or aesthetic, the dangers of the street and its vulgar commodities which contaminate.[76]

Implicit in this poem, then, is this notion of contagion and contamination (carried by the rat) which, just as the gaze in 'Les Yeux des pauvres' corrupts the idyll, transgresses the reasonable limits of the respectable. Baudelaire's 'morale désagréable' is, of course already transgressive of these limits, which is almost certainly why, in 1865, 'Assommons les pauvres!', along with three other poems, was rejected by Charpentier of the *Revue nationale et étrangère* as 'impubliable'.[77] The respectable is, of course, a bourgeois obsession, and the bourgeois subject repeatedly defines itself through the exclusion of what is considered 'low', by its rejection of the repugnant and the contaminating. In this respect, the moral truisms represent more than just the 'anthologization of idiocy';[78] they represent the discursive bastion of all that which presents

---

[75] The narrator clearly speaks from the perspective of the aristocrat and this interesting parallel has been drawn by Jonathan Monroe: ibid. 107 and esp. n. 23.

[76] The rat is obviously associated with disease but, in the 19th cent. particularly, is seen as a contaminating force, a link with the sewers, a phobic mediator between high and low. See Peter Stallybrass and Allon White, *The Politics and Poetics of Transgression* (London: Methuen, 1986), 143–8.

[77] Noted by Claude Pichois (*OC* i. 1349). The other poems rejected were 'Mademoiselle Bistouri', 'Le Galant Tireur' and 'La Soupe et les nuages'.

[78] Terdiman, *Discourse/Counter-Discourse*, 200.

itself as respectable, the *hygiène, conduite,* and *morale* which circumscribe conduct in codification and militate against all excess (and difference). But, as Baudelaire shows with his reinvention of these discursive carriers of bourgeois culture, such moral discourse conceals indecency since, in its ambiguity, it contains its own contradictions and opposing possibilities. Not only does this mean that the authority of the discourse is undermined (and recognition of its truth withdrawn), it also implies the reframing of the moral context in which it circulates. What Baudelaire's prose poems do is to textualize what is otherwise repressed. 'Assommons les pauvres!' releases, then, the bourgeois fear and hatred of the poor within the acceptable confines of a philosophical maxim about the nature of equality. And 'Le Joujou du pauvre' shows that equality to exist but only in its base desires. The transcoding and displacement of this discourse plays upon the same problematic of sameness and difference we have seen operating elsewhere. In ironizing the discourse by means of which the bourgeoisie consolidates itself as a respectable and conventional body, Baudelaire seeks to expose the bourgeois exclusion of the low as constitutive of class identity. This baseness is what links 'pauvreté' and 'médiocrité', and is implicit in the discursive representation, since what constitutes the *already said* comes to be seen as debased, as impoverished, as commonplace.

This is characterized in its most explicit way in those poems which have been described as 'poèmes-boutades'. In 'Un plaisant', for example, the cliché 'Je vous la souhaite bonne et heureuse!', a ritualized, seasonal figure of exchange, is offered, in an elaborate display of deference, to an ass. The citational technique is combined with the other readable codes (here specifically a dress code) to place the speaker who is immediately and obviously recognizable as a bourgeois, fatuous and self-satisfied. The ass is unmoved, but the narrator is not: 'je fus pris subitement d'une incommensurable rage contre ce magnifique imbécile, qui me parut concentrer en lui tout l'esprit de la France' (*OC* i. 279). In this poem, the 'fine' mess in which France finds itself ideologically is characterized by this sort of 'esprit'. Baudelaire is clearly playing on both 'beau' and 'esprit' here. In fact, the repetition of 'beau' draws attention to itself as it slips from an attribute associated with the man's clothes to one associated with his nature. In this slippage, the ironies already implicit in the man's beauty, in his magnificence, are fully worked out in the word's antiphrastic meaning: 'C'est du beau!'[79] In the same way, 'esprit' evokes the meanings of intellect and thought, of character and identity (especially, perhaps, 'esprit de corps'), and of a 'mot d'esprit', a 'boutade'. It is precisely the 'esprit' of this text, its 'sens profond', which reveals the form of the poem to be a caricature of the attitudes and discourse it displays.[80] The 'boutade' *in* the poem becomes the 'boutade' *of* the poem. The most wilfully prosaic of all the forms of prose poem in the collection thus reproduces the prosaism and the ideological lowliness of the group it opposes. Ross Chambers has described the way in which such discursive irony functions:

> From the split that irony introduces between *what is said* and *what is meant*, a double source of oppositionality arises, as an 'anamnestic' realization of discursive mediation, according as irony works as a 'negation' of the ideological discourse it cites and ironizes, or as an 'appropriation' of that discourse. In the first instance, the ironic meaning is inferred simply as being 'not' the meaning specified in the discourse that is ironically 'mentioned'. The negation does not necessarily imply a relation of 'oppositeness' (as in the classic definition of irony as 'saying one thing but meaning the opposite'), but it does imply a meaning of *otherness* in which ironic *oppositionality* arises.[81]

The otherness of the form as adopted in the prose poem is an elaborate otherness of the discourse with which it engages and in which it presents itself. In the 'poèmes-boutades', the obviousness of the oppositionality has mystified some critics. But what is being offered is the equivalent of 'des ordures soigneusement choisies' ('Le Chien et le flacon', *OC* i. 284): a caricatural representation of the discursive/artistic exchange. In the powerful exaggerations of these poems, Baudelaire lays bare the mechanisms that more stylized parodies will exploit so that our intelligence of it is brought closer as its difference is accentuated. In exploiting these strategies to emphasize ironic oppositionality, Baudelaire engages with the hegemonic discourse. The outcome of this engagement is almost always highly ambiguous, but in showing the narrator in

---

[79] Cf. another popular expression which is also evoked by this: 'en faire, en dire de belles' where the feminine refers specifically to 'des sottises'.

[80] For a reading of this poem as caricature, see Steve Murphy, 'Le Complexe de supériorité et la contagion du rire: 'Un Plaisant' de Baudelaire', *Travaux de Littérature*, 7 (1994), 257–85. [81] Ross Chambers, *Room for Maneuver*, 239.

these prose poems as fundamentally unaware, grotesque, or exaggerated, Baudelaire insists upon their comic status. This is brought into still greater relief by his emphasis on 'low' forms which, like the prose poem itself, are representative of particular forms of (potentially subversive) comic art.

4

The Prose Poem and the
Dualities of Comic Art

Il [Baudelaire] était caricaturiste dans le sens précis du mot,
avec les deux facultés maîtresses de la pénétration et de
l'imagination, et un don d'expression vivant et sommaire.

Auguste de Poulet-Malassis[1]

IN turning to the way in which the *Petits Poèmes en prose* explore
the comic, and particularly the paradox of the comic, we should
concentrate briefly on the 'poèmes boutades'. As this name suggests, these poems present themselves as comic 'babioles'.[2] The
poems which we might categorize as 'poèmes-boutades' — 'Un
plaisant', 'Le Chien et le flacon', 'Le Miroir', 'Laquelle est la
vraie?', 'Perte d'auréole', and 'La Soupe et les nuages'[3] are generically the most difficult to situate of the fifty *Petits Poèmes en prose*.

---

[1] A. de Poulet-Malassis, 'Baudelaire', in *Sept Dessins de gens de lettres, MM. Victor Hugo,
Prosper Mérimée, Edmond et Jules de Goncourt, Charles Baudelaire, Théophile Gautier, Charles
Asselineau* (Paris: Rouquette, 1874), 7.

[2] The term 'boutade' carries the meaning both of wit and of triviality. A boutade can
either be a whim or a joke.

[3] David H. T. Scott does not include 'Le Chien et le flacon' and categorizes it instead as
'moralité', no doubt because of its epigrammatic nature. And he includes 'La Femme
sauvage et la petite maîtresse' and 'Le Galant Tireur' because of their 'threatened and indirect violence' and their 'bizarre tonality'. See Barbara Wright and David H. T. Scott, *La
Fanfarlo and Le Spleen de Paris* (London: Grant & Cutler, 1984), 76–80. I have not included
these poems in this category because of their longer length and because, as Scott himself
suggests, they participate in the same sort of development (albeit not as narrativized) as
poems like 'Assommons les pauvres!' and 'Le Mauvais Vitrier'. They have, in other words,
the same tendency to work with a moral epigram, and the same explosive violence, but they
do not have the same generic strangeness and explosive brevity.

These are poems which are shorter than most, are purposefully allegorical, and offer only minimal narrative. They are forced but suggestive allegories which invoke a sort of *raillerie*, offering both the attack of a *pointe* and the literary deftness and unexpectedness of a *saillie*. As Lemaître, who first described these poems in this way, remarks: 'nous rencontrons ici une sorte de genre littéraire auquel il semble Baudelaire ait aimé s'exercer [. . .] où tout un monde de désillusions et de rancœurs se ramasse dans une incisive brièveté. [. . .] Généralement, ces boutades baudelairiennes prennent pour cible les diverses formes de la sottise moderne.'[4] What this suggests is a form of satire, but one which, although specifically related to the formal qualities of the poem itself (for Lemaître is here trying to define the genre) neglects the formal, but for brevity, and privileges the thematic.

It is primarily their form which is striking, however. These are poems which operate on the very limits of formal experimentation, on the borderline. These poems figure the duality of the prose poem, existing in a tension between the poetic suggestiveness of allegory and the prosaic rootedness of the language and situations. 'Laquelle est la vraie?' (*OC* i. 342) explores this tension by representing the poet caught between the two antithetical Bénédictas, one ideal, the other real. A poem in two halves, 'Laquelle est la vraie?' was, in fact, published under the title 'L'Idéal et le Réel' in the *Revue nationale et étrangère*.[5] The buried Bénédicta is ideal, not only because of her immortalized purity ('elle était trop belle pour vivre longtemps'),[6] but because, in death, she is entombed 'dans une bière d'un bois parfumé et *incorruptible* comme les coffres de l'Inde' (my emphasis). The 'image même d'une poésie de l'idéal',[7] the buried Bénédicta has, however, a prosaic double who dances on

---

[4] *Petits Poèmes en prose (Le Spleen de Paris)*, ed. Lemaître, 185.

[5] 7 Sept. 1867. Noted by Claude Pichois (*OC* i. 1344), who also remarks that 'la construction en deux parties antinomiques est à rapprocher de "La Chambre double"'.

[6] This is, as Hiddleston rightly notes, a send-up of the Romantic cliché of death visited upon the young and innocent heroine. *Baudelaire and Le Spleen de Paris*, 77. It is also worth remarking, however, the irony of the poet-narrator's comment 'aussi est-elle morte quelques jours après que j'eus fait sa connaissance'.

[7] Barbara Johnson, *Défigurations du langage poétique*, 76. See also Etienne Gilson, who sees in this idealized Bénédicta and her coffin the poetic text or *Les Fleurs du mal*. 'Baudelaire and the Muse', in Henri Peyre (ed.), *Baudelaire: A Collection of Critical Essays* (Englewood Cliffs, NJ: Prentice Hall, 1962), 82. Margery Evans also discusses this poem in *Baudelaire and Intertextuality*, 28–30.

the grave and laughingly taunts the poet: 'C'est moi la vraie Bénédicta! C'est moi, une fameuse canaille! Et pour la punition de ta folie et de ton aveuglement, tu m'aimeras telle que je suis!'[8] The poet, in his fury, stamps the ground and ends up knee-deep in the freshly dug grave. This poem, thematically and stylistically, characterizes the poet's inability to distinguish between the poetic and the prosaic, and comically and caricaturally has him with one foot in each camp 'attaché, pour toujours peut-être à la fosse de l'idéal'. This elaboration and shift in signification of the locution 'un pied dans la tombe' is, of course, highly comic and self-ironic and the tension of the poem seems to implode in 'le vertige de l'hyperbole' (*OC* ii. 539).

In caricaturally figuring figurality, the poem draws attention to its form and its discourses. This is, of course, exactly the point and it works in more or less the same way in 'Un plaisant', 'Le Chien et le flacon', 'Le Miroir', 'Perte d'auréole', and 'La Soupe et les nuages'. These poems are, in their form, grotesque exaggerations of their own meaning and represent aspects of comic art as Baudelaire explains it in his essays on the subject. In this respect, 'la vraie Bénédicta' represents all that is vulgar (*la canaille*) and is opposed to the aesthetic ideal of her dead *sosie*. In their conjunction, however, they are, like the prose poem, representative of the central paradox of art, a paradox Baudelaire understands to be present in the caricatural: 'Chose curieuse et vraiment digne d'attention que l'introduction de cet élément insaisissable du beau jusqu'à dans les œuvres destinées à représenter à l'homme sa propre laideur morale et physique! Et, chose non moins mystérieuse, ce spectacle lamentable excite en lui une hilarité immortelle et incorrigible' (*OC* ii. 526). 'Le Miroir', too, stages this paradox, since the mirror can only offer the reflection of ugliness (' — Pourquoi vous regardez-vous au miroir, puisque vous ne pouvez vous y voir qu'avec déplaisir?'), whilst framing the aesthetic object. This, as we have already seen, is a poem about self-awareness and the man described as 'épouvantable' resolutely refuses to subscribe to the

---

[8] Claude Pichois notes a variant in the published version of 1863: 'piétinant sur la terre fraîche avec une violence frénétique et bizarre, disait, dans ce patois familier de la canaille que ma pudeur ne saurait reproduire' (*OC* ii. 1344). This emphasizes the prosaism of the second Bénédicta and marks more clearly the poet's assumed distance from such language. In fact, this variant offers a sort of commentary on the rôle of the citational in the prose poems.

representation the narrator offers: ' — Monsieur, d'après les immortels principes de 89, tous les hommes sont égaux en droits; donc, je possède le droit de me mirer; avec plaisir ou déplaisir, cela ne regarde que ma conscience.' Instead, he continues to contemplate his reflection, as the narrator and the reader look on. In his indulgent self-contemplation and his dismissal of the narrator's intervention, the 'homme épouvantable' refuses to be directly implicated in self-examination; he exempts himself and pleads his legal rights. The satirical attack launched by the narrator does not appear to touch him and his attitude of distant superiority seems to reflect the generalized bourgeois response to caricatural *charge*. The very same mechanism is employed by Daumier in the caricature entitled 'La Lecture du *Charivari*' (1 Apr. 1840) in which two men are behind an open copy of the newspaper. Terdiman's reading of this lithograph (as a *mise en abyme* of contemplation) offers a useful critical parallel to a reading of Baudelaire's 'Le Miroir':

There is a risk that our contemplation may imitate their own. And if our reading should tend toward the same detachment as theirs, the satirical hook to the caricature is present to expose it to the challenge to which they are themselves subjected. The embedded metalanguage of the representation thus seeks to devaluate an attitude toward the image by which the consumers of a critical artifact manage, *in the very exercise of their power to acquire it*, to absorb or evade its ideological implications and the threatening bearing of its mockery.[9]

'Le Miroir' stages a discursive combat in which each party asserts superiority without any resolution (other than the paradoxical deadlock of the narrator's conclusion), alongside the prevalent caricatural interrogation of self-image which often frames people and their portraits.[10]

   In their heavy-handed symbolism, these poems do seem to carry a *charge* and to be experimenting formally with a caricatural model. The 'poèmes-boutades' demonstrate a particular kind of caricatural technique which Baudelaire is experimenting with in this collection: a closed, or 'lisible' form in which the anecdotal is reduced to the symbolic; a distillation of a technique he exploits in longer prose poems. It is not surprising, then, that a close relationship

[handwritten margin note: poèmes -boutades + caricature]

---

[9] Terdiman, *Discourse/Counter-Discourse*, 179.
[10] See, for example, some of Daumier's *Croquis d'expressions* or his depictions of the public at the *Salons*.

between some of the prose poems and certain images emerges. It is possible to imagine each of the 'poèmes-boutades' as caricatures. There is, in fact, a Daumier drawing, 'Le Nouvel An', which reproduces the ceremonious greeting of 'Un plaisant' in image and in caption and which may have triggered Baudelaire's treatment of a related motif.[11] But whereas Daumier chose so often to use direct speech in his captions,[12] Baudelaire, in this poem, seeks out a title which can complement the citation of such a pleasantry. There is deliberate play upon the title which refers both to the poem itself and to the joker at its centre, the noun having the meaning of both 'ce qui' and 'celui qui plaît, qui amuse'.[13] This elaborate joke is, in fact, underpinned by what Baudelaire has to say about the important role of amusement in its relation with the serious, and this with specific reference to Daumier, 'un homme qui, tous les matins, divertit la population parisienne, qui, chaque jour, satisfait aux besoins de la gaieté publique et lui donne sa pâture'. He continues: 'Jusqu'à présent les artistes seuls ont compris tout ce qu'il y a de sérieux là-dedans, et que c'est vraiment matière à une étude.' The title of 'Le Chien et le flacon' is evocative of the poem's theme, characterizing the relationship between the public (here personnified by a dog and, etymologically, a *canaille*) and poetic form, since figuratively the term *flacon* evokes the container rather than its contents. This is emphasized in the imagined alternative offering, 'un paquet d'excréments', which reproduces the pattern of the container and what it contains while proposing a gift more suited to the recipient.[14] 'La Soupe et les nuages', by the same

---

[11] This lithograph was published in *Le Charivari* in February 1852.

[12] On this subject, see Terdiman, *Discourse/Counter-Discourse*, ch. 3, 'Counter-Images: Daumier and *Le Charivari*', pp. 149–97. Particularly significant to my argument here is the point that he makes on 183–4: 'It is thus particularly significant that the overwhelming majority of Daumier's captions report speech. They comprise an effort to record the class and situation-specific utterances which—along with bodily attitude, costume, facial expression, and the other non-verbal languages which could be represented in a drawing — carry the image of the satirized world. With a logic which parallels Balzac's perception that the multiple languages of a social formation are the levers by which one might seize its inner articulations, the language of these lithographs—and the verbal, paradoxically, most powerful among them— are indispensable elements in the generic innovation which the caricatures constituted.'

[13] It is, of course, also possible to read 'plaisant' as an adjective in this title and it is more than possible that Baudelaire was aware of the ironic and antiquated meaning '(en épithète devant le nom ou en attribut). Qui fait rire à ses dépens.' Cf. *Fusées*, XII: 'Ce qu'il y a de d'enivrant dans le mauvais goût, c'est le plaisir aristocratique de déplaire' (*OC* i. 661).

[14] Cf. the coffin of 'Laquelle est la vraie?' and the last stanza of 'Une charogne': 'Alors, ô

token, speaks of its form in the *choc* of the prosaic and the poetic. Baudelaire is master of the title, and is perfectly well aware of the role it plays in shaping the text. This we have already seen in relation to the *Petits Poèmes en prose* in general, but it is in the *inter-titres*[15] that this awareness is most suggestively played out with Baudelaire offering the same sort of *défilé* he describes in the *Salon de 1859*: 'Je pourrais faire défiler sous vos yeux le titre comique à la manière des vaudevillistes, le titre sentimental auquel il ne manque que le point d'exclamation, le titre calembour, le titre profond et philosophique, le titre trompeur, ou titre à piège' (*OC* ii. 614). In this essay, Baudelaire offers a list of examples of titling which he systematically derides, concluding 'Je me suis senti sincèrement affligé de voir qu'un homme d'un vrai talent cultivât *inutilement* le rébus' (*OC* ii. 615, my emphasis). We are, in other words, to read Baudelaire's titles as significantly, or meaningfully, cultivating such enigma. Or, more specifically, we are to understand that, in many of the titles chosen, the thematic evocation often conceals a density of meaning and contains or suggests a *titre rhématique* which discloses the centrality of a formal imperative, thereby highlighting the paradigmatic variations which occur within the text.[16]

This is no less true of the central essay which articulates Baudelaire's ideas on the forms of the comic. In *De l'essence du rire et généralement du comique dans les arts plastiques*, Baudelaire announces a grand project whilst simultaneously stating quite clearly that he does not intend to write an impersonal survey, a 'traité de la caricature'. However, as is so often the case with Baudelaire's literary and art criticism, what starts out as 'quelques réflexions', soon becomes a statement of personal creative principles in an 'article de philosophe et d'artiste'. Bemoaning the lack of serious studies of this art form and dismissing existing criticism as 'guère que des matériaux', Baudelaire is credited as being the first

---

ma beauté! dites à la vermine | Qui vous mangera de baisers, | Que j'ai gardé la forme et l'essence divine | De mes amours décomposés!' (*OC* i. 32).

[15] This is Genette's term and designates titles occurring within a work where that work is subdivided. See *Seuils*, 271–93 for a discussion of these and particularly pp. 287–90 for a consideration of their occurrence in the *recueil*.

[16] In this respect, Baudelaire's own hesitations over the titling of the work, which were explored in Ch. 1, and the large number of titles (63 in all) he noted for future elaboration into prose poems (*OC* i. 366–74) underline his awareness of the significance of these in establishing a contract.

to stress the importance of this popular art for an understanding of the period, its politics, and its aesthetic values,[17] clearly stating that 'une histoire générale de la caricature dans ses rapports avec tous les faits religieux et politiques, graves ou frivoles, relatifs à l'esprit national ou à la mode, qui ont agité l'humanité, est une œuvre glorieuse et importante' (*OC* ii. 525). The importance of caricature as an art form is asserted only in the nineteenth century, perhaps because, with the advent of *modernité*, its peculiar mixture of the frivolous and the meaningful, its simplicity of form and its universal appeal, it was an art form which spoke to the people of things it could understand; it was readily available and was no longer primarily for the rich or the Church.[18] Until this period, the form's contemporaneity, the very aspect which made it successful in the new era of change, was what had condemned it to long-term oblivion and had prevented it from ever coming out of the *atelier*, where it was a private joke shared only by artists. Baudelaire describes caricature as essentially fleeting, blowing constantly away in the winds of journalistic change (*OC* ii. 525), but the theories he sets down and his conception of a history of the genre represent the aestheticization of a popular, 'low' art form. More than ten years after Baudelaire's article on the subject, and perhaps even as many as twenty since the first version of his thoughts was set down on paper,[19] Champfleury, in his history of caricature, was more overtly stating the case for this art form as a valid historical document:

La caricature tient un rôle très bas dans l'histoire, peu d'écrivains s'étant préoccupés de ses manifestations; mais aujourd'hui que l'érudit ne se contente plus des documents historiques officiels, et qu'il étudie par les monuments figurés tout ce qui peut éclairer les événements et les

[17] See Yoshio Abé, 'Une nouvelle esthétique du rire: Baudelaire et Champfleury entre 1845 et 1855', *Annales de la Faculté des Lettres*, Chûô University, 35 (1964), 20. See also Pichois's statement that Baudelaire, 'en donnant droit de cité artistique à la caricature et en définissant le grotesque comme une catégorie esthétique, est [. . .] en France un novateur' (*OC* ii. 1345).

[18] Edward Lucie-Smith notes that two practical circumstances contributed to the development of caricature in the 19th cent.: the alliance of the art form with the press (whereas previously drawings had been distributed on separate sheets); and the invention, in 1798, of lithography: *The Art of Caricature* (London: Orbis, 1981), 77.

[19] Pichois discusses the difficulty of dating these essays exactly in *OC* ii. 1342, and suggests that by placing them at the first date of publication (i.e. 1855) critics undermine the originality of these texts. In *Baudelaire: Études et témoignages* (Neuchâtel: La Baconnière, 1967), 80–94, Pichois dates the work to 1846 at the latest.

hommes, la caricature sort de sa bassesse et reprend le rôle puissant qu'elle fut chargée de jouer de tout temps.

La caricature est avec le journal le cri des citoyens. Ce que ceux-ci ne peuvent exprimer est traduit par des hommes dont la mission consiste à mettre en lumière les sentiments du peuple.[20]

Baudelaire is fully aware of the significance and originality of this study of the comic, and with respect to a body of critical work including *De l'essence du rire* and *Quelques caricaturistes français*, writes in a letter to Julien Lemer, 'j'ai une assez vive envie de montrer ce que j'ai su faire en matière de critique' (*C* ii. 442). It is with considerable irony and disingenuousness, then, that Baudelaire begins *De l'essence du rire* with these statements regarding his modest ambitions and personal obsession. Indeed, there is some similarity between the techniques used to introduce this essay and the elaboration of the prose poem project in the *lettre-dédicace*, except that here, instead of his claims that he remains 'bien loin de [s]on mystérieux et brillant modèle', Baudelaire makes no claims for the project other than those (highly theoretical ones) implicit in the title itself. In fact, quite the opposite, so that, as Michèle Hannoosh has shown, the opening sentence takes issue with the title, 'deflating with one stroke the swollen seriousness of its excessive length and the enormous project which it announces'.[21] In fact, so many of the techniques of Baudelaire's irony are brought into action here that it is impossible not to see this essay as reproducing in its formal expression the theories of the comic it seeks to elucidate. Like the strategies of 'Le Miroir', then, this essay on the comic plays up to the reader in a way which both flatters the reader's superiority over the 'charlatans de la gravité' and makes him or her the butt of the joke with a seductive reference: 'rien de ce qui sort

---

[20] Champfleury [J. F. F. Husson-Fleury], *Histoire de la caricature moderne* (Paris: Dentu, 1868), vii–viii. Baudelaire refers to a project on a grand scale and specifically mentions that it would be produced collaboratively (*OC* ii. 525). This work by Champfleury, the second of two volumes, both of which appeared in 1865 and which cite Baudelaire frequently is, no doubt, the work in question. See Pichois's 'Notice' to *De l'essence du rire* (*OC* ii. 1345).

[21] *Baudelaire and Caricature. From the Comic to an Art of Modernity* (University Park: Pennsylvania State University Press, 1992), 12. Part of this deflation is a parody not just of the sort of treatise Baudelaire invokes here, but of a specific treatise on the comic, Joubert's *Traité du ris, contenant son essence, ses causes et mervelheus effais, curieusement recherchés et observés*, which was published in 1597. This similarity is pointed out by Giovanni Maccia in *Baudelaire critico* (Florence: Sansoni, 1939) and cited by Hannoosh, in 13 n. 2.

de l'homme n'est frivole aux yeux du philosophe' (*OC* ii. 526).[22] In the very next section, however, and no more than a few lines after this literary reference, Baudelaire reverts to his other favoured citational technique, italicizing the maxim 'Le Sage ne rit qu'en tremblant', after which he engages in a protracted questioning of the origin and a detailed reading of its meaning, which is patently at odds with the concision of the quotation itself (*OC* ii. 526–7). In his heavy-handed placing of this quotation ('Cette singulière maxime me revient sans cesse à l'esprit depuis que j'ai conçu le projet de cet article, et j'ai voulu m'en débarrasser tout d'abord'), there is the critical equivalent of the prose poem which ironically elaborates a narrative from such a saying. In both cases, the result is the same. Rather than being a mere starting point, the saying becomes the focus of the text and reveals the tactics of the philosopher who simultaneously attracts authority to himself and comically undermines it. But like Baudelaire's use of maxims elsewhere, this one is turned inside out (critically) and is then put to work reinvested with new meaning.[23] Baudelaire uses this essay to present and to formulate caricaturally his theories on the comic, using the tactics of exaggeration, complication, citation, duplicity, and deception, all tactics we have seen with respect to his style in the prose poem and which are themselves the very essence of the comic.

In this essay Baudelaire elaborates a theory of the comic which, it will be seen, revolves around two different kinds of comedy: the *comique ordinaire* or *significatif* and the *comique absolu*. The *comique significatif* is a referential and imitative art, where that imitation is disposed to be comic. It derives from a sense of superiority over others and presents itself as double. Baudelaire writes: 'Le comique significatif est un langage plus clair, plus facile à comprendre pour le vulgaire, et surtout plus facile à analyser, son élément étant visiblement double: l'art et l'idée morale' (*OC* ii. 536–7).

---

[22] With great irony, Baudelaire here takes on the 'professeurs jurés de sérieux' and the 'académiciens', playing them at their own game by setting up this classical resonance. The words are, in fact, Terence's: 'Humani nil a me alienum puto'. Baudelaire uses this same quotation, again somewhat ironically, in his 'notice' on Gautier (*OC* ii. 127–8).

[23] Cf. Hannoosh's reading of the rôle of this maxim, *Baudelaire and Caricature*, 16–20, which shows Baudelaire's appropriation of and distance from this maxim as a joke which 'foregrounds the metaphoricity of the theology on which the entire theory depends, exposes it, and ironically makes it the vehicle of an apologia for the very genre it most prescribes'.

This, Baudelaire argues, is the 'esprit dominant' of French comic art, and he cites, as examples, Rabelais, 'qui garde [. . .] quelque chose d'utile et de raisonnable', and Voltaire, who is 'essentielle- ment français',[24] whose raison d'être is this idea of superiority and who is 'tout à fait significatif'.

The *comique absolu*, on the other hand, is highly creative and artistic, a grotesque transformation of the real into something quite new which terrifies and challenges. It cannot be grasped by reason, only by intuition. It is profound, axiomatic, and primitive and provokes excessive and spontaneous laughter. Few French artists aspire to the *comique absolu*. Molière and Callot both have moments when they attain this ideal, but for the most part its expo- nents are German or English. Baudelaire insists upon spontaneity as a feature which enables us to distinguish between the two forms of the comic: 'Il n'y a qu'une vérification du grotesque, c'est le rire, et le rire subit; en face du comique significatif, il n'est pas défendu de rire après coup; cela n'arguë pas contre sa valeur; c'est une ques- tion de rapidité d'analyse'. And whereas the *comique significatif* is dual, the *comique absolu* 'se présente sous une espèce *une*' (*OC* ii. 536, original emphasis) because of a unity in form and content.[25] Baudelaire argues that 'le rire est l'expression d'un sentiment double, ou contradictoire' (*OC* ii. 534), because it is both innocence and knowledge.

Both these forms of the comic, Baudelaire sums up, are based on the dominant idea of superiority. Moreover, for the comic to occur, two people are required and it is primarily the *rieur*, the spectator, who experiences the comic (rather than the victim). The part of innocence can be feigned by those whose job it is to develop the comic and to use it for the diversion of other people, a phenomenon

[24] Cf. *Mon cœur mis à nu*, XVIII: 'Je m'ennuie en France, surtout parce que tout le monde y ressemble à Voltaire. Emerson a oublié Voltaire dans ses Représentants de l'humanité. Il aurait pu faire un joli chapitre intitulé: Voltaire, ou l'anti-poète, le roi des badauds, le prince des superficiels, l'anti-artiste, le prédicateur des concierges, le père Gigogne des rédacteurs du Siècle.'

[25] Indeed, Baudelaire's understanding of the two different kinds of the comic has been shown to be readable in his formal treatment of them. Rosemary Lloyd argues that 'La puis- sance du comique absolu se ressent dans la transformation de perspective dans l'essai: le cri- tique se tient à l'écart du comique significatif, il le juge, il l'analyse; le vertige du comique absolu, au contraire, l'entraîne, le bouleverse, il ne peut plus le disséquer, il ne peut que le décrire.' *Baudelaire et Hoffmann: Affinités et influences* (Cambridge: Cambridge University Press, 1979), 181.

which, Baudelaire clarifies, 'rentre dans la classe de tous les phénomènes artistiques qui dénotent dans l'être humain l'existence d'une dualité permanente, la puissance d'être à la fois soi et un autre' (*OC* ii. 543).[26] The truly comic artist, then, is the one who uses his power to be other and to demonstrate otherness in all beings; the one who recognizes the otherness within the self as well as the others which have constituted that self. The comic artist is, for Baudelaire, the artist who, in all self-awareness, capitalizes on that dual nature both to instruct and entertain others; he is a mirror for their duality and their ugliness; and through comic art, he brings the spectator-reader to a consciousness of his or her superiority (in relation to the butt of the joke),[27] and inferiority (in relation to the superior artistry of the comic display).

The response to the comic fascinates Baudelaire, then. Set apart from the rational world of recognizable features, persons, or situations, he can fully explore the interface of art and the fantastic in the grotesque and exaggerated figures; 'quelque chose qui ressemble à ces rêves périodiques ou chroniques qui assiègent régulièrement notre sommeil' (*OC* ii. 568).[28] The *comique significatif*, in complete contrast to this 'création absurde, étrangère à toute signification morale',[29] is a constant reminder of man's condition, not only in terms of Original Sin, but also of a broader social reality. We find both elements of the comic in the *Petits Poèmes en prose* and, given the some of the formal aspects which are so readily attributable to the caricatural, it seems appropriate to conduct a more thorough investigation into the ways in which the prose poem exploits Baudelaire's theory of the comic and its formal requirements.

The way in which the text is structured already suggests something of the same framework since, as we have noted, the model of

---

[26] For a fuller discussion of this in a broader literary context, see Hannoosh, *Baudelaire and Caricature*, 68–74.

[27] The exemplary tale of Virginie (*OC* ii. 528–30) serves as an illustration of the theory.

[28] Although many of Goya's etchings in *Los Caprichos* could be described in this way, the one which most readily springs to mind is 'El Sueño de la razón produce monstruos'. It is interesting to note that Goya's commentary on this etching states that only when imagination is coupled with reason can the impossible thoughts be turned into art and beauty. Although Baudelaire might not choose the word reason, preferring perhaps something akin to *volonté*, the idea is certainly shared. *The Complete Etchings of Goya* (New York: Crown Publishers, 1962 [1943]).

[29] Charles Mauron, 'Le Rire baudelairien', *Europe*, 45/456–7 (Apr.–May 1967), 59.

the *chose vue* and Baudelaire's engagement with the logic of the newspaper layout already suggest a work which, like caricature, is fragmented and journalistic in nature, something which is always changing, 'un art léger, fugace qui a contre lui la mobilité même de la vie' (*OC* ii. 556). It is a genre born of observation and the productive interaction with the urban crowd. As Baudelaire asserts in the *lettre-dédicace*, 'c'est surtout de la fréquentation des grandes villes, c'est du croisement de leurs innombrables rapports que naît cet idéal obsédant' (*OC* i. 276). This engagement with the everyday is a way of portraying and taking issue with the values, beliefs, and social practices of the bourgeoisie. Caricature is an ideal art form for this, 'car les images triviales, les croquis de la foule et de la rue, les caricatures, sont souvent le miroir le plus fidèle de la vie' (*OC* ii. 544). Baudelaire's prose poems appear to be caricatural in several fundamental ways: they are comic and exaggerated representations of a certain social realism; they are brief, sketchily drawn, anecdotes always with some kind of a moral, implicitly or explicitly encapsulated in the text; they are mongrel in their form, a distinct move away from the restrictions of artistic or poetic traditions, with the revolutionary power to bring about a new art form; they are suggestive in their brevity, indicating deliberate ambiguity and contradiction, just as meaning in caricature springs from the lines of the drawing and then surpasses them in meaning; in their self-disparaging irony, they mock the artist as well as his society; and, in their distortion of the real, they are sometimes supernatural.

For Baudelaire, it was Daumier who best exemplified the art of caricature, for he drew it away from the purely political and into the realm of the novel and participated in the Balzacian ideal of a human comedy.[30] Both were involved with the classification of Parisian types in their social context and it was primarily as a result of Balzac's *Comédie humaine* that a new repertory of such types emerged, creating a 'satire générale des citoyens' (*OC* ii. 555).[31]

---

[30] Baudelaire goes as far as to say that 'la véritable gloie et la vraie mission de Gavarni et de Daumier ont été de compléter Balzac, qui d'ailleurs le savait bien, et les estimait comme des auxiliares et des commentateurs' (*OC* ii. 560).

[31] From 1831 caricature suffered terrible fines and intensifying prosecution, almost forcing *La Caricature* into liquidation. In 1832 Daumier was imprisoned for portraying Louis-Philippe as Gargantua. After 1835 censorship laws forbade direct reference to real persons or institutions, so caricaturists were forced to invent more subtle ways of attacking these,

The combination of careful observation, deep understanding, and skilled expression is what, Baudelaire believes, characterizes Daumier's mastery of his subject. Daumier produced almost four thousand lithographs and these do build, and not only because of their number, to a kind of social completeness. Like Baudelaire's prose poems, however, they are born of discrete and instantaneous encounters or situations with anonymous others (representing generalized types). The anonymity of the prose poems is striking. 'L'Étranger' clearly works this motif as its central preoccupation, using other classifying codes to attempt to situate the stranger. This anonymity is a feature of all the figures we encounter as we move through the poems: a *petite vieille*, a *beau Monsieur ganté, verni, cruellement cravaté, plusieurs hommes de lettres, un être affligé*, the *tels qui* of 'Le Mauvais Vitrier', *directeurs de théâtre et de journaux, une sauteuse*, widows, *saltimbanques*, the poor, the mad, and various unnamed friends and anonymous pronouns. Daumier uses his anonymous figures and types to explore, between the upper and lower limits of the urban bourgeoisie, his recurrent moral themes:

wishful thinking, role-playing; affectation, sometimes pathetic and sometimes arrogant; wariness of cultural novelty; ambition, resentment, envy, vanity; powerlessness and indifference to the powerless; complacency and complaisance, towards the status quo; embarassment and obsequiousness; snobbery, self-righteousness, dissimulation, disingenuousness and hypocrisy.[32]

It is possible to find all of these themes represented by the anonymous characters of the *Petits Poèmes en prose*, but what is particularly striking is the way in which those latter elements, self-righteousness, dissimulation, disingenuousness, and hypocrisy, are also a central technique of comic art. This relationship between

usually through imaginary characters endowed with many of the physical characteristics which had come to be associated with those same persons and institutions. Hence Daumier's Ratapoil and Macaire; Monnier's M. Prudhomme and Traviès's Mayeux. See Michèle Hannoosh, *Baudelaire and Caricature*, 114–18; Edward Lucie-Smith, *The Art of Caricature*, 77; and Judith Wechsler, *A Human Comedy. Physiognomy and Caricature in 19th-Century Paris* (London: Thames & Hudson, 1982), 71. The repertory of types which emerges in the 19th-cent. novel (caricaturally) includes the bureaucrat, the confidence man, the social climber, the banker, the moneylender, the stock-market player, the industrialist, the journalist, and the commercial writer. See Wechsler, *A Human Comedy*, 26.

[32] The list is from Wechsler, *A Human Comedy*, 136.

the form and its moral content is what leads Baudelaire to speak of
the unity of comic art and to say of Daumier that 'l'idée se dégage
d'emblée' (*OC* ii. 556). Whereas those caricaturists, like Charlet,
who represent 'niaiseries nationales' (*OC* ii. 549) seek to flatter the
spectator,[33] Daumier's ironic representations have 'un fonds
d'honnêteté et de bonhomie' which shape the seriousness and the
virulence of his attack on his complacent bourgeois subject. The
Petits Poèmes en prose participate in the same desire to represent 'la
triviale et terrible réalité' (*OC* ii. 552), to hold up that representation as a mirror of physical and moral ugliness and to counter the
notion that Baudelaire so ironically cites: 'Dans les arts, *il ne s'agit
que de plaire*, comme disent les bourgeois' (*OC* ii. 547).

As we saw with respect to 'Un plaisant', Baudelaire is interested
in the notion of pleasing, and in 'Les Dons des fées' he works the
idea in a way which is suggestive both of the *comique significatif* and
the *comique absolu*. The poem is set in the world of the marvellous,
in the world of fairy tales. In this world, fairies of all ages, dressed
in 'robes de vapeurs multicolores' are distributing marvellous gifts
to new-born children in an elaborate narrativization of providence.
At the centre of this poem is the moral absurdity and fundamental
inequality of the world. The distribution is compared to a school
prize-giving, a comparison which removes us from the world of the
fantastic and evokes the real, while at the same time emphasizing
the inappropriateness of the comparison on even moral grounds:
'Ce qu'il y avait ici de particulier, c'est que les Dons n'étaient pas
la récompense d'un effort, mais tout au contraire une grâce
accordée à celui qui n'avait pas encore vécu, une grâce pouvant
déterminer sa destinée et devenir aussi bien la source de son malheur que de son bonheur' (*OC* i. 305). It is precisely this moral
incongruity and disproportion which Baudelaire reproduces in the
characters, environment, and tone of this poem, for, as he says in
his literary criticism: 'La disproportion du ton avec le sujet, disproportion qui n'est sensible que pour le sage désintéressé, est un
moyen de comique dont la puissance saute à l'œil; je suis même
étonné qu'il ne soit pas employé plus souvent' (*OC* ii. 185).

---

[33] Baudelaire is candid in his attack on Charlet, stating overtly that 'Charlet a toujours
fait sa cour au peuple. Ce n'est pas un homme libre, c'est un esclave: ne cherchez pas en lui
une vérité; c'est presque toujours une câlinerie adressée à la caste préférée' (*OC* ii. 547).

'Les Dons des fées' draws all of its comic effect from such incongruity and disproportion. The physical appearance of the fairies, but for their dresses, is firmly rooted in the real and, in the situation described, they display all the human weaknesses of those invested with similar office in the real world. They are *ahuries*, like ministers when parliament is sitting or like state pawnbrokers caught in a rush to release valuables on a public holiday; they are conscious of the time and anxious to get home to their families, their dinner, and their slippers (*OC* i. 306). Each and every one of these terms of comparison is caricatural and, in its incongruity, is comic. But the incongruity finds a form of unity in the parallel inequalities of supernatural and earthly justice and in the appeal to the reader's judgement. The end result of the distribution of gifts is, precisely, such injustice, with no right of appeal. Wealth attracts wealth and poetry and beauty are gifts that cannot flourish in the wrong environment. Baudelaire exploits at every level the comic that emerges from the inappropriate treatment of subjects,[34] and synthesizes the incongruity of the gifts with his own inappropriate metaphors—metaphors which enact the caricatural process of vulgarization—so that here 'l'idée qui se dégage d'emblée' is precisely incongruity and disproportion.

After the distribution is completed, one father is without a gift for his child. His intervention in the proceedings reinforces the wordliness of these fairies (he calls out 'Eh! Madame' as he grabs hold of her 'robe de vapeurs') and, in its prosaism and conversational inflection, represents, at one and the same time, a stark contrast to and a reinforcement of the incongruous tone of the narration. This marks a further comic development of the narrative, with the enumeration of different kinds of fairies,[35] and the evocation of the laws which govern the *merveilleux*, and which enable the fairy to grant an extra gift, provided that she herself is endowed with sufficient imagination. It is in this turn of the narrative that the ultimate incongruity and disproportion emerges for the fairy comes up with an idea which is 'le meilleur des lots', 'le

[34] Hannoosh notes Baudelaire's awareness of this comic technique in the *Salon de 1859*. *Baudelaire and Caricature*, 77.

[35] Claude Pichois lends some weight to Eigeldinger's suggestion that the list comes from Monfaucon de Villars's *Comte de Gabalis ou Entretiens sur les sciences secrètes* which Baudelaire had borrowed from Poulet-Malassis in 1861 (*OC* i. 1325). The intention in reproducing the list in this way is clearly parodic.

Don de plaire', but which does not meet with appropriate approval. The shopkeeper, his profession itself caricaturally charged, is incapable of grasping 'la logique de l'Absurde' and questions the gift: 'Mais plaire comment? plaire. . . ? plaire pourquoi?' (*OC* i. 307). In accordance with the *comique significatif*, the fable's moral is clearly drawn by the fairy at the end of the poem: 'Comment trouvez-vous ce petit Français vaniteux, qui veut tout comprendre, et qui, ayant obtenu pour son fils le meilleur des lots, ose encore interroger et discuter l'indiscutable?' Art is not explicable in this way and needs no justification. Baudelaire here plays upon the notion of art as an ability to charm, while at the same time overturning that bourgeois saying that 'Dans les arts, *il ne s'agit que de plaire.*' This poem seeks not only to please (or amuse) but to criticize and bring the reader-victim to awareness. It does so by emphasizing the superiority of art (as *indiscutable*) and by caricaturing the recipient's self-interest and, as in 'Le Chien et le flacon', his ability to distinguish good art from bad, a good gift (or talent) from a bad one.[36]

In its comic techniques, this poem also indicates to us the ways in which we might read the vulgarity and trivialization of other prose poems as a form of caricature. The stereotyping and anonymity of characters is, for example, complemented by the cliché and the *lieu commun* which, in contrast to art, represent the *déjà dit* and appear incongruous in a poetic context. In addition to this, their association with the *légende* is both contextual, evoking the cited idiocies which appeared beneath caricatures, and textual in the sense that they are often constitutive of the poem's meaning. Baudelaire, in fact, rejects the value of Daumier's captions, arguing that the comic effect is constitutive and needs no explanation: 'Les légendes qu'on écrit au bas de ses dessins ne servent pas à grand-chose, car ils pourraient généralement s'en passer. Son comique est, pour ainsi dire, involontaire' (*OC* ii. 556). Within a literary caricature, however, it is *volontaire* for such a linguistic device becomes the means to formulate the trivial, to exaggerate the prosaic, to determine the stereotype, to introduce variations

[marginal annotation: other pps]

[marginal annotation: literary caricature]

[36] This reading of the poem allows for an additional interpretation of the conclusion as an attack on the editorial intrusions of Houssaye and *La Presse*, intrusions which led to a dispute between Baudelaire and the newspaper and which meant that the group of poems in which 'Les Dons des fées' was to appear was never published. See Pichois's bibliographical notice to 'Les Tentations' (*OC* i. 1325) for further details.

within the type, and to accentuate self-ignorance and pomposity. In such formulations, 'toutes les pauvretés de l'esprit, tous les ridicules, toutes les manies de l'intelligence, tous les vices du cœur se lisent [. . .] et en même temps, tout est dessiné et accentué largement (*OC* ii. 552).

The final remark is not an afterthought. For Baudelaire, Daumier's stereotyping is 'accentué largement' and his many types thrive because of the suggestiveness of their exaggeration. The same technique in a lesser artist is not, however, so successful. Prudhomme, created and acted by Henri Monnier, appeared as a theatrical caricature in 1830 in a play entitled *La Famille improvisée*.[37] He is a significant phenomenon, if only because of his durability and scope, exemplifying the way in which theatre attracted journalists who, in turn attracted greater audiences to the performances, thereby establishing the figure as a cultural commonplace. Once the cultural reference has been established, its symbolism spreads and the exaggerated proportions of the stage character can be adapted, reinforcing at every turn the currency of the stereotype. Prudhomme soon became an emblem of the bourgeoisie, helped along towards recognition not only by the theatrical performances, but by Monnier's publication of the fictional character's *mémoires* in 1857[38] and by the numerous caricatures drawn by Daumier between 1852 and 1870.[39] Daumier's lithographs of Prudhomme project all the fatuousness and pretension of the class he comes to embody, symbolizing narrow-mindedness, dull routine, mediocrity, and a complete lack of imagination. In keeping with this, Monnier's art very much relied on the platitudes and clichés of bourgeois conversation, as his character's name ironically declares.[40] Given Baudelaire's passion for the *lieu commun*, it is significant that he can find nothing to admire in Joseph Prudhomme, the speaker of platitudes *par excellence*:

---

[37] For a literary account of this performance, see Alexandre Dumas, *Mes Mémoires*, viii (Paris: M. Lévy, 1869), 173–4.

[38] H. Monnier, *Les Mémoires de M. Joseph Prudhomme* (Paris: Librairie nouvelle, 1857), 2 vols.

[39] J. Wechsler estimates that there were around sixty drawings of Prudhomme during this period, *A Human Comedy*, 112.

[40] This point is made by Wechsler, who adds that the name also generated a number of other terms which emerged out of the character's prolixity: *Prudhommeries*, *Prudhommesque*, *Prudhommade* and even *Josephprudhommiser*. *A Human Comedy*, 117–18.

Ainsi Monsieur Prudhomme, ce type monstrueusement vrai, Monsieur
Prudhomme n'a pas été conçu en grand. Henri Monnier l'a étudié, le
Prudhomme vivant, réel; il l'a étudié jour à jour, pendant un très long
espace de temps. [. . .] Après l'avoir étudié, il l'a traduit; je me trompe; il
l'a décalqué. A première vue, le produit apparaît comme extraordinaire;
mais quand tout Monsieur Prudhomme a été dit, Henri Monnier n'avait
plus rien à dire.   (*OC* ii. 557)

Monnier's art is pure imitation, 'la limpidité du miroir, d'un miroir
qui ne pense pas et qui se contente de réfléchir les passants' (*OC* ii.
558); a copy of the real with no creative attributes. This passive
reflection represents a sort of seamlessness between art and the real
which, far from counter-discursively representing the bourgeois by
introducing difference within the constant return of the same,
instead offers more and more of the same, so that life and art,
world and stage, become the same thing. Baudelaire knows instinc-
tively that Monnier's talent is a 'talent essentiellement bourgeois'
(*OC* ii. 557) and a talent to be dismissed, as indeed he dismisses
Pinelli, as 'le poncif dans l'allure et la conduite qui s'introduit dans
la vie des artistes comme dans leurs œuvres' (*OC* ii. 572).

It is bourgois art because it remains consistently within the
confines of obsessive self-image, without any accretion of self-
awareness. As a result it confirms the prejudices and self-delusions
of dominant discourse, rather than counter-discursively challeng-
ing them, with the end result that bourgeois 'culture' comes to
appear more dominant, more real, and more truthful. Monnier,
says Baudelaire, 'ne sait rien créer, rien idéaliser, rien arranger', 'il
n'a jamais connu le grand art'. He offers, then, only the poorest of
imitations, a 'calque', the artistic equivalent of the *daguerréotype*
(*OC* ii. 557–8), a narcissistic self-contemplation in the 'triviale
image sur le métal' (*OC* ii. 617). Baudelaire, it is well known, was
no friend to photography, and in likening Monnier's art to a
daguerréotype, he saw it as the *contrepartie* of art itself, an 'absolue
exactitude matérielle' (*OC* ii. 618). Baudelaire considers photography as the equivalent to 'l'imprimerie' and 'la sténographie', as a
servant of the arts.[41] Like the cliché and the stereotype (both terms

---

[41] In an anecdote recounted by Champfleury, Baudelaire is said to have met with Monnier
and to have characterized his works as 'sténographies bourgeoises'. *La Vie Parisienne*, 10
Sept. 1864. This anecdote also appears, in a slightly altered version, in his *Histoire de la caricature moderne*, 243–4. Cited by Hannoosh, who describes Monnier's production in terms
of just another dictionary, *Baudelaire and Caricature*, 156.

born of printing and mass reproduction),[42] photography is naturally appealing to 'la sottise de la multitude'.[43] Baudelaire elaborates the relationship clearly in *Le Public moderne et la modernité* in
a passage which draws upon stereotyped images and evokes clichéd
discourses to hold up the bourgeois and industry as responsible
for the degradation of art: 'La Fatuité moderne aura beau rugir,
éructer tous les borborygmes de sa ronde personnalité, vomir tous
les sophismes indigestes dont une philosophie récente l'a bourrée
à gueule-que-veux-tu, cela tombe sous le sens que l'industrie,
faisant irruption dans l'art, en devient la plus mortelle ennemie'
(*OC* ii. 618). Monnier's art is, like photography, *exact et froid*,
vétilleux, and producing merely *du chic d'après nature* (*OC* ii. 557).
Baudelaire's objection to it is that, like the 'triviale image sur le
métal', it is endlessly reproducible but with nothing new to say. His
own use of the commonplace bears no relation to this for, like
Daumier's caricatures, the stereotyping impulse seeks to expose
psittacism by exploring the relations between the patterns themselves, to grasp a higher understanding of the self, of others, and
of form than the social convention immediately reveals. It is, like
the best in comic art, a proper application of form to content and
meaning.

Monnier's art stops short of the comic because it is just a
'calque'; it is 'monstrueusement vrai'. Rather than holding up a
mirror to show the monstrous, it monstrously reflects the ordinary.
Daumier is the *contrepartie* of Monnier (*OC* ii. 557), suggesting
details to the mind, rather than giving them to the eye. Baudelaire
is attracted in Daumier to a more ideal art; an art which, though
rooted in the *significatif*, is creatively developed into something
approaching the *comique absolu*. It is an art of 'vivantes monstruosités', like Goya's 'monstrueux vraisemblable' (*OC* ii. 569–70), in
contrast to Monnier's art of the 'monstrueusement vrai'. In the
passage where Baudelaire describes Daumier's monstrous reality
—a passage which is remarkable for the ways in which it describes

---

[42] See Amossy and Rosen, *Discours du cliché*, 5–6, and Isabelle Rieusset-Lemarié
'Stéréotype ou reproduction de langage sans sujet', in Alain Goulet, (ed.), *Le Stéréotype:
Crise et transformations*, Actes du colloque de Cerisy-la-Salle, 1993 (Caen: Presses universitaires de Caen, 1994), 15–18.
[43] It is interesting to note that Baudelaire emphasizes the received wisdom of bourgeois
tastes in art by referring to it as a Credo and by elaborating it (re-citationally and parodically) as such. See *OC* ii. 616–17.

Baudelaire's own prose poetry project—he systematically ties Daumier's art to the referential or *significatif*, while at the same time describing the impact of this art in the terms of the *absolu*:

> Feuilletez son œuvre, et vous verrez défiler devant vos yeux, dans sa réalité fantastique et saisissante, tout ce qu'une grande ville contient de vivantes monstruosités. Tout ce qu'elle renferme de trésors effrayants, grotesques, sinistres et bouffons, Daumier le connaît. Le cadavre vivant et affamé, le cadavre gras et repu, les misères ridicules du ménage, toutes les sottises, tous les orgueils, tous les enthousiasmes, tous les désespoirs du bourgeois, rien n'y manque.   (*OC* ii. 554–5)

Despite its referentiality, Daumier's *comique significatif* approaches the *absolu* because of the fear it inspires and the grotesque images it presents. Indeed, the artists Baudelaire most respects are those who achieve this blend. Certain of Hoffmann's tales (Baudelaire provides a reading list) are, for example, a 'catéchisme de haute esthétique', blending as they do a certain amount of the *significatif* with *le comique le plus absolu*: 'Ses conceptions comiques les plus supra-naturelles, les plus fugitives, et qui ressemblent souvent à des visions de l'ivresse, ont un sens moral très visible' (*OC* ii. 542). Goya's art, for all that it is neither *significatif* nor *absolu*, is the expression of 'l'Absurde possible' and the 'grotesques horreurs' he represents are 'pénétrées d'*humanité*'(*OC* ii. 570, original emphasis). The 'vivantes monstruosités' are born, then, of a comic which is 'une création mêlée d'une certaine faculté imitatrice d'éléments préexistants dans la nature' (*OC* ii. 535). The *dose* of each kind of comic varies from artist to artist and from work to work. On Baudelaire's scale of *mixité*, Daumier remains at the *significatif* end, within 'la réalité fantastique', never exceeding certain self-imposed limits which might 'blesser la conscience du genre humain' (*OC* ii. 556–7). At the other end are the artists of the *comique absolu* who, whilst retaining something of the *significatif*, depict the truly fantastic monstrous, the excessive, and the violent.[44]

Baudelaire's discussion of the *comique absolu* also extends, then, and quite naturally, into a discussion of the *fantastique* and the

---

[44] Violence is almost a synonym of the *comique absolu* in *Quelques caricaturistes étrangers*. It is the 'signe distinctif' of the English pantomime (*OC* ii. 539) and characterizes the work of Hogarth, Seymour, Cruikshank, and 'les autres Anglais'. It is 'l'explosion dans l'expression' (*OC* ii. 565–6). It is a pity, therefore, that Jérôme Thélot's far-reaching study of this theme, *Baudelaire: Violence et poésie*, does not address violence as comic, particularly in the prose poems he analyses.

merveilleux. Indeed, he draws attention to the distinction he makes between these supernatural forms when he describes the pantomime actors 'qui s'élancent à travers l'œuvre fantastique, qui, à proprement parler, ne commence que là, c'est à dire sur la frontière du merveilleux' (*OC* ii. 541). Baudelaire's description here would seem to suggest a kind of gradation through an ever-decreasing sense of the real into a world where the only structuring principles are determined by the imagination. Rosemary Lloyd proposes a distinction between the two forms.[45] 'La frontière du merveilleux', is the threshold where the context ceases to be coherently recognizable, or where grotesque symbolism becomes a pure signifier;[46] where the *fantastique* may subsist, but where it is pre-eminently hallucinatory rather than socially symbolic. This, as Baudelaire defines it, is where 'la ligne de suture, le point de jonction entre le réel et le fantastique est impossible à saisir; c'est une frontière vague que l'analyste le plus subtil ne saurait pas tracer, tant l'art est à la fois transcendent et naturel' (*OC* ii. 570). This is the landscape of 'Chacun sa chimère', as many critics have pointed out.[47] The 'coupole spleenétique du ciel' (*OC* i. 282) is a vast, grey emptiness comparable only with the barren land: 'une grande plaine poudreuse, sans chemin, sans gazon, sans un chardon, sans une ortie' (*OC* i. 282). This landscape, which Kopp compares to Dante's limbo,[48] is very much like Baudelaire's description of Goya's world, 'un paysage fantastique, un coin de Sierra inconnue et infréquentée, un échantillon du chaos, l'horreur du vague et de l'indéfini' (*OC* ii. 569). This world is reflected in the figures which traverse it, directionless and oppressed, not just by the weight upon them, but by its strong grip around them:

la monstrueuse bête n'était pas un poids inerte; au contraire elle enveloppait et opprimait l'homme des ses muscles élastiques et puissants; elle

---

[45] 'Dans le monde merveilleux, l'auteur invente des mondes que régissent des lois qui ne sont pas celles de la vie quotidienne, tandis que le fantastique, pour employer l'expression de R. Eminescu, est "le lieu d'interpénétration des normes de la vie réelle avec des normes qui n'appartiennent pas à celle-ci"', *Baudelaire et Hoffmann*, 33.

[46] David Scott, *Pictorialist Poetics: Poetry and the Visual Arts in Nineteenth-Century France* (Cambridge: Cambridge University Press, 1988), 68.

[47] See J. Prévost, *Baudelaire: Essai sur la création et l'inspiration poétiques* (Paris: Mercure de France, 1968 [1953]); Rosemary Lloyd, *Baudelaire et Hoffmann*, 37; and J. A. Hiddleston, *Baudelaire and Le Spleen de Paris*, 42.

[48] *Petits Poëmes en prose (Le Spleen de Paris)* ed. R. Kopp (Paris: Corti, 1969), 203.

s'agraffait avec ses deux vastes griffes à la poitrine de sa monture; et sa tête fabuleuse surmontait le front de l'homme comme un de ces casques horribles par lesquels les anciens guerriers espéraient ajouter à la terreur de l'ennemi. (*OC* i. 282)

The relationship between the men and their chimera is one of both unity and struggle, and it is no coincidence that, symbolic of the life of the imagination, the fantastic monster's head crowns the very part of human anatomy associated with dream and prevents its carrier from seeing it.

Prévost's association of this poem with Goya's *capricho*, 'Tu que no puedes' in which two men move across an empty landscape, burdened by the weight of two asses is a convincing one and is particularly valuable in bringing to the fore Baudelaire's response to Goya and the impact of this response on the poet's conception of the comic: 'La puissance de Goya dans le fantastique lui sert à railler un assez médiocre réel. La pensée de Goya reste en deçà de ses visions. Baudelaire au contraire va au-delà: il entrevoit dans ce dessin une vérité humaine et immense.'[49] Goya's etching is clearly satirical, whereas Baudelaire's poem owes much more to the world of metaphysics. If Spain is groaning under the oppression of fools (the aristocracy and the clergy, particularly), Baudelaire's men are oppressed by their own desires, their own hopes, and, not least of all, the very burden of having to keep living until they reach their journey's end, driven by their monstrous chimera. This is the realm of the mysterious and the fantastic, the twilight world of death and nightmare: 'le cortège se passa à côté de moi et s'enfonça dans l'atmosphère de l'horizon, à l'endroit où la surface arrondie de la planète se dérobe à la curiosité du regard humain (*OC* i. 283). The horizon is, at one and the same time, the end of life as we know it in death and the end of tangible reality as it melts into the world of nightmare. The narrator is as if transfixed a moment by what he sees, a fusion of external and internal worlds, the representation of his own 'écrasante chimère'—boredom or indifference—and the mystery of universal man's condition. Then, he too, unable to contemplate the mystery any longer (gripped by 'l'irrésistible indifférence'), is pushed to continue to tread life's path. The nightmare of the men enveloped by their chimera is another

---

[49] Prévost, *Baudelaire. Essai sur la création et l'inspiration poétiques*, 127.

brutal intrusion on the private life of the mind, an extrapolation of a personal condition which intensifies the experience. The narrator of the poem looks into the nightmarish apparition as Baudelaire engages with a visual representation. Except that here, the narrator turns away, and in his refusal to contemplate the monstrousness of his own existence for long, becomes himself framed in the grotesque representation.

This nightmarish image of men weighed down by existence recurs in 'Enivrez-vous'. The same visual impact of Goya's 'Tu que no puedes' imprints itself upon the poem, this time the *chimère* being time, that inexorable taskmaster. Except that here, rather than indifferently accepting his own indifference, the poet recommends that the shackles be cast off and that the imagination be allowed to reign: 'Pour ne pas sentir l'horrible fardeau du Temps qui brise vos épaules et vous penche vers la terre, il faut vous enivrer sans trêve' (*OC* i. 337). The opposition of the dream-world and of reality is here established, the temporary victory over time—by whatever means—holding the key to the frontier of the fantastic. Time is the antithesis of the supernatural but, as Baudelaire reminds us in 'Les Dons des fées', still reigns in 'le monde intermédiaire, placé entre l'homme et Dieu'. 'La Chambre double', where the spectre of reality is dispatched, only to reappear with its interruption of the 'éternité de délices' of the dream-world, plays out this confrontation of imagination and reality, of time and timelessness, in a way which evokes the thematics of enslavement:

> Oh! oui! le Temps a reparu; le Temps règne en souverain maintenant; et avec le hideux vieillard est revenu tout son démoniaque cortège de Souvenirs, de Regrets, de Spasmes, de Peurs, d'Angoisses, de Cauchemars, de Colères et de Névroses. [. . .]
> Oui! le Temps règne; il a repris sa brutale dictature. Et il me pousse, comme si j'étais un bœuf, avec son double aiguillon.—'Et hue donc! bourrique! Sue donc, esclave! Vis donc, damné!'   (*OC* i. 281–2)

Baudelaire explores in these poems, and in the etching 'Tu que no puedes', the way in which the nightmarish figures can be exploited both metaphysically and as the exaggerated and grotesque symbols of an oppressive, and peculiarly Baudelairean, reality. In this respect, his treatment of all visual sources is alike.[50] The imagina-

---

[50] Cf. David Scott on Puget, *Pictorialist Poetics*, 58.

tion plays with the exaggerated fictions of spectres from the real world. At the interface of everyday circumstances and the fantastic, the 'frontière du merveilleux', there is essentially a conflict between the desired fictions of the imagination—the quest for an ideal or sustained illusion—and the grotesque and exaggerated fictions of reality which haunt the poet's imagination.

Whilst Baudelaire's transposition of 'Tu que no puedes' shifts the original emphasis from the *significatif* to the *absolu* in order to exploit the image's suggestiveness and to raise questions of metaphysical significance, it is in no way to be seen as resistance to grounding such explorations of the fantastic in the everyday, as we saw in 'Les Dons des fées'. Rather, Baudelaire plays with inversions of the real and the fantastic, of nightmare and reality, to blur the boundaries between the two.

A relaxation of the will, or what Goya calls the sleep of reason, results in fictions of the imagination and exaggerated scenarios. In the celebrated etching entitled 'El Sueño de la razón produce monstruos', Goya depicts an artist neglecting his pens for dream-making activity, represented in the background by a host of different creatures. The format is, according to George Levitine, a cliché, parodied here by Goya, of 'the type of book illustration in which the depiction of the sleeping author introduces a dream sequence'.[51] Goya reworked the theme, changing it subtly on each occasion,[52] but each version contained the same dreaming artist surrounded by creatures of a fantastic nature and always with the lynx, 'the supernatural penetration of the mental eye of *fantasía*'.[53] But, as with Baudelaire, the fantastic is firmly rooted in the vulgarity of the real, in a complex network of equivalences and reversals, for as Goya was to write as a caption to the second version of the etching, 'El autor soñando. Su yntento sólo es desterrar bulgaridades perjudiciales, y perpetuar con esta obra de caprichos, el testimonio sólido de la verdad' (The author dreaming. His intention is only to banish harmful vulgarities and, with this work of extravagant fantasies, to bear sure and everlasting witness to

---

[51] 'Some Emblematic Sources of Goya', *Journal of the Warburg and Courtauld Institutes* (1959), 114. The specific example given occurs in a 1726 edition of Quevedo's *Obras*.

[52] See José Manuel B. Lopez Vasquez, *Los Caprichos de Goya y su significado* (Santiago de Compostela: Universidad de Santiago, 1982), 171.

[53] G. Levitine, 'Some Emblematic Sources of Goya', 121.

truth).[54] The etching was to become the frontispiece, the signifying threshold of the fantastic world of the *caprichos*, creating a sense of visual space which could be explored by the fantasy of the spectator or which established the other *caprichos* as products of Goya's dream-work.

Although Baudelaire does not specifically mention this etching in his discussion of Goya, he clearly demonstrates an awareness of those techniques and themes Goya exploits in it and which emerge from his work as a whole. Hannoosh points out that there is, in Baudelaire's appreciation of Goya, an awareness of 'a dual, equivocal quality' and further suggests that this essay demonstrates his clear understanding of the interplay between the rational and the irrational, and their reciprocal value:

As the title states, the sleep of reason produces the monsters of superstition, prejudice, ignorance and oppression; but at the same time, only *through* the sleep of reason are the monsters exposed and the immense power of the irrational brought to light—through the equally monstrous creations of the *Caprichos* themselves.[55]

Baudelaire's awareness of this interplay is still more clearly revealed by his application of it in the prose poem 'Les Tentations'. This poem is an elaborate play on the sleep of reason[56] and in it the poet-narrator is witness to a fantastic enactment of the socially monstrous. In this way the poem plays upon the notion of the creative process as the enactment of the imagination's gremlins (the irrational, supernatural, and grotesque) as well as caricaturing the process of enlightenment.

The poem recounts a dream:

Deux superbes Satans et une Diablesse, non moins extraordinaire, ont la nuit dernière monté l'escalier mystérieux par où l'enfer donne assaut à la faiblesse de l'homme qui dort, et communique en secret avec lui. Et ils sont venus se poser glorieusement devant moi, debout comme sur une estrade. Une splendeur sulfureuse émanait de ces trois personnages, qui se détachaient ainsi du fond opaque de la nuit. Ils avaient l'air si fier et si plein de domination, que je les pris d'abord tous les trois pour de vrais Dieux.   (*OC* i. 308)

---

[54] Cited in J. M. B. Lopez Vazquez, *Los Caprichos de Goya*, 171 (my translation).
[55] Hannoosh, *Baudelaire and Caricature*, 212.
[56] The *Caprichos* were, at one stage, to be entitled *Sueños*, ibid. 213.

There is a notion of theatrical illusion implicit in the assault on the imagination, the stage, the effects of the light, and, most importantly perhaps, in the mistaking of the actors for something they are not. It is particularly in this respect that the full complexities of grotesque and fantastic iconography become apparent, since tangible elements mingle with absurd monsters and sleep and waking mingle with the same lack of clarity as theatrical illusion. The fusion of diverse iconographic elements is particularly marked where there is some form of logical discontinuity, or where there is ironic incongruity. This is most apparent in 'Les Tentations', where devils are confused with deities as they come to offer an earthly paradise. The first of these, an androgynous Eros, adorned with the accoutrements of Original Sin, of sex and surgery, and of Christian faith, appears in the traditional form and red tunic of the Devil:[57]

Autour de sa tunique de pourpre était roulé, en manière de ceinture, un serpent chatoyant qui, la tête relevée, tournait langoureusement vers lui ses yeux de braise. A cette ceinture vivante étaient suspendus, alternant avec des fioles pleines de liqueurs sinistres, de brillants couteaux et des instruments de chirurgie. Dans sa main droite il tenait une autre fiole dont le contenu était d'un rouge lumineux, et qui portait pour étiquette ces mots bizarres: 'Buvez, ceci est mon sang, un parfait cordial'; dans la gauche, un violon qui lui servait sans doute à chanter ses plaisirs et ses douleurs, et à répandre la contagion de sa folie dans les nuits de sabbat.

À ses chevilles délicates traînaient quelques anneaux d'une chaîne d'or rompue, et quand la gêne qui en résultait le forçait à baisser les yeux vers la terre, il contemplait vaniteusement les ongles de ses pieds, brillants et polis comme des pierres bien travaillées. (*OC* i. 308)

The fantastically grotesque presentation of Eros as a devil who uses a perfumed sensuality of tropical fragrance to win over the poet is combined with the rather terrifying image of insects fluttering from his fiery lips, described as incense-burners.

There is a highly complex interplay of imagery and iconography in this poem, as the bacchant reveller hawks his sexual temptation with the traditional image of an aroused snake, but also with the subverted religious symbol of blood as a *parfait cordial*, suggestive of sexual stimulation and exchange, but in the image of a very

[57] This is itself an inversion. The colour *pourpre* is associated with high office, royalty, and the Church.

different kind of communion to which it is clearly a reference. The knives and surgical instruments, the *mystérieuse coutellerie*, are another reference to the Bistouri-like fantasy of submission and aggression, and here combine with the shackles of human sexual relationships and the all-pervading cruelty associated with the lacerating effect on the flesh that the manicured nails, so carefully described, might have. The diverse elements come together in the compound image of sexual love, as the erotic devil makes the poet the following promise, coaxing him gently with the persuasive repetition of *si tu veux* and the insistence upon it being his own desire:

'Si tu veux, si tu veux, je te ferai le seigneur des âmes, et tu seras le maître de la matière vivante, plus encore que le sculpteur peut l'être de l'argile; et tu connaîtras le plaisir, sans cesse renaissant, de sortir de toi-même pour t'oublier dans autrui, et d'attirer les autres âmes jusqu à les confondre avec la tienne.'   (*OC* i. 308)

Sexual communion, with all its attendant cruelty and power-play, becomes fused with the clichés of Catholicism, subverted in language and iconography, so that Eros can tempt with a dramatic reinvention of the all-too-familiar icons of Christian faith. This complex fusion of religious and grotesque iconographic elements is representative of Baudelaire's attempts to render the iconographic impact of grotesque art (and particularly of Goya's grotesque) on his creative imagination, in that the mosaic of symbols and connotations assumes the appearance of a terrifying fantasy. Its references and associations are reassuringly familiar, but it is through the combination and incongruity of these that the fantastic assumes its power and impact.

The same is true of the use of traditional iconography in the works of Goya. In the etching 'Todos caerán', for example, the old woman prays for the demise of the men at the hands of the young prostitutes, the women forming a threesome at the foot of a crucifix-like composition. The picture space would seem, therefore, to be making ironic use of religious and artistic associations, the women's waiting for the men being a reinvention of the deposition of Christ in the presence of the three Marys, here subverted into an act of greed and lust, rather than one of maternal and spiritual generosity. The *caprichos* 'Duendecitos' (demonic creatures, but also monks)[58] and 'Se repulen' show devil-like creatures with the same nails as Eros in the prose poem, helping each other in some dubious design. The satire of portraying monks as devils involved in shady operations (hence the way one of those present in 'Se repulen' hides the group with his bat-like wings) points to the many occasions when Goya treats the theme of religious and governmental hypocrisy,[59] describing these figures in his somewhat ironic commentary of 'Duendecitos' as 'ya otra gente. Alegres, juguetones, serviciales y un poco golosos, amigos de pegar chascos, pero muy hombrecitos de bien' (an altogether different sort of person. Happy, playful, obliging and rather greedy, given to playing tricks, but for all that good and honest little fellows).[60]

The devils in Baudelaire's *Petits Poèmes en prose* play a similar role to Goya's imp-like creatures, then, for they combine grotesque fantasy with a sense of socio-religious satire. 'Les Tentations' is a parody of the temptation of Christ, the three temptations here appearing as the three separate creatures of the poem's subtitle *Eros, Plutus et la Gloire*. The first, as we have seen, is the temptation of physical love; the second of money; and the third, fame. These three desired objectives are mentioned directly by Baudelaire in a letter to his mother which, written in November 1856, is of interest not only because of their occurrence here, but also because of the terms in which Baudelaire describes his longing for them. He writes: 'J'ai une soif diabolique de jouissance, de gloire et de puissance' (*C* i. 360). In the fantasy as it is played out in 'Les Tentations', however, the three demons are presented as unattractive, for one reason or another. Just as Eros's offer of love, or physical *jouissance*, is presented as trickery, cruelty, and a shackle (despite the perfumed exoticism), so power is presented as synonymous with money, here essentially bourgeois, overweight, showy, and all gained at the expense of others. In contrast with Eros, Plutus appears in a more earthly form, the representative over-fed bourgeois fixed by nineteenth-century iconography:[61]

---

[58] Lopez Vasquez points out that, in the second half of the 18th cent., *duende* was often used as a synonym of *fraile*, *Los Caprichos de Goya*, 194.

[59] See, for further examples of this, *Caprichos* 11, 'Están calientes', and 8, '¡Que se la llevaron!'   [60] Cited by Lopez Vasquez, *Los Caprichos de Goya*, 194.

[61] The fat paunch and small eyes was to become a fixed characteristic of the stupidity, indifference, and arrogance of the bourgeois. See Judith Wechsler, *A Human Comedy*, 76–8.

C'était un homme vaste, à gros visage sans yeux, dont la lourde bedaine surplombait les cuisses, et dont toute la peau était dorée et illustrée, comme d'un tatouage, d'une foule de petite figures mouvantes représentant les formes nombreuses de la misère universelle. Il y avait de petits hommes efflanqués qui se suspendaient volontairement à un clou; il y avait de petits gnomes difformes, maigres, dont les yeux suppliants réclamaient l'aumône mieux encore que leur mains tremblantes; et puis de vieilles mères portant des avortons accrochés à leurs mamelles exténuées. Il y en avait encore bien d'autres.

Le gros Satan tapait avec son poing sur son immense ventre, d'où sortait alors un long et retentissant cliquetis de métal, qui se terminait en un vague gémissement fait de nombreuses voix humaines. Et il riait, en montrant impudemment ses dents gâtées, d'un énorme rire imbécile, comme certains hommes de tous les pays quand ils ont trop bien dîné. (*OC* i. 309)

In this temptation, the imagery is much closer to the *significatif* than that of Eros, although there is a similar confluence of grotesque iconographic elements. More than in the first temptation, the representation of this second one is a combination of modern characterizations of a certain class or type, owing much to Daumier's 'Gargantua' who swallows favours and bribes and defecates medals and money as he is surrounded by the needy who serve him, but also to the fantastic grotesque. The tattoos on the skin of the devil are the physical manifestation of the devil's guilt, 'un papier de tenture de tous les malheurs' (*OC* i. 309) with skeletal creatures reminiscent of Hogarth's 'Gin Lane' hanging from the skin, emaciated and ugly, disgustingly grotesque in their misery.[62] It is the skin, crawling with the needs and miseries of those dependent on it, which is the projection of the fantastic imagination, the perception of something so horrifying and yet so real. This external visual trace is interesting also in that it represents an elaboration of the principles of physiognomy, the classification of character types according to outward bodily signs, by imprinting

---

[62] Baudelaire mentions this engraving only briefly (*OC* ii. 565), but he does so to comment on the 'cas terribles qui sont peu comiques à notre point de vue français'. Baudelaire's poem evokes 'vieilles mères portant des avortons accrochés à leurs mamelles exténuées' (*OC* i. 309) and in both 'Gin Lane' and 'Gargantua' there are equivalent grotesque representations of infants at the breast of the defiled mothers. Some of the grotesque images of 'Les Tentations' would seem an attempt to incorporate the horrors of this kind of splenetic and violent comic art into a broader framework represented both by Baudelaire's essay and his application of these theories in the prose poem.

on the features the impact of that character on other individuals. There is, in fact, a Goya etching, 'El Coloso durmiente', which represents a human form as mass of tiny creatures, and it is possible that this 'tatouage' in Baudelaire is a reworking of the motif; a reworking which emphasizes the dream-work implicit in the Goya drawing which shows only the head of a sleeping man composed of a myriad of tiny figures which constitute its features.

The same mixture of the real and the fantastic grotesque is to be found in the person of the third temptation, Fame, who again is representative of some kind of gain for favours. As in the narrative's biblical equivalent, the third temptation is the hardest to resist, since the courtesan arrives blowing a reinterpreted *heavenly* trumpet, the trumpet of worldly renown. The herald of the modern age is the press, 'enrubannée comme un mirliton' [63] with the names of the world's newspapers, powerful institutions which make and break reputations. The *trompette* is, like the woman herself in the narrator's view, *prostituée*. Again, the temptation appears as an allegory, but one which fuses very real characteristics—such as her voice, hoarse through too much *eau-de-vie*—with the symbol of the desired objective. With each temptation comes a refusal, culminating in the *Va-t-en* of powerful biblical connotations.

The narrator is impressed and, therefore, tempted, punningly interjecting 'Diable!', but he is only 'à moitié subjugué'. It is paradoxical that, in the sleep of reason, he can triumph over such temptation, for the extravagant creations of his imagination offer enlightenment when, in a conscious state, the reality is more tempting:

Certes, d'une si courageuse abnégation j'avais le droit d'être fier. Mais malheureusement je me réveillai, et toute ma force m'abandonna. 'En vérité, me dis-je, il fallait que je fusse bien lourdement assoupi pour montrer de tels scrupules. Ah! s'ils pouvaient revenir pendant que je suis éveillé, je ne ferai pas tant le délicat!'

Et je les invoquai à haute voix, les suppliant de me pardonner, leur offrant de me déshonorer aussi souvent qu'il le faudrait pour mériter

---

[63] The image of the *mirliton* has interesting connotations since it is suggestive of the cheap kazoo-like instrument given to children at carnivals. That is to say, coarse and transient instruments which make a lot of noise. See the *Dictionnaire de l'Académie française* (1878), which describes the *mirliton* as a 'roseau bouché par les deux bouts avec une pelure d'oignon ou un morceau de baudruche'.

leurs faveurs; mais je les avais sans doute fortement offensés, car ils ne sont jamais revenus. (*OC* i. 310)

His resistance to temptation upholds the othodoxy, but with none of the Christian virtue one might expect. Indeed, it is out of pride that the narrator of 'Les Tentations' refuses on each occasion, showing himself to be superior to the Tempters. The inversions here become more apparent. The devil-like creatures are like 'de vrais Dieux' and the narrator, in his proud responses to each temptation, betrays superiority—'idée satanique s'il en fut jamais! Orgueil et aberration!', as Baudelaire points out in *De l'essence du rire* (*OC* ii. 530). If Goya's images suggest 'the *impossibility* of defeating evil other than through the *irrational*, that is, the extraordinary, extravagant creations of the imagination',[64] 'Les Tentations' takes this a step further by simultaneously defeating the evil Tempters in sleep, and recalling them in waking, so that the grotesque hallucination can be properly re-enacted as rational acceptance of what is properly monstrous.

This dream of the gratification of desire recurs in 'Le Joueur généreux', where once again the Devil appears, with the strongly recognizable characteristics of some munificent bourgeois, and in a fantastic underground world (readily accessible from the streets of Paris). This dream-world is hell, but is represented here as the land of Tennyson's lotus eaters[65] or the billows of 'Déjà', which the poet strives to attain through the imagination and through which he seeks to intoxicate his senses.[66] It resembles Baudelaire's *enfer* in a very specific sense, however, for the narrator says 'jamais je ne vis d'yeux brillant plus énergiquement de l'horreur de l'ennui et du désir immortel de se sentir vivre' (*OC* i. 325).

The narrator stakes his soul in a card game and loses, but the cliché is subverted when the Devil generously gives his partner the prize he would have won only to prove the truth of the popular expression that he is *bon diable*. He may not return the lost soul

---

[64] Hannoosh, *Baudelaire and Caricature*, 212–13.

[65] The Baudelairean paradise of 'calme, ordre et volupté' here transposed in the context of hell, with its peace and tranquillity and the sibilant music of the waterfalls, is a direct borrowing from Tennyson's 'The Lotus Eaters'.

[66] It is usually with the verb *s'enivrer* that this spiritual and sensual *emportement* is expressed and Baudelaire's careful avoidance of this verb and his choice of the coarser alternative *se soûler* is, no doubt, significant, suggesting the direct materialism of the devil's offer.

but, with an ironic reference to fate, the autocratic Devil does offer the fantasies of the temptations represented by Eros, Plutus, and Fame:

'Je vous donne l'enjeu que vous auriez gagné si le sort avait été pour vous, c'est-à-dire la possibilité de soulager et de vaincre, pendant toute votre vie, cette bizarre affection de l'Ennui, qui est la source de toutes vos maladies et de tous vos misérables progrès. Jamais un désir ne sera formé par vous, que je ne vous aide à le réaliser; vous régnerez sur vos vulgaires semblables; vous serez fourni de flatteries et même d'adorations; l'argent, l'or, les diamants, les palais féeriques, viendront vous chercher et vous prieront de les accepter, sans que vous ayez fait un effort pour les gagner; vous changerez de contrée et de patrie aussi souvent que votre fantaisie vous l'ordonnera; vous vous soûlerez de voluptés, sans lassitude, dans des pays charmants où il fait toujours chaud et où les femmes sentent aussi bonnes que les fleurs, — et cætera, et cætera...'. (OC i. 328)

This is a list of the things the poet most longs for, and the Devil's unwillingness to continue the list is a sort of pact between himself and the narrator (and man, more generally) by which we understand that he knows our every desire. The narrator is overwhelmed by his generosity, but his pride prevents him from showing humble appreciation by kneeling before this benefactor. In every gesture, the narrator challenges social and religious convention. In praying for the Devil to keep his promise, the narrator makes a gesture as ridiculous as the one for which Baudelaire criticizes his mother when she prays for the success of his theatrical enterprises or when he himself wishes Poe to be an intercessor.[67] Subsumed in this comic paradox is the oblique reference to the importance of faith for the accomplishment of God's work, twisted in 'Le Joueur généreux' into an inability (yet overwhelming desire) to put trust in the Devil, in the Satanic illusion: 'Mais peu à peu, après que je l'eus quitté, l'incurable défiance rentra dans mon sein; je n'osais plus croire à un si prodigieux bonheur' (OC i. 328). The yearning for faith is challenged by a deep-rooted disbelief which, when it challenges God's word, is traditionally considered to be the work of the Devil. Here, a lack of faith asserts itself at a level distinct from diabolic persuasion, so profound is the *esprit de révolte* of the

---

[67] 10 Oct. 1859: Ton idée de prier Dieu pour mes affaires de théâtre est très comique: mais tout ce qui vient de toi est toujours très bien' (C i. 607); and *Hygiène*, VII (OC i. 673).

narrator. Alternatively, what the *défiance* reveals is the attraction to the worldly promises of satanism, but an irretrievable anchor in the doctrines of traditional Christianity which remind the narrator that the Devil can never be trusted.

This jesting at the interface of good and evil, the inversions, the punning, the complex twisting of conventional expectations, and the incongruous iconography all contribute to a sense that the imagination elaborates upon situations which are not only profoundly rooted in the psyche, but which have significant ramifications for an interpretation of the artist's relationship with his social context. In 'Le Joueur généreux' and 'Les Tentations', the exchanges which occur suggest that, through the comic grotesque, Baudelaire is not simply exploring the fantastic grotesque, but also attempting to raise central theological and social questions through this exploration. The statement in 'Le Joueur généreux' that the greatest ruse of the Devil is to pretend that he does not exist (*OC* i. 326–7) remains intimately linked with the idea of Original Sin and orthodox Christian values, but there is clearly more to what becomes, in the hands of Baudelaire, an ironic joke. Here, Satan's presence is assured (even if it is only in the imagination of the narrator) and his world so vividly evoked within the urban reality that the narrator is astonished that he had not noticed it before (*OC* i. 325). But, where the Devil does not appear in person, he appears as an incitement to action, as an enactment in the imagination. In this way, the satanic experience becomes a drive or impulse, rather like Goya's *duendecitos* who accomplish acts of grotesque foolery in the imagination in the same way as the *démon d'action* or *démon de combat* of 'Le Mauvais Vitrier' and 'Assommons les pauvres!': the enactment of a grotesque fantasy through fictionalization of the *impulsion mystérieuse et inconnue*. This enactment in the imagination is not so much a complete escape from the realities of everyday existence, but rather like the comic, a way of representing and exorcizing the profound dissatisfactions and of conquering them with imaginary scenarios. The more grotesque these scenarios, the greater the sense of victory.

The grounding of grotesque nightmare in recognizable nineteenth-century social stereotypes demonstrates Baudelaire's own ideal of a fusion of the *significatif* and the *absolu*, even if that occurs in the synthetic vision of the spectator (*OC* ii. 568). In this way, 'Les Tentations' can be seen as a way of anchoring the *absolu* in the *significatif*; and 'Chacun sa chimère' as an embodiment, or an aestheticization, of the process Baudelaire suggests in his description of Daumier's art, where the *significatif* is raised to the *absolu* by the epithets Baudelaire applies to it. A large number of the prose poems can be seen, then, as the sort of *défilé* of 'vivantes monstruosités' that he associates with Daumier and, indeed, all comic art. It is the 'chaos des vivantes cités' (*OC* i. 91) reproduced in disorder and discontinuity, but in all its grotesqueness and humanity.

The prose poem, like comic art, is perfectly adapted to such representation, for it is the formal combination of the prosaic and the extraordinary, the eccentric within the banal and tragic extracted from the trivial. Indeed, T. J. Clark has remarked upon the uneasy insertion of the metaphorical in plainness of diction and on the way in which, in 'Le Vin des chiffonniers', this effects a shift from the ordinary to the fantastic.[68] This ordinariness of expression, this grotesque prosaism of artistic form, is itself the expression, the evolving discourse, of the nineteenth-century city.[69] In its most prosaic form, it is the *locution vulgaire*. It is in this context that what Baudelaire says about that form of clichéd discourse seems to take on new life: 'Profondeur immense de pensée dans les locutions vulgaires, trous creusés par des générations de fourmis' (*OC* i. 650). The ant image occurs again in *Tableaux parisiens*, in those poems which frame the monstrous encounters of the modern city. Baudelaire's 'fourmillante cité' releases, as Richard Burton has so eloquently argued, 'a whole Pandora's box of urban monstrosities' and 'suggests a writhing mass of ant-like creatures, all identical to each other, a magma of barely differentiated shapes and forms'.[70] But what emerges from such forms is chiasmic creativity, since the 'fourmillante cité', the city of endlessly reproducible sameness, soon becomes the 'cité pleine de rêves'.[71] Reading this as a

---

[68] *The Absolute Bourgeois: Artists and Politics in France 1848–1851* (London: Thames & Hudson, 1978 [1973]), 161–2. Clark, in fact, looks closely here at the different versions of this poem, in prose and verse, which was initially dedicated to Daumier and which, in his view, remains, in its different forms, his poem and a reflection of his interests and methods.

[69] On this point, see Terdiman, *Discourse/Counter-Discourse*, 266–8.

[70] *Baudelaire in 1859. A Study in the Sources of Poetic Creativity* (Cambridge: Cambridge University Press, 1988), 108.

[71] Pichois notes this in his formal appreciation of this line: 'Admirable coup d'archet initial que cet alexandrin, en forme de chiasme et d'accent circonflexe, distribuant autour de la césure le mot cité répété' (*OC* i. 1012).

grotesque creative fertility (*pleine* as pregnant), the city 'engenders
a never-ending progeny of freaks and monsters, spawning them in
an uncanny and uncontrollable manner';[72] it is like 'la ville en son
ampleur', viewed from the mountain in the 'projet d'épilogue' as
an inclusive panorama of the degraded human condition: 'Hôpital,
lupanar, purgatoire, enfer, bagne, | Où toute énormité fleurit
comme une fleur' (*OC* i. 191). Paris as monster is a cliché. Balzac
reworks the image in a number of ways, but describes it, for
example, as 'le plus délicieux des monstres' and as 'cette monstrueuse merveille',[73] terms which Baudelaire seems to echo in his
variations on the poetry of the grotesque in comic art. In
Baudelaire, however, as in the best examples of comic art, the stock
image is always reinvested or inverted. So it is, then, that
Baudelaire harnesses the clichéd monstrosity of the city (that
which makes it surreal), or indeed any other stock image of monstrosity, with other commonplace *parisianismes*. In this conjunction
and inversion, the degraded humanity of the city become monstrous and the monsters of the imagination become bourgeois
stereotypes. Paris is, for example, figured (and repeatedly) as a
monstrous prostitute, *Paris-Putain*,[74] or an 'énorme catin'. This
formula, reminiscent of Baudelaire's assertion that poetry can rival
the visual (and other) arts 'par l'accouplement de tel substantif
avec tel adjectif, analogue ou contraire' (*OC* i. 183), reproduces, in
the vulgar deformation and defamation of a name (Catherine), the
monstrosity (*énormité*) of the figure.[75] The slippage from Paris as
monster to Paris as prostitute (another cliché) is almost natural in
the discourses of the nineteenth century,[76] and the prostitute body

---

[72] Burton, *Baudelaire in 1859*, 108.

[73] *Ferragus, La Comédie humaine* (Paris: Pléiade, 1951–65), v. 18–19. Cited by Prendergast, *Paris and the Nineteenth Century*, 246 n. 136.

[74] The term is Burton's, *Baudelaire in 1859*, 108

[75] Cf. Prendergast's analysis of the irony of *énorme* in this context: 'it is é-norme, that which transgresses and exceeds the norm, not just as subversion of the morally normative, but also as distressingly beyond the norms of intelligibility, as that which defeats the sense-making powers of the artist', *Paris and the Nineteenth Century*, 162.

[76] Dr Alexandre Jean Baptiste Parent-Duchâtelet was largely responsible for this. His major study on prostitution, *De la prostitution dans la Ville de Paris*, created a taxonomy of the prostitute which became the source of all 19th-cent. commonplaces regarding the prostitute, as well as a source of inspiration for artists and writers who, in their turn and with their stereotypes, may even have shaped the behaviours of prostitutes themselves. See Bernheimer, *Figures of Ill Repute*. Baudelaire himself plays on this cliché when, in his discussion of Gavarni, he remarks: 'Gavarni a créé la Lorette [. . .] et quelques-unes de ces filles se sont perfectionnées en se l'assimilant' (*OC* ii. 560).

becomes synonymous with urban space, 'not just a figure in the city, but a figure of the city'.[77]

'Quelles bizarreries ne trouve-t-on pas dans une grande ville, quand on sait se promener et regarder?' asks, rhetorically, the narrator of 'Mademoiselle Bistouri', before asserting the monstrosity of urban reality: 'La vie fourmille de monstres innocents.' The poem recounts the encounter between the poet-narrator and a prostitute who accosts him at nightfall 'à l'extrémité du faubourg'. Both the time and the topography emphasize marginality, the frontiers between one condition and another.[78] The poem builds its humour on a case of mistaken identity which Baudelaire plays out in a dramatization of the events and the dialogue, itself comically reproducing the failure of the encounter in a 'dialogue de sourds':

'Vous êtes médecin, Monsieur?' [. . .]

'— Non; je ne suis pas médecin. Laissez-moi passer. — Oh! si! vous êtes médecin. Je le vois bien. Venez chez moi. Vous serez bien content de moi, allez!—Sans doute, j'irai vous voir, *après le médecin*, que diable! . . .— Ah! ah!—fit-elle, toujours suspendue à mon bras, et en éclatant de rire,— vous êtes un médecin farceur, j'en ai connu plusieurs dans ce genre-là. Venez.' (*OC* i. 353)

The narrator's joke, italicized to draw attention to the pun, plays creatively with the cliché of public health and prostitution and appeals to the reader who, with the narrator, adopts a certain superiority, a *quant-à-soi*. The joke is not, however, lost on her and is, indeed, compounded by her insistence that he is a doctor of the joking sort. With this insistence, in fact, she gains the upper hand because, both as a result of her refusal to take no for an answer and the narrator being 'hooked' on the enigma of her already apparent obsession, he allows himself to be escorted back to her place. The self-correction of the narrator is, here, significant, for the rejection of the term *compagne* in favour of *énigme* installs a degree of distance in the transaction which he will continue to exploit ironically. The distance, in fact, increases as the narrator delivers, in Bistouri's direct speech, more and more of her medical fantasies

---

[77] Prendergast, *Paris and the Nineteenth Century*, 161.

[78] This sets up the poem's central concerns. The 'extrémité du faubourg' is a metaphor for eccentricity and the socially marginal, and, as we know from 'Le Crépuscule du soir', 'le crépuscule excite les fous' (*OC* i. 311). These limits also mark the limits of their encounter and they are a metaphor for the protagonists' indistinguishability.

involving him, without intervention on his part until she, so sure of the identity she has created for him, slips into *tutoiement* and causes him to object to the fiction. Like his first intervention, his second is again a joke at her expense, but Bistouri has closed the distance between them, and the narrator himself is seduced into the familiarity of the *tu* form.

Since he is still resisting all her attempts to implicate him in her fantasies, Bistouri changes tactic, reaching for images, 'des portraits des médecins illustres de ce temps'. This is a bid on her part to implicate him by seducing him into admitting recognition. The narrator plays along, to the delight of Bistouri, who is not duped and who herself draws attention to the fact that the name is printed beneath the lithograph. At this point the game develops into physiognomic reflection:

'Tiens! voilà Z., celui qui disait à son cours, en parlant de X.: 'ce monstre qui porte sur son visage la noirceur de son âme!' [. . .] Tien, voilà K., celui qui dénonçait au gouvernement les insurgés qu'il soignait à son hôpital. C'était le temps des émeutes. Comment est-ce possible qu'un si bel homme ait si peu de cœur?' (*OC* i. 354)

The purpose of this is not only to parody the clichés drawn from Lavater's encyclopaedia of characters, which included a chapter entitled 'Observations sur les signes physiognomiques des professions',[79] but to frame the characters' reading of each other (reciprocal portraits) and to bring into focus the paradoxes of this poem. Bistouri takes the narrator for a doctor because he is 'si gentil et si bon pour les femmes'. This gentleness, which matches Bistouri's own, contrasts sharply with the doctor as 'un homme qui aime couper, tailler et rogner' and the fantasy of the doctor-lover 'avec sa trousse et tablier, même avec un peu de sang dessus'. This poem is the elaboration of ideas on sexuality which are more tersely formulated in the *Journaux intimes*. In *Fusées*, for example, Baudelaire writes: 'il y a dans l'acte de l'amour une grande ressemblance avec

---

[79] Wechsler cites an extract from this which is particularly relevant here: 'Skilful and very experienced surgeons have in their physiognomy a particular dominant trait, which comes from a habitual movement of raising the upper lip—which can be attributed to the effort they make to resist the impression caused by the sight of suffering and pain which they have before their eyes during major operations'. Prostitutes, like politicians, require their observer to exercise both physiognomic discrimination and dissimulation.' *A Human Comedy*, 25–6.

la torture, ou avec une opération chirurgicale' (*OC* i. 659); and in *Mon cœur mis à nu* 'Quant à la torture, elle est née de la partie infâme du cœur de l'homme, assoiffé de voluptés. Cruauté et volupté, sensations identiques, comme l'extrême chaud et l'extrême froid' (*OC* i. 683). The paradox is resolved in the fundamental duality of humanity. This is just one of a series of paradoxes and rôle reversals. Bistouri pays the doctors when it turns out she has troubled them '*inutilement*' and offers her services free of charge to a polite 'petit interne', as well as hospitality to the narrator. The narrator is feminized and Bistouri masculinized, in her name, physique, and in her fantasy which, the narrator says, is spoken like a man's desire to see his actress-lover in costume.[80] Indeed, it is at the point where Bistouri confesses her male fantasy, that the narrator reasserts his *idée-fixe*, but as if transfixed (seduced) by these confessions, he falls into the rôle he has so far resisted and speaks like a doctor: 'Peux-tu te souvenir de l'époque et de l'occasion où est née en toi cette passion si particulière?' Suddenly the magic is broken. Mademoiselle Bistouri disconnects and becomes vacant, hesitant, and inarticulate and the narrator, too, turns away to seek answers elsewhere.

The prayer at the end of the poem, with its complex ironies, questions the very notions of the monster and the monstrous and leaves uncertain the narrator's ability to understand the mysteries of man's moral ugliness:[81]

Seigneur, mon Dieu! vous, le créateur, vous le Maître; vous qui avez fait la Loi et la Liberté; vous, le souverain qui laissez faire, vous, le juge qui pardonnnez; vous qui êtes pleins de motifs et de causes, et qui avez peut-être mis dans mon esprit le goût de l'horreur pour convertir mon cœur, comme la guérison au bout d'une lame; Seigneur, ayez pitié, ayez pitié des fous et des folles! Ô Créateur! peut-il exister des monstres aux yeux de Celui-là seul qui sait pourquoi ils existent, comment ils *se sont faits* et comment ils auraient pu *ne pas se faire*? (*OC* i. 356)

The narrator's obsession with understanding the monstrous other, with penetrating the mystery of her condition, ends in the frozen

---

[80] For a fuller discussion of the masculine/feminine dialectic in this prose poem, see Marie Maclean's excellent analysis, *Narrative as Performance*, 148–60.
[81] As Prévost notes, this questioning of intelligibility becomes almost blasphemous. *Baudelaire: Essai sur la création et l'inspiration poétiques*, 122.

image of his own monstrosity, his own 'goût de l'horreur' embodied in his fascination with Bistouri. Despite the punning reference to this poem's inversions in 'la guérison au bout d'une lame', we are left wondering how much self-knowledge the narrator really has. His appeal to God asserts recognition of the monstrous as a human condition, but seeks to ensure *differentiation* in that recognition.[82] This is ironic, not least because the Divine Creator, too, is monstrous and, as Baudelaire writes in *Mon cœur mis à nu*, he is 'l'être le plus prostitué' (*OC* i. 692). The paradoxes of this text are the same as those at the heart of Baudelaire's comic theory. The narrator, despite his passion for deciphering the mysterious, is left with no answers, either from Bistouri or from his entreaty. In his desire to distinguish himself from the monstrous, he too becomes an unwitting victim of the grotesque comic for, in accordance with the *comique absolu*, the object of the comic can only be comic 'à la condition d'ignorer sa nature' and, 'par une loi inverse, l'artiste n'est artiste qu'à condition d'être double et de n'ignorer aucun phénomène de sa nature double' (*OC* ii. 543). This is an aspect of the comic in the prose poems to which we shall return, but for the moment we should remain with the monstrous others which the text parades.

Most often, Baudelaire uses the term *monstre* (and its variations) with respect to women and, indeed, this is one of the characteristics that most attracts him in Goya's work: 'toutes les débauches du rêve, toutes les hyperboles de l'hallucination, et puis toutes ces blanches et sveltes Espagnoles que de vieilles sempiternelles lavent et préparent, soit pour le sabbat, soit pour la prostitution du soir, sabbat de la civilisation' (*OC* ii. 568). It is the need to fix these haunting female creatures in grotesque iconography that Baudelaire explores in 'Le Désir de peindre', where the object of his interest is dark, mysterious, and touched by a moon which is 'sinistre et enivrante' and where the vision of laughter brings about the urge to paint, or describe it:

---

[82] The narrator prays for those touched by madness and monstrosity in a way which is clearly not self-inclusive. Shoshana Felman argues that 'to talk about madness is always, in fact, to deny it. However one represents madness to oneself or others, to represent madness is always, consciously or unconsciously, to play out the scene of the denial of one's own madness'. *Writing and Madness* (Ithaca, NY: Cornell University Press, 1985), 252. Cited by Evans, *Baudelaire and Intertextuality*, 73.

Dans son petit front habitent la volonté tenace et l'amour de la proie. Cependant, au bas de ce visage inquiétant, où des narines mobiles aspirent l'inconnu et l'impossible, éclate, avec une grâce inexprimable, le rire d'une grande bouche, rouge et blanche, et délicieuse, qui fait rêver au miracle d'une superbe fleur éclose dans un terrain volcanique.   (*OC* i. 340).

The hallucinatory fantasies which Baudelaire selects in Goya are precisely those which represent witchcraft. Baudelaire refers specifically to the etching '¿Quien lo creyera?', of which he says: 'toute la hideur, toutes les saletés morales, tous les vices que l'esprit humain peut concevoir sont écrits sur ces deux faces, qui, suivant une habitude fréquente et un procédé inexplicable de l'artiste, tiennent le milieu entre l'homme et la bête' (*OC* ii. 569). The monstrous, like the *chimère*, is always double, half-human, half-beast. David Scott has shown how this particular etching is transposed in 'Duellum' into a struggle between the poet and his mistress,[83] and this motif is further exploited in the *Petits Poèmes en prose*, where no fewer than ten poems explore female monstrosity in some form or other. These *Sorcières thessaliennes* are reminiscent of other Goya etchings, the prostitutes who subjugate men and pluck them like chickens in 'Todos caerán' and 'Ya van desplumados' . Even maternal love is portrayed as corrupt when, in 'La Corde', a poem perhaps inspired by 'A Caza de dientes',[84] the hanged son's rope is sought by the mother so that she might make some money out of human superstition (*OC* i. 331). For Baudelaire, however, what is lost in the seduction is not just the purse (as with Goya's plucked males), but something far more atavistic, deeply spiritual and creative. Baudelaire exploits the duality of the monstrous, either, as in 'Mademoiselle Bistouri', 'Portraits de maîtresses', and 'Un cheval de race', by masculinizing the female, or by showing that grotesqueness to be part of a binary ideal. There is a microcosm of this duality in 'La Chambre double' where woman is seen as a remedy for *Ennui* and where the poet's dream of 'l'Idole, la souveraine

---

[83] *Pictorial Poetics*, 67–8.
[84] It seems remarkable, if not intended, that there should be such a close parallel between this etching and 'La Corde', particularly since the latter is known to be based on the suicide of Manet's model Alexandre who hanged himself sometime between the spring of 1859 and the summer of 1860. See Robert Kopp, *Petits Poëmes en prose* (Paris: Corti, 1969), 305. Both the etching and the prose poem bear witness to the same horror of false grief, superstition, and the commercialization of both.

des rêves' suddenly yields to the grotesque reality of an 'infâme concubine qui vient crier misère et ajouter les trivialités de sa vie aux douleurs de la [sienne] (*OC* i. 281). In 'Un cheval de race', too, with its echo structure of time and beauty, there is a sense of the grotesque, despite the deep-rooted tenderness and love the poem betrays:

Elle est bien laide. Elle est délicieuse pourtant!

Le Temps et l'Amour l'ont marqué de leurs griffes et lui ont cruelle-ment enseigné ce que chaque minute et chaque baiser emportent de jeunesse et de fraîcheur.

Elle est vraiment laide; elle est fourmi, araignée, si vous voulez, squelette même; mais aussi elle est breuvage, magistère, sorcellerie! en somme, elle est exquise.   (*OC* i. 343)

Here the paradoxical combinations of adjectives evoke the mixed emotions and responses that sexual love provokes in the poet, recalling 'Le Galant Tireur', where the partner is both 'délicieuse et exécrable', nagging wife and muse (*OC* i. 349), doubly double since she is reproduced in effigy.

Most often, however, the women of the prose poems are shown in their monstrous incarnations. They are violent and grotesque, thumping the dreamy poet into action, as the vulgar and hysterical 'petite folle monstrueuse' does in 'La Soupe et les nuages' (*OC* i. 350); or they are wicked enchanters, as in 'Les Tentations'; or grotesquely rapacious, as in 'Portraits de maîtresses' and 'La Femme sauvage et la petite maîtresse'. Woman is monstrous and grotesque because she represents all that is bestial, natural, and instinctive, she is a 'phénomène vivant', representing 'du comique dans l'amour', like Goya's 'monstres viables'. For this reason she is represented as having rapacious appetites, and Baudelaire plays upon the commonplace of an equivalence between ingestion and sexual hunger. Indeed, in both 'La Femme sauvage et la petite maîtresse' and 'Portraits de maîtresses' Baudelaire engages in an elaborate and inverted joke by, in the former, representing the caged woman voraciously tearing apart her prey, itself a *bête féroce*, so the poet is forced to clarify that he is using the term to describe the woman; and, in the latter, by suggesting that the *monstre polyphage* requires (the rations of) seven soldiers to sat-isfy her needs. An entry in *Mon cœur mis à nu* underscores the connection:

La femme est le contraire du Dandy.
Donc elle doit faire horreur.
La femme a faim et elle veut manger. Soif, et elle veut boire.
Elle est en rut et elle veut être foutue.
Le beau mérite!
La femme est *naturelle*, c'est-à-dire, abominable.   (*OC* i. 677)

She is the opposite of the dandy-narrator's reasonableness and subtle suggestion in 'Portraits de maîtresses' and of the narrator's ironic *sage parole* (expressed by the conventional wisdom *il ne faut pas manger tout son bien en un jour*),[85] in 'La Femme sauvage et la petite maîtresse'.[86] She is unleashed animality with which her male counterpart, always feminized by her power, must struggle. Another entry in the *Journaux intimes*, this time in *Fusées*, further clarifies the diabolic monstrosity evoked by the reference, in 'La Femme sauvage', to 'un de ces animaux qu'on appelle générale-ment "mon ange"':

Minette, minoutte, minouille, mon chat, mon loup, mon petit singe, grand singe, grand serpent, mon petit âne mélancolique.

De pareils caprices de langue, trop répétés, de trop fréquentes appella-tions bestiales témoignent d'un côté satanique dans l'amour; les satans n'ont-ils pas des formes de bêtes?   (*OC* ii. 660).

Here diabolic creatures (including the serpent) become one with the bestial female. The women of Baudelaire's prose poems are, then, all 'femmes déchues'. It is interesting to note, in this respect, the number of women in the prose poems who laugh.[87] Laughter is, first and foremost, the feature that characterizes madness. But it is also the mark of the satanic, for 'le Verbe incarné n'a jamais ri' (*OC* ii. 527). In Baudelaire's caricatural story depicting the satanic essence of laughter, Virginie, 'l'ange immaculée', does not laugh when presented with the comic grotesque. Instead she is fearful. Only when her Fall has occurred, 'quand elle aura baissé d'un degré

---

[85] For a full exploration of the significance of this, see Maclean, *Narrative as Performance*, 102–3.
[86] For a close examination of savagery in the prose poems, see Evans, *Baudelaire and Intertextuality*, 110–20.
[87] The grotesque Bénédicta laughs in 'Laquelle est la vraie?'; Bistouri laughs; the wife of the 'galant tireur' laughs at her husband's *maladresse*; and the poet-painter of 'Le Désir de peindre' strives to record the face of laughter.

en pureté', will she be able to laugh (*OC* ii. 530). Laughter is temptation, it is 'une dégradation physique et morale', the Fall and the distortion of human features gripped in uncontrollable impulse. All of the representations of women in the prose poems are initially *significatif*; that is to say that they are firmly rooted in their social context. They laugh, either out of madness, or out of weakness, and their laughter is spontaneous. This confirms their ignorance (or their madness), for the Sage 'y regarde de bien près avant de se permettre de rire comme s'il devait lui en rester je ne sais quel malaise et quelle inquiétude' (*OC* ii. 527). What is more, woman in the prose poems laughs at the male narrator or another male protagonist, and mostly she laughs at his weakness. The framing of this laughter makes it, in its turn, the object of the comic and poses the question raised in *De l'essence du rire*: 'Est-il phénomène plus déplorable que la faiblesse se réjouissant de la faiblesse?' (*OC* ii. 530). The representations, the framing, occurs both in the poem, where woman is presented as a portrait, an effigy, or a side-show, and with the poem which, as we saw in 'Mademoiselle Bistouri', subjects the analysing subject's looking or portraiture to scrutiny. So it is that in 'La Femme sauvage et la petite maîtresse' and in 'Portraits de maîtresses' that the monstrousness of the male ('l'autre monstre, c'est un mari') is subjected to the same framing. This is, of course, exactly the purpose of the story of Virginie in *De l'essence du rire* (*OC* ii. 529–30) which engages (seduces) the reader in a contemplation of spectacle which amounts to a kind of voyeurism, before bringing us to awareness of it with the final words of the section: 'Mais, pour le moment, nous, analyste et critique, qui n'oserions certes pas affirmer que notre intelligence est supérieure à celle de Virginie, constatons la crainte et la souffrance de l'ange immaculée devant la caricature.' It is precisely this notion of superiority which the comic spectacle of the *Petits Poèmes en prose* explores and exploits, so that, as Maclean has shown, the text becomes a reflective trap in which each audience is reflected in another audience, just as each relationship of desire or power is mirrored in another.[88]

Nowhere is the significance of this for comic art better exemplified than in 'Une mort héroïque' a poem representing pantomime which, Baudelaire asserts, is 'l'épuration de la comédie; c'en est la

---

[88] *Narrative as Performance*, 107.

quintessence; c'est l'élément comique pur, dégagé et concentré'
(*OC* ii. 540). The poem frames a performance which is watched by
the Prince of the kingdom (who has demanded it), by an audience,
and by our narrator. The reader, in turn, becomes the extended
audience of the textual act. Fancioulle is presented to us as both
activist and actor. Arrested for his part in a political conspiracy, he
is forced by the Prince to perform in a 'grand spectacle' which
some of the subjects interpret as a royal pardon. Our narrator, on
the other hand, offers a different explanation: 'Il voulait profiter de
l'occasion pour faire une expérience physiologique d'un intérêt
capital, et vérifier jusqu'à quel point les facultés habituelles d'un
artiste pouvaient être altérées ou modifiées par la situation extraordinaire où il se trouvait' (*OC* i. 320). The self-congratulatory
insight, closely followed by a pun which acts in the same way, alerts
us to the performance of the narrator and, therefore, to his rôle in
filtering (and interpreting) the text. The narrator is both artist
(producer of text) and audience. This emphasizes our experience
of the events portrayed as a fictional *text*, as a framed narrative, and
has important implications for our response to it. The analytical
credentials and the pun are seductive and we are taken in by the
performance of the narrator who, in his turn is taken in by the performance of Fancioulle. The stage is set, then. Narrative power
over the reader slips gently into the political power deployed in
stage setting:

Enfin, le grand jour arrivé, cette petite cour déploya toutes ses pompes, et
il serait difficile de concevoir, à moins de l'avoir vu, tout ce que la classe
privilégiée d'un petit Etat, à ressources restreintes, peut montrer de
splendeurs pour une vraie solennité. Celle-là était doublement vraie,
d'abord pour la magie du luxe étalé, ensuite par l'intérêt moral et mystérieux qui y était attaché. (*OC* i. 320–1).

This, along with the narrative, places the Prince and the theatrical
setting in competition with the talents of Fancioulle, for what we
have in 'Une mort héroïque' is, in fact, a power play, not only political, in fact not essentially political at all. The real conflict between
the Prince and Fancioulle (and the narrator) is one of artistic
power. The Prince, 'véritable artiste lui-même', wishes to be
admired for the show he is putting on. Fancioulle, for his part, is
such a good actor, that he can aspire to and, on this occasion
achieve, the 'parfaite idéalisation'.

Fancioulle, as his name suggests, is a *bouffon* and his art is properly that of the pantomime; a performance that is the essence of the *comique absolu*, exaggerated and grotesque, which plumbs the depths of human experience. Baudelaire devotes some pages to the significance of this art form and his interest in it is recorded in a letter to his mother in which he writes of his dream to 'fondre des *qualités littéraires* avec la *mise en scène tumultueuse* du boulevard' (*C* ii. 98). Pierrot had been a popular figure of early eighteenth-century *fêtes foraines*, and survived even the shock of the Revolution by entertaining the mixed crowds of the *théâtre à quatre sous*.[89] Indeed, it was in the Théâtre des Funambules, in operation since 1816 as a forum for performing dogs and other such acts,[90] that Pierrot—and the art of mime—was transformed in 1830. It was Jean-Baptiste Deburau who carried the role of Pierrot to its apotheosis, transforming the role from that of a foolish lout[91] into the astute *pícaro* who only feigns stupidity. Not only did the stupidity become self-disparaging irony, enabling Deburau to deal rather than receive the blows, the whole repertoire of theatrical gesture was to be expanded to incorporate movement more specific to the contemporary context.[92] There are strong similarities between the caricatural and mime. Both found support amongst writers and critics, both were addressed to a broad and daily audience, both engaged with human types and their bodily expressions, and both sought to break down dividing lines between moral and high art.[93] In exactly the same way as Baudelaire coined the term *argot plastique* to describe caricature, Champfleury was to talk of Deburau as miming *argot*.[94] This was an expression of the incorporation into the figure of Pierrot of new roles (métiers),[95] gestures associated with those roles, and even the vernacular of the artisan classes.[96] As Jules Janin described him, Deburau was 'l'acteur du peuple, l'ami du peuple, bavard, gourmand, flâneur, faquin, impas-

[margin annotation: Caricature + mime]

---

[89] See Enid Welsford, *The Fool: His Social and Literary History*, 304–5.
[90] This is when it was nothing more than a basement, known as *Les Chiens savans*. See Jules Janin, *Deburau: Histoire du théâtre à quatre sous pour faire suite à l'histoire du Théâtre-Français* (Paris: Librairie des Bibliophiles, 1881 [1832]), 47.
[91] See Maurice Wilson Disher, *Clowns and Pantomimes* (London: Constable, 1925), 135.
[92] See Judith Wechsler, *A Human Comedy*, 45.   [93] Ibid. 42.
[94] *Souvenirs et portraits de jeunesse* (Paris: E. Dentu, 1872), 64–5.
[95] Edmond Texier, *Tableau de Paris* (Paris: Paulin et Le Chevalier, 1852–3), i. 122.
[96] Deburau would himself have had first-hand experience of these trades. There is a

sible, révolutionnaire comme l'est le peuple'.[97] Pierrot became more aware, a combination of false and real, exceeding the simple joys of *enfantillages* (what Baudelaire would see as the unity of 'la joie') and engaging more and more in the the grotesque energy of the satirical clown and the verbal.[98] This tradition is clearly apparent in the figure of Fancioulle, who excels 'dans les rôles muets ou peu chargés de paroles'. He is also revolutionary, but as befits his elevation to high literary status here, he is elevated socially, too, and becomes le sieur Fancioulle, 'presqu'un des amis du Prince'.

In keeping, then, with Baudelaire's expressed interest in popular forms, there are elements, in Fancioulle's performance, of the English pantomime Baudelaire records in *De l'essence du rire*. In a passage from this essay, for example, Baudelaire describes the relationship between the performers and the audience in a way which is remarkable for its similarity to 'Une mort héroïque':

> Une des choses les plus remarquables comme comique absolu, et, pour ainsi dire, comme métaphysique du comique absolu, était certainement le début de cette belle pièce, un prologue plein de haute esthétique. Les principaux personnages de la pièce, Pierrot, Cassandre, Harlequin, Colombine, Léandre, sont devant le public, bien doux et bien tranquilles. Ils sont à peu près raisonnables et ne diffèrent pas beaucoup des braves gens qui sont dans la salle. Le souffle merveilleux qui va les faire se mouvoir extraordinairement n'a pas encore soufflé sur leurs cervelles. Quelques jovialités de Pierrot ne peuvent donner qu'une pâle idée de ce qu'il fera tout à l'heure. [. . .]
>
> Aussitôt le vertige est entré, le vertige circule dans l'air; on respire le vertige; c'est le vertige qui remplit les poumons et renouvelle le sang dans le ventricule.
>
> Qu'est-ce que le vertige? C'est le comique absolu; il s'est emparé de chaque être. (*OC* ii. 540)

---

great deal of information available on the different trades practised by Deburau and his fellow performers at the Théâtre des Funambules in Louis Péricaud, *Le Théâtre des Funambules, ses mimes, ses acteurs et ses pantomimes depuis sa fondation jusqu'à sa démolition* (Paris: Léon Sapin, 1897).

[97] *Deburau*, 69.

[98] See Louisa E. Jones, *Sad Clowns and Pale Pierrots*, and Robert Storey, *Pierrots on the Stage of Desire. Nineteenth-Century French Literary Artists and the Comic Pantomime* (Princeton: Princeton University Press, 1985) for an examination of the changing face of pantomime, the new roles of the clown, and the effects of both of these on the iconography of mid-19th-cent. culture.

The relationship between Fancioulle and the audience and that of the actors and audience in the English pantomime are almost identical, as indeed is the development in performance from calm gentleness of the prologue. Fancioulle transports the crowds away from the reality of the impending death sentence and the theatre towards 'la frontière du merveilleux', inspiring in them, first, a sense of *douceur* and pardon and secondly of frenetic joy or *vertige*. There is a sense of total freedom to express physically the vertigo of art and life, with pratfalls, arms swinging like windmills and guffawing laughter; the ultimate expression not only of the comic, but of a physical response to it. It is, moreover, the physical nature of the *comique absolu* which Baudelaire stresses most keenly, seeing it as life-giving, a refreshing dizziness like a rush of air to the lungs or blood to the heart. This is all the more poignant in Fancioulle's performance, given his subsequent death, and given that some part of the audience which shares in the *vertige* comprises his fellow conspirators: 'Personne ne rêva plus de mort, de deuil, ni de supplices. Chacun s'abandonna, sans inquiétude, aux voluptés multipliées que donne la vue d'un chef-d'œuvre d'art vivant.'

On the night of the 'grand spectacle', Fancioulle surpasses himself in what is already established as one of his best rôles.

Fancioulle fut, ce-soir là, une parfaite idéalisation, qu'il était impossible de ne pas supposer vivante, possible, réelle. Ce bouffon allait, venait, riait, pleurait, se convulsait, avec une indestructible auréole autour de la tête, auréole invisible pour tous, mais visible pour moi, et où se mêlaient, dans un étrange amalgame, les rayons de l'Art et la gloire du Martyr. Fancioulle introduisait, par je ne sais quelle grâce spéciale, le divin et le surnaturel, jusque dans les plus extravagantes bouffonneries.   (*OC* i. 321)

The narrator, again drawing attention to his own exceptional vision, sanctifies the performance and, in so doing, crowns Fancioulle with the halo of the martyr and the laurel of the great artist. This crowning is textual, but the audience's appreciation is equivalent, expressed in their 'explosions de la joie et de l'admiration' and in their applause. The Prince, however, is more restrained and, in the power struggle, he retains an awareness of the situation, if not a complete control over it. The narrator speculates on the cause: 'Se sentait-il vaincu dans son pouvoir de despote? humilié dans son art de terrifier les cœurs et d'engourdir les esprits? frustré de ses espérances et bafoué dans ses prévisions?' (*OC* i. 322).

The Prince is right to be concerned for his power. With silence and gesture, Fancioulle captivates his audience, reducing them to the grotesque spectacle of convulsive laughter which he so cleverly mimes on stage. And he appears to transcend the impending death sentence, miming it with mockery, 'l'étrange bouffon bouffonnait si bien la mort'.

At this moment the Prince intervenes, sending a page to put an end to the performance, just as Fancioulle is at his dramatic peak and, with the shrill intrusion of the *coup de sifflet*, Fancioulle falls down dead. The clown dies upon the stage as a climax to his dramatic art and to his political idealism and, with this intrusion, the Prince reasserts his power and control over the assembled people. His act raises unanswerable questions, not the least of which is why he interrupts the performance in this way. Is it indeed jealousy and vengeful hostility in his eyes? Our narrator continues to speculate, and is unable to resist the opportunity to offer answers: 'Le sifflet, rapide comme un glaive, avait-il réellement frustré le bourreau? Le Prince avait-il lui-même deviné toute l'homicide efficacité de sa ruse? Il est permis d'en douter. Regretta-t-il son cher et inimitable Fancioulle? Il est doux et légitime de le croire.' (*OC* ii. 323).

What is certain is that Fancioulle is indeed inimitable, and unparalleled, as the last paragraph of the poem makes clear. The reason for this is the reason for his death. It is no longer an act. Fancioulle is such a perfect idealization of the role that he becomes it. This is, as the narrator suggests, a divine comedy, and as Chambers defines it, a sort of sacred theatre:[99]

Fancioulle me prouvait, d'une manière péremptoire, irréfutable, que l'ivresse de l'Art est plus apte que tout autre à voiler les terreurs du gouffre; que le génie peut jouer la comédie au bord de la tombe avec une joie qui l'empêche de voir la tombe, perdu, comme il est, dans un paradis excluant toute idée de tombe et de destruction.   (*OC* i. 321)

Fancioulle's power over the audience is absolute. It is the incarnation of a rôle taken to such a level that Fancioulle forgets himself

---

[99] 'À la relation de Dieu au monde correspond une relation des hommes au spectacle. Ainsi, un monde fortement sacralisé, où la divinité est présente dans la vie, se retrouve dans le théâtre sacré où règne une communion entre spectateurs et spectacle et se résume dans le comédien possédé, investi par le dieu et confondu, par conséquent, avec son rôle.' '"L'Art sublime du comédien" ou le regardant et le regardé. Autour d'un mythe baudelairien', *Saggi e Ricerche di Letteratura Francese*, NS II (1971), 191.

in *la joie* and, in so doing, passes into the 'absolu définitif'. He loses sight of the necessary duality of all representation ('l'humanité déchue'), thereby transgressing the limits of the comic. As Hannoosh has persuasively argued, Fancioulle's 'parfaite idéalisation' fails to fulfil the conditions of comic art; his performance destroys art's dualism because it fails to represent man's relative inferiority to an omnipotent absolute (death).[100] Unlike the superior, ironic, artistic stance of the Prince, and that of our dualistic narrator, who frames the performance with analysis and constantly reminds us of the textual performance, Fancioulle does not sustain the necessary *dédoublement*.

The framing of the text, the version of the narrator (which embeds a version purporting to be that of the Prince), enables us to read the poem as comic art whilst simultaneously perceiving the comic failure which is Fancioulle's unified performance. This *dédoublement* is, as we have seen, at the very heart of Baudelaire's poetic practice and it is the very essence of Baudelaire's theory of the comic, as he confirms in his conclusion to *De l'essence du rire*:

> Les artistes créent le comique; ayant étudié et rassemblé les éléments du comique, ils savent que tel être est comique, et qu'il ne l'est qu'à condition d'ignorer sa nature; de même que, par une loi inverse, l'artiste n'est artiste qu'à la condition d'être double et de n'ignorer aucun phénomène de sa double nature. (*OC* ii. 543)

'Une mort héroïque' stages the necessary *dédoublement* of art by doubling the performance of Fancioulle with the carefully constructed narrative of the poem in which 'la puissance d'être à la fois soi et un autre' is elaborately inserted. The 'parfaite idéalisation' of Fancioulle's performance is translated by the pen in a way which is clearly designed to suggest the inferiority of the medium as well as the dualism of the process (appreciation and analysis). The narrator says: 'ma plume tremble, et les larmes d'une émotion toujours présente me montent aux yeux pendant que je cherche à vous décrire cette inoubliable soirée'. In *De l'essence du rire*, where the critical process is in fact the same as our narrator's, he says more or less the same thing of the English pantomime: 'Avec une plume tout cela est pâle et glacé. Comment la plume pourrait-elle rivaliser avec la pantomime?' (*OC* ii. 540). In both cases, the writer is sepa-

---

[100] *Baudelaire and Caricature*, 53–8.

rated, situationally and temporally, from the performance that his own art re-enacts and this reinforces his duality as both spectator and spectacle. This, in its turn, and as we have seen elsewhere, frames distinct audiences. The reader of this text has to take account of distinct staged instances of spectatorship, that is to say a generalized audience which includes the other conspirators, the Prince and the narrator. But, as readers, we are also forced into a *dédoublement* by the different levels of representation which themselves are mirrored in the strategies of a *discours double* (constituted by the *énoncé* and the *énonciation*).

Baudelaire illustrates this problematic relationship between narrator and narratee and spectator and spectacle with the story of Virginie, as we have seen, but he also adapts the theory of superiority (which occurs in both the *comique significatif* and the *comique absolu*) by insisting on the rôle of the laugher, or the receiver of a comic spectacle. Laughter arises as a result of a feeling of superiority over someone or something, as Baudelaire further exemplifies his point with respect to the stock image of a fall (*OC* ii. 532). But this form of superiority is a lack of self-awareness ('un orgueil inconscient') and is simultaneously symptomatic of a 'grandeur infinie' (in relation to lesser beings) and 'misère infinie' (with respect to 'l'Être absolu'). This is *faiblesse*. The real essence of the comic is self-ironic awareness, the rare case of 'la force de se dédoubler rapidement et d'assister comme spectateur désintéressé aux phénomènes de son *moi*' (*OC* ii. 532). This is where Fancioulle fails and where the poet (who is *dédoublé*) succeeds.[101] At this point in his essay on the comic, Baudelaire slips almost imperceptibly from the negative form of superiority (such as Voltaire's) to the theorized superiority of a comic artist such as Hoffmann, artists 'qui ont en eux la réceptibilité suffisante de toute idée absolue' (*OC* ii. 536). The play on the epithet *suffisante*, in fact, characterizes that receptiveness as dualistic and self-ironic, not least because of the way in which it is related to, and here brings about, an explanation of the application of theory to method: 'Il [Hoffmann] a cherché souvent à résoudre en œuvres artistiques les théories savantes qu'il avait émises didactiquement, ou jetées sous la forme de conversations inspirées et de dialogues critiques' (*OC* ii. 536). Theory (science) enables the superior artist to avoid the pitfalls of

---

[101] In Baudelaire's comic, it is, I think, also that to which the ideal reader must aspire.

ignorant laughter; it enables the self-ironic philosopher to frame the paradox of the comic.

Comic art (and its theorization) itself provides a framework which accommodates the prose poem's *double postulation* which is to account, on the one hand, for the 'chose vue', the spectacle of modern life and of man's moral ugliness and, on the other, to develop the comic grotesque as an art of the *absolu*. The prose poems represent the poetic equivalent of caricatural and comic technique. They play with the possibilities of the fragmented and the journalistic; they isolate an image and from it generate new meaning; they are dynamic rather than stable; and they distort and exaggerate. The prose poems produce ironic perspectives on stereotyped characters, situations, and discourses; they are engaged in a comic that is clearly *significatif*, but always combine with this some element of the *absolu*. Baudelaire translates the visual world of a social gallery into his prose poetry. Playing upon the techniques of 'low' art, exploiting the commonplace and the pun as caricature exploits its models, demanding a knowledge of context and a sympathy to its distortion, and, requiring, like irony, the participation of an observer in the process, Baudelaire presents us with a verbal caricature not only of contemporary French society, but of more universal human truths. Here, more than anywhere else in Baudelaire's work, we have a sense of the visual artist, combining mastery of observation in a complex play of form and message. The prose poems bear witness to the compound impact of comic and grotesque iconography of the visual and performing arts, communicating with power and imagination the trivialization of and victory over social tensions. The trivialization of these repressive forces through a grotesque humour allows for a duality of acceptance and rejection: 'the faculty of seeing apparently incongruous elements as part of a scheme for supra-logical necessity'.[102] This tension lies at the core of Baudelaire's theory of the comic according to which humour is essentially human (and therefore contradictory), caught, as we have seen, in a perpetual tension between the Supreme Being and animal-like *Bêtise*.

Baudelaire's experimentation was to take many forms and to extend over a period of twenty years, from his early caricatural

---

[102] R. Graves, *Mrs. Fisher or the Future of Humour* (London: Kegan Paul, Trench & Trubner, 1928), 55.

self-portraits or sketches begun in 1843 and his theories of comic art developed throughout his career, to this innovative prose project which bears so many traces of the philosopher as comic artist. The theory and the practice are always one, so that, despite his attempt to cultivate an appearance of the trivial, Baudelaire's excursion into a properly comic art is utterly conscious.[103] As Baudelaire himself puts it with respect to what is perhaps caricature's most dominant image ('la pyramidale et olympienne *Poire* de processive mémoire'): 'Le symbole avait été trouvé par une analogie complaisante. Le symbole dès lors suffisait. Avec cette espèce d'argot plastique, on était le maître de dire et de faire comprendre au peuple tout ce qu'on voulait' (*OC* ii. 550). By adapting the *analogie complaisante* of caricature to his prose poetry, Baudelaire could further explore the possibilities of discursive duplicity and artistic paradox by using his own version of that *argot plastique.* This term is itself heavily charged with significance, suggesting the transience, the malleability, and the lowliness of the art form.[104] It is, however, precisely this combination of covert textual practices and the reinvention of the coded discourses and forms on which these depend which was to result in the generation of a new art form. The prose poem is the formal expression of the *comique absolu,* the *vertige de l'hyperbole,* the *dédoublement* of the comic-lyric artist and the ultimate *miroir à alouettes* for the spectator-reader.

[103] Cf. Poulet-Malassis: 'Pour rapides et cursifs que soient ses croquis, ils résultaient d'une élaboration mentale inconsciente et lente; ses modèles étaient ceux que l'habitude ou le courant de la vie imposait à son attention: figures littéraires obsédantes, physionomies d'amis intimes, visages de créatures singulières, et, plus rarement, visage d'un homme sur qui son regard s'était concentré dans quelque circonstance mémorable', 'Baudelaire', in *Sept Dessins,* 7–8.

[104] See Ainslie Armstrong McLees for a discussion of both the interrelation of the verbal and visual in this image, as well as the subversive nature of this interaction. 'Baudelaire and Caricature: Argot plastique', *Symposium,* 38/3 (Fall 1984), p.222 and *Baudelaire's Argot plastique. Poetic Caricature and Modernism* (Athens, Ga., and London: University of Georgia Press, 1989), 148.

Select Bibliography

Works by Baudelaire

Œuvres complètes, ed. Claude Pichois, 2 vols. (Bibliothèque de la Pléiade; Paris: Gallimard, 1975–6).

Petits Poëmes en prose, in *Œuvres complètes*, vol. iv (Paris: Michel Lévy, 1869).

Petits Poëmes en prose (Le Spleen de Paris), ed. J. Crépet (Paris: Conard, 1934).

Petits Poèmes en prose (Le Spleen de Paris), ed. Daniel-Rops (Paris: Les Belles Lettres, 1962).

Petits Poèmes en prose (Le Spleen de Paris), ed. H. Lemaître (Paris: Garnier, 1962).

Petits Poèmes en prose (Le Spleen de Paris), ed. M. Ruff (Paris: Garnier–Flammarion, 1967).

Petits Poëmes en prose, ed. M. Zimmermann (Manchester: Manchester University Press, 1968).

Petits Poëmes en prose, ed. R. Kopp (Paris: Corti, 1969).

Petits Poëmes en prose (Le Spleen de Paris), ed. R. Kopp (Coll-Poésie; Paris: Gallimard, 1973).

Salon de 1846, ed. David Kelley (Oxford: Clarendon Press, 1975).

Le Spleen de Paris (texte de 1869), ed. C. Roy (Paris: Livre de Poche, 1964).

Le Spleen de Paris: Petits Poèmes en prose, ed. M. Milner (Paris: Imprimerie nationale, 1979).

Le Spleen de Paris (Petits Poèmes en prose). La Fanfarlo, ed. David Scott and Barbara Wright (Paris: Flammarion, 1985).

Other Works

ABÉ, Y., 'Une Nouvelle esthétique du rire: Baudelaire et Champfleury entre 1845 et 1855', *Annales de la Faculté de Lettres*, Chûô University, 35 (1964), 18–30.

ACTON, W., *Prostitution Considered in its Moral, Social and Sanitary*

Aspects in London and Other Large Cities and Garrison Towns [1857] (London: Frank Cass, 1870).

ADHÉMAR, J., 'Baudelaire critique d'art', *Revue des sciences humaines* (1958), 111–19.

ALCANTER DE BRAHM, *L'Ostensoir des ironies* (Paris, 1899).

ALFORD, S. E., *Irony and the Logic of the Romantic Imagination* (New York: P. Lang, 1984).

ALLEMAN, B., 'De l'Ironie en tant que principe littéraire', *Poétique*, 36 (Nov. 1978), 385–98.

ALMANSI, G., 'L'Affaire mystérieuse de l'abominable tongue-in-cheek', *Poétique*, 36 (Nov. 1978), 419–26.

AMOSSY, R., and ROSEN, E., *Les Discours du cliché* (Paris: CDU/SEDES, 1982).

ASSELIN, H., 'Baudelaire critique d'art', *Chantiers*, 20/3 (Jan. 1956), 15–17.

ASSELINEAU, C., *et al.*, *Hommage à C. F. Denecourt. Fontainebleau. Paysages, légendes, souvenirs, fantaisies* (Paris: Hachette, 1855).

AUSTIN, J. L., *How to Do Things with Words* [1962] (Oxford: Oxford University Press, 1975).

AVICE, J.-P., and PICHOIS, C. (eds.), *Baudelaire, Paris, l'Allégorie* (L'Année Baudelaire, 1; Paris: Klincksieck, 1995).

BABUTS, N., *Baudelaire at the Limits and Beyond* (Newark: University of Delaware Press, 1997).

BALZAC, H. de, *Ferragus*, *La Comédie humaine* (Bibliothèque de la Pléiade; Paris: Gallimard, 1951–65), Vol. V.

BANDY, W. T., *Baudelaire Judged by his Contemporaries (1845–1867)* (New York: Columbia University Press, 1933).

—— and PICHOIS, C., *Baudelaire devant ses contemporains* (1st edn. Monaco: editions du Rocher, 1957; Paris: Klincksieck, 1995).

BARRELL, J., *Poetry, Language and Politics* (Manchester: Manchester University Press, 1988).

BARTHES, R., *S/Z* (Paris: Seuil, 1970).

—— *Littérature et Réalité* (Paris: Seuil, 1982).

BECQ, A., 'Baudelaire et 'l'amour de l'art': La Dédicace 'aux bourgeois' du *Salon de 1846*', *Romantisme*, 17–18 (1977), 71–8.

BEDOLLIÈRE, É. de la, *Les Industriels: Métiers et professions en France* (Paris: A. Pigoreau, 1842).

BEHLER, E., *Irony and the Discourse of Modernity* (Seattle and London: University of Washington Press, 1990).

BELL, S., *Reading, Writing and Rewriting the Prostitute Body* (Bloomington and Indianapolis: Indiana University Press, 1994).

BENJAMIN, W., *Charles Baudelaire: A Lyric Poet in the Era of High Capitalism* (London: NLB, 1979).

BERCOT, M., 'La Seconde Esthétique de Baudelaire', *L'Information littéraire*, 5 (1953), 204–11.

BERGSON, H., *Le Rire: Essai sur la signification du comique* [1900] (Paris: Presses universitaires de France, 1983).

BERNARD, S., *Le Poème en prose de Baudelaire jusqu'à nos jours* [1959] (Paris: Nizet, 1994).

BERNHEIMER, C., *Figures of Ill Repute: Representing Prostitution in Nineteenth-Century France* (Cambridge, Mass., and London: Harvard University Press, 1989).

BERRANGER, M.-P., *Dépaysement de l'aphorisme* (Paris: Corti, 1988).

BERSANI, L., *Baudelaire and Freud* (Berkeley and Los Angeles: University of California Press, 1977).

BERTRAND, A., *Gaspard de la Nuit: Fantaisies à la manière de Rembrandt et de Callot* (Paris: Renduel, 1842).

BIARD, J. D., 'Baudelaire et Pierre Dupont', *Nineteenth-Century French Studies*, 16 (1987–8), 95–110.

BLANC, L., *Questions d'aujourd'hui et de demain*, 5 vols. (Paris: E. Dentu, 1873–84).

BLIN, G., *Le Sadisme de Baudelaire* (Paris: Corti, 1948).

BLOOD, S., *Baudelaire and the Aesthetics of Bad Faith* (Stanford: Stanford University Press, 1997).

BLOOM, H., *The Anxiety of Influence: A Theory of Poetry* (Oxford and New York: Oxford University Press, 1973).

BONHEIM, H., *The Narrative Modes: Techniques of the Short Story* (Cambridge: D. S. Brewer, 1982).

BOOTH, W. C., *The Rhetoric of Fiction* (Chicago: University of Chicago Press, 1961).

—— *A Rhetoric of Irony* (Chicago and London: University of Chicago Press, 1974).

BORNEQUE, J.-H., 'Les Poèmes en prose de Baudelaire', *L'Information littéraire*, 5 (1953), 77–182.

BREMOND, C., *Logique du récit* (Paris: Seuil, 1973).

—— 'Le Meccano du conte', *Magazine littéraire*, 150 (July–Aug. 1979).

BRINSMEAD, A.-M., 'A Trading of Souls: Commerce as Poetic Practice in the *Petits Poèmes en prose*, *Romantic Review*, 79 (1988), 452–65.

BROOKS, C., *The Well-Wrought Urn: Studies in the Structure of Poetry* (New York: Reynal & Hitchcock, 1947).

—— 'Irony as a Principle of Structure', in Morton Dauwen Zabel (ed.), *Literary Opinion in America* (New York: Harper and Brothers, 1951).

BUGLIANI, I., 'Baudelaire tra Fourier e Proudhon', *Critica Storica*, 4 (1973), 591–659.

—— *Baudelaire: L'Armonia e la discordanza* (Roma: Bulzoni, 1980).

BURTON, R. D. E., *Baudelaire in 1859: A Study in the Sources of Poetic Creativity* (Cambridge: Cambridge University Press, 1988).

—— *Baudelaire and the Second Republic: Writing and Revolution* (Oxford: Clarendon Press, 1991).

—— 'Destruction as Creation: "Le Mauvais Vitrier" and the Poetics and Politics of Violence', *Romanic Review*, 83/1 (Jan. 1992), 297–322.

—— 'Baudelaire's Indian Summer: A Reading of "Les Bons Chiens"', *Nineteenth-Century French Studies*, 22/3–4 (1994), 466–86.

CARGO, R. T., *Concordance to Baudelaire's Petits Poëmes en prose* (Alabama: University of Alabama Press, 1971).

CAWS, M. A., and RIFFATERRE, H., *The Prose Poem in France* (New York: Columbia University Press, 1983).

CELLIER, L., 'D'une rhétorique profonde: Baudelaire et l'oxymoron', in *Parcours initiatiques* (Neuchâtel: La Baconnière, 1977).

CHAMBERS, R., 'The Artist as Performing Dog', *Comparative Literature*, 23 (Fall 1971) 312–24.

—— '"L'Art sublime du comédien" ou le regardant et le regardé'. Autour d'un mythe baudelairien', *Saggi e Ricerche di Letteratura Francese*, NS 11 (1971), 189–260.

—— 'Change and Exchange? Story Structure and Paradigmatic Narrative', *Australian Journal of French Studies*, 12 (1975), 326–42.

—— '"Frôler ceux qui rôdent": Le Paradoxe du saltimbanque', *Revue des sciences humaines*, 42/167 (1977), 347–63.

—— 'Trois paysages urbains: les poèmes liminaires des *Tableaux Parisiens*', *Modern Philology*, 80 (1983) 372–89.

—— *Story and Situation: Narrative Seduction and the Power of Fiction* (Minneapolis: University of Minnesota Press, 1984).

—— 'Baudelaire's Street Poetry', *Nineteenth-Century French Studies*, 13/4 (1985), 244–59.

—— *Mélancolie et opposition: Les Débuts du modernisme en France* (Paris: Corti, 1987).

—— 'Are Baudelaire's "Tableaux parisiens" about Paris?', in Anna Whiteside and Michael Issacharoff, *On Referring in Literature* (Bloomington and Indianapolis: Indiana University Press, 1987), 95–110.

—— 'Baudelaire's Dedicatory Practice', *SubStance*, 56 (1988), 5–17.

—— *Room for Maneuver: Reading (the) Oppositional (in) Narrative* (Chicago and London: University of Chicago Press, 1991).

CHAMPFLEURY, J. F. F., *Souvenirs des Funambules* (Paris: M. Lévy, 1859).

—— *Histoire de la caricature moderne* (Paris: E. Dentu, 1868).

—— *Souvenirs et portraits de jeunesse* (Paris: E. Dentu, 1872).

—— 'Henry Monnier', *Gazette des beaux-arts*, 15 (Apr. 1877), 363–81.

—— *Henry Monnier: Sa vie et son œuvre* (Paris: E. Dentu, 1889).

CHAR, R., *Le Marteau sans maître*, suivi de *Moulin premier* (Paris: Corti, 1970).

CHATMAN, S., *Story and Discourse: Narrative Structure in Fiction and Film* (Ithaca, NY: Cornell University Press, 1978).

CHÉREL, A., *La Prose poétique française* (Paris: L'Artisan du livre, 1940).

CHESTERS, G., 'The Transformation of a Prose Poem: Baudelaire's "Crépuscule du soir"', in *Baudelaire, Mallarmé, Valéry: New Essays in Honour of Lloyd Austin* (Cambridge: Cambridge University Press, 1982).

—— 'A Political Reading of Baudelaire's "L'Artiste inconnu"', *Modern Language Review*, 79/1 (Jan. 1984), 64–76.

—— *Baudelaire and the Poetics of Craft* (Cambridge: Cambridge University Press, 1988).

CITRON, P., *La Poésie de Paris dans la littérature française de Rousseau à Baudelaire*, 2 vols. (Paris: Minuit, 1961).

CLARK, P. P., 'Stratégies d'auteur au XIXe siècle', *Romantisme*, 17–18 (1977), 92–102.

CLARK, T. J., *Image of the People: Gustave Courbet and the 1848 Revolution* (London: Thames & Hudson, 1972).

—— *The Absolute Bourgeois: Artists and Politics in France 1848–1851* [1973] (London: Thames & Hudson, 1978).

—— *The Painter of Modern Life: Paris in the Art of Manet and his Followers* (London: Thames & Hudson, 1985).

COHEN, J., *Structure du langage poétique* (Paris: Flammarion, 1967).

COLLOT, M., 'Le Sujet lyrique hors de soi', in Dominique Rabaté (ed.), *Figures du sujet lyrique* (Paris: Presses universitaires de France, 1996), 113–25.

COMBE, D., 'La Référence dédoublée: Le Sujet lyrique entre fiction et l'autobiographie', in Dominique Rabaté (ed.), *Figures du sujet lyrique* (Paris: Presses universitaires de France, 1996), 39–63.

COMPAGNON, A., *La Seconde Main ou le travail de la citation* (Paris: Seuil, 1979).

CRÉPET, E.-J., *Baudelaire* (Paris: Messein, 1906).

CRUIKSHANK, G., *Humorous Illustrations* (London: Simpkin, Marshall, Hamilton, Kent & Co., n.d.).

CULLER, J., *The Pursuit of Signs: Semiotics, Literature, Deconstruction* (London: Routledge & Kegan Paul, 1981).

—— *Flaubert: The Uses of Uncertainty* (Ithaca, NY, and London: Cornell University Press, 1985).

—— (ed.), *On Puns: The Foundation of Letters* (Oxford: Blackwell, 1988), esp. 1–16.

—— 'Baudelaire and Poe', *Zeitschrift für französische Sprache und Literatur*, 50 (1990), 61–73.

DANIEL-ROPS, 'Baudelaire, poète en prose', *La Grande Revue*, 136 (1931), 534–5.

DAUMIER, H., *Les Gens de médecine* (Paris: Sauret, 1966).

—— *Les Gens de justice* (Paris: Sauret, 1974).

—— *Locataires et propriétaires* (Paris: Sauret, 1977).

—— *L'Œuvre lithographique*, 2 vols. (Paris: Hubschmid, 1978).

—— *120 Great Lithographs* (New York: Dover; London: Constable, 1978).

—— *Les Tracas de Paris* (Paris: Vilo, 1978).

—— *Les Gens d'affaires (Robert Macaire)* (Paris: Vilo, 1979).

—— *Les Gens du spectacle* (Paris: Sauret, 1982).

—— *Mœurs politiques* (Paris: Sauret, 1982).

DELABROY, J., and CHARNET, Y., *Baudelaire: Nouveaux chantiers* (Lille: Presses universitaires du Septentrion, 1995).

DELEUZE, G., *Différence et répétition* (Paris: Presses universitaires de France, 1968).

—— and GUATTARI, F., *Mille Plateaux* (Paris: Minuit, 1980).

DELVAU, A., *Dictionnaire de la langue verte* (Paris: Dentu, 1867).

DEMERS, J., 'L'Art du conte écrit ou le lecteur complice', *Études françaises*, 9/1 (1972), 3–13.

—— and GAUVIN, L., Le Conte écrit, une forme savante', *Études françaises*, 12/1–2 (1976) 3–24.

DERRIDA, J., *Donner le temps*, 1: *La Fausse Monnaie* (Paris: Galilée, 1991).

DIDIER, B. 'Une économie de l'écriture: "Fusées" et "Mon Cœur mis à nu"', *Littérature*, 10 (May 1973), 57–64.

—— *Le Journal intime* (Paris: Presses universitaires de France, 1976).

DISHER, M. W., *Clowns and Pantomimes* (London: Constable, 1925).

DOLLÉANS, E., *Histoire du mouvement ouvrier*, 2 vols. (Paris: Colin, 1939).

DROST, W., 'Baudelaire between Marx, Sade and Satan', in *Baudelaire, Mallarmé, Valéry: New Essays in Honour of Lloyd Austin* (Cambridge, Cambridge University Press, 1982)

DUMAS, A. (père), *Mes Mémoires*, 7 vols. (Paris: M. Lévy, 1865–9).

DURANTY, E., 'Sur la physiognomie', *La Revue libérale*, 2 (1867), 499–523.

—— 'Promenades au Louvre', *Gazette des Beaux Arts*, (Jan. 1877), 15–37; (Feb. 1877), 172–80; (Mar. 1877), 281–9.

—— 'Daumier', *Gazette des Beaux Arts*, (May 1878), 429–43; (June 1878), 528–44.

DYSON, A. E., *The Crazy Fabric: Essays in Irony* (New York: St Martin's Press, 1965).

ECO, U. 'Looking for a Logic of Culture', in T. Seboek (ed.), *The Tell-Tale Sign: A Survey of Semiotics* (Lisse: Peter de Ridderness, 1975).

—— *The Rôle of the Reader: Explorations in the Semiotics of Texts* (Bloomington: Indiana University Press, 1979).

EIGELDINGER, M., 'A propos de l'image du thyrse', *Revue d'histoire littéraire de la France*, 85 (1975), 110–112.

—— '"Le Thyrse", lecture thématique', *Études baudelairiennes*, viii (Neuchâtel: La Baconnière, 1976).

ELLIOTT, R. C., *The Literary Persona* (London: University of Chicago Press, 1982).

EMPSON, W,. *Seven Types of Ambiguity* [1930] (Harmondsworth: Penguin, 1977).

ENCINA, J. DE LA, *Goya, su mundo histórico y poético* (Mexico: La Casa de la España en México, 1939).

ENRIGHT, D. J., *The Alluring Problem: An Essay on Irony* (Oxford: Oxford University Press, 1986).

EVANS, D. O., *Social Romanticism in France 1830–1848* (Oxford: Oxford University Press, 1981).

EVANS, M. A., 'Laurence Sterne and the *Spleen de Paris*', *French Studies*, 42 (1987), 165–76.

—— *Baudelaire and Intertextuality:. Poetry at the Crossroads* (Cambridge: Cambridge University Press, 1993).

FAIRLIE, A., 'Observations sur les *Petits Poëmes en prose*' and 'Quelques Remarques sur les *Petits Poëmes en prose*', in *Imagination and Language: Collected Essays on Constant, Baudelaire, Nerval and Flaubert* (Cambridge: Cambridge University Press, 1981).

FELMAN, S., *Writing and Madness* (Ithaca, NY: Cornell University Press, 1985).

FERGUSON, P. P., *Paris as Revolution: Writing the 19th-Century City* (Berkeley, Los Angeles, and London: University of California Press, 1994).

FIELDING, H., *Joseph Andrews*, ed. M. Batterstin (Oxford: Oxford University Press, 1967).

FIETKAU, W., *Schwanengesang auf 1848: Ein rendezvous au Louvre: Baudelaire, Marx, Proudhon und Victor Hugo* (Reinbek bei Hamburg: Rowohlt 1978).

FLAUBERT, G., *Dictionnaire des idées reçues, Œuves complètes*, ed. A. Thibaudet and R. Dumesnil (Bibliothèque de la Pléiade; Paris: Gallimard, 1952), ii. 999–1023.

FLUCHÈRE, H., 'Maurice Chapelan, Anthologie du poème en prose', review in *French Studies*, 2, (1948), 188.

FONDANE, B., *Baudelaire et l'expérience du gouffre* (Paris: Seghers, 1947).

FOURIER, C., *Œuvres*, 6 vols. (Paris: Bureaux de la Phalange, 1841–5).

—— *Théorie de l'unité universelle*, vol. i (Paris: Anthropos, 1966).

Les Français peints par eux-mêmes, 8 vols. (Paris: L. Curner, 1841–2).

FRANCE, H., *Dictionnaire de la langue verte: Archaïsmes, néologismes, locutions étrangères, patois* (Paris: Librairie du Progrès, 1907).

FREDKIN, G. R., 'Poétique et politique: Baudelaire et le paradoxe autoréférentiel', *Nineteenth-Century French Studies*, 16 (1987–8), 95–110.

FREUD, S., *Wit and its Relation to the Unconscious*, trans. A. A. Brill (London: Kegan Paul, Trench & Trubner, n.d.).

FRIED, M., 'Painting Memories: On the Containment of the Past in Baudelaire and Manet', *Critical Inquiry*, 10 (Mar. 1984), 510–42.

FRISBY, D., *Fragments of Modernity* (Cambridge: Polity Press, 1985).

FROIDEVAUX, G., *Baudelaire: Représentation et modernité* (Paris: Corti, 1989).

FÜGLISTER, R. L., 'Baudelaire et le thème des bohémiens', *Études baudelairiennes*, ii (Neuchâtel: La Baconnière, 1977).

GASARIAN, G., *De loin tendrement: Étude sur Baudelaire* (Paris: Champion, 1996).

GENETTE, G., *Figures III* (Paris: Seuil, 1972).

—— *Introduction à l'architexte* (Paris: Seuil, 1979).

—— *Palimpsestes: La Littérature au second degré* (Paris: Seuil, 1982).

—— *Nouveau Discours du récit* (Paris: Seuil, 1983).

—— *Seuils* (Paris: Seuil, 1987).

GILSON, E., 'Baudelaire and the Muse', in H. Peyre (ed.), *Baudelaire: A Collection of Critical Essays* (Englewood Cliffs, NJ: Prentice Hall, 1962).

GODFREY, S., 'Baudelaire's Windows', *L'Esprit Créateur*, 22/4 (Winter 1982), 83–100.

GONCOURT, J. and E. DE, *Journal*, ed. Robert Ricatte (Paris: Fasquelle & Flammarion, 1956).

GORDON, R. B., 'The Lyric Persona: Nerval's "El Desdichado"', in C. Prendergast (ed.), *Nineteenth-Century French Poetry: Introductions to Close Reading* (Cambridge: Cambridge University Press, 1990), 86–102.

GOULET, A., (ed.), *Le Stéréotype: Crise et Transformations*, Actes du colloque de Cerisy-la-Salle (Caen: Presses universitaires de Caen, 1994).

GOYA, F. DE, *The Complete Etchings* [1943] (New York: Crown, 1962).

—— *Los Caprichos*, facsimile ed. E. Lafuente Ferrari (Barcelona: Gili, 1977).

—— *Goya's Drawings* (New York: Dover; London: Constable, 1986).

GRAVES, R., *Mrs. Fisher or the Future of Humour* (London: Kegan Paul, Trench, Trubner & Co., 1928).

GREIMAS, A., *Du sens: Essais sémiotiques* (Paris: Seuil, 1970).

—— 'Les Actants, les acteurs et les figures', in C. Chabrol (ed.), *Sémiotique narrative et textuelle* (Paris: Larousse, 1973).

—— and COURTÉS J., *Sémiotique: Un dictionnaire raisonné de la théorie du langage* (Paris: Hachette, 1979).

GROUPE μ, 'Ironique et Iconique', *Poétique*, 36 (Nov. 1978), 427–42.

GUINARD, P., 'Baudelaire, le musée espagnol et Goya', *Revue d'histoire littéraire de la France*, special Baudelaire no. (Apr.–May 1967), 321–8.

GUREWITCH, M., *Comedy: The Irrational Vision* (Ithaca, NY, and London: Cornell University Press, 1975).

GUTWIRTH, Marcel, 'A propos du *Gâteau*: Baudelaire, Rousseau et le recours à l'enfance', *Romanic Review*, 80/1 (Jan. 1989), 75–87.

HAIDU, P., 'Au début du roman, l'ironie', *Poétique*, 36 (Nov. 1978), 443–66.

HAMBLEY, P. S., 'Baudelaire et l'utopie', *Bulletin baudelairien*, 6/1 (31 Aug. 1970), 5–7.

—— 'Littérature et fouriérisme', *Australian Journal of French Studies*, 11/3 (Sept.-Dec. 1974), 237–52.

—— 'Idéologie et poésie: Notes sur Baudelaire et ses contemporains', *Australian Journal of French Studies*, 16/1 (Jan.-Apr. 1979), 191–213.

HAMON, P., *L'Ironie littéraire: Essai sur les formes de l'écriture oblique* (Paris: Hachette, 1996).

HANDWERK, G. J., *Irony and Ethics in Narrative: From Schlegel to Lacan* (New Haven: Yale University Press, 1985).

HANNOOSH, M., 'Baudelaire, Etching and Modern Art', *French Studies*, 43 (1984), 42–55.

—— 'The Reflexive Function of Parody', *Comparative Literature*, 41/2 (Spring 1989), 113–27.

—— *Baudelaire and Caricature: From the Comic to an Art of Modernity* (University Park: Pennsylvania State University Press, 1992).

HARRINGTON, K. A., 'Fragmentation and Irony in *Les Fleurs du Mal*', *Nineteenth-Century French Studies*, 20/1–2 (1991–2), 177–86.

HASKELL, F., LEVI E., and SHACKLETON, R. (eds.), *The Artist and the Writer in France: Essays in Honour of Jean Seznec* (Oxford: Clarendon Press, 1970).

HAUGEN, A. K., 'Baudelaire, le rire et le grotesque', *Littérature*, 72 (1987), 12–29.

HAXELL, N. A., 'The Name of the Prose: A Semiotic Study of Titling in the Pre-Baudelairean Prose Poem', French Studies, 44 (1990), 156–69.

HECK, F. S., 'Baudelaire's *Confiteor* and the Reader', *Kentucky Romance Quarterly*, 31/1 (1984), 23–30.

HEMMINGS, F. W. J., *Culture and Society in France 1848–1898: Dissidents and Philistines* (London: Batsford, 1971).

HIDDLESTON, J. A., 'Baudelaire and the Poetry of Prose', *Nineteenth-Century French Studies*, 12/1–2 (Fall–Winter 1983–4), 124–37.

—— 'Baudelaire and "la critique de l'identification"', *French Forum*, 9/1 (Jan. 1984), 33–41.

—— 'Baudelaire, Manet and "La Corde"', *Bulletin baudelairien*, 19/1 (1984), 7–11.

—— 'Fusée, maxim and commonplace in Baudelaire', *Modern Language Review*, 80/3 (July 1985), 562–70.

—— 'Baudelaire et le rire', *Études baudelairiennes*, xii (Neuchâtel: La Baconnière, 1987), 85–98.

—— *Baudelaire and Le Spleen de Paris* (Oxford: Clarendon Press, 1987).

—— 'Chacun son *Spleen*: Some Observations on Baudelaire's Prose Poems', *Modern Language Review*, 86 (Jan. 1991), 66–9.

—— '"Le Spleen de Paris" et la caricature', *Romantisme*, 74 (1991), 57–64.

HIRSCH, E. D., *Validity in Interpretation* (New Haven: Yale University Press, 1967).

HOLLAND, E., *Baudelaire and Schizoanalysis: The Sociopoetics of Modernism* (Cambridge: Cambridge University Press, 1993).

HOUSSAYE, A., *Poésies complètes* (Paris: Charpentier, 1850).

HOWELLS, B., 'Baudelaire: Portrait of the Artist in 1846', *French Studies*, 37/4 (Oct. 1983), 426–39.

—— *Baudelaire: Individualism, Dandyism and the Philosophy of History* (Oxford: Eurpean Humanities Research Centre, *legenda*, 1996).

HUNT, H. J., *Le Socialisme et le romantisme en France: Étude de la presse socialiste de 1830 à 1848* (Oxford: Clarendon Press, 1935).

HYSLOP, L. B., 'Baudelaire, Proudhon and "Le Reniement de Saint Pierre"', *French Studies*, 30/3 (1976), 273–86.

—— *Baudelaire, Man of his Time* (New Haven: Yale University Press, 1980).

ISER, W., *The Implied Reader: Patterns of Communication in Prose Fiction from Bunyan to Beckett* [1972] (Baltimore: Johns Hopkins University Press, 1974).

—— *The Act of Reading: A Theory of Aesthetic Response* [1976] (Baltimore: Johns Hopkins University Press, 1978).

—— 'Interaction between Text and reader', in S. Suleiman and I. Crosman (eds.), *The Reader in the Text* (Princeton: Princeton University Press, 1982).

JACKSON, J. E., and PICHOIS, C., *Baudelaire: Figures de la mort, figures de l'éternité* (L'Année Baudelaire, 2; Paris: Klincksieck, 1996).

JAMESON, F., *The Political Unconscious: Narrative as a Socially Symbolic Act* (Ithaca, NY, and London: Cornell University Press, 1981).

JANIN, J., *Deburau: Histoire du théâtre à quatre sous pour faire suite à l'histoire du Théâtre-Français* (Paris: Librairie des Bibliophiles, 1881).

JENNY, L., 'Fictions et figurations du moi', in Dominique Rabaté (ed.), *Figures du sujet lyrique* (Paris: Presses universitaires de France, 1996), 99–111.

JENSON, V., *Genèse du Spleen baudelairien* (Rome: Edizioni dell'Ateneo, 1982).

JOHNSON, B., 'Quelques conséquences de la différence anatomique des textes: Pour une théorie du poème en prose', *Poétique*, 28 (1976), 450–65.

—— *Défigurations du langage poétique: La Seconde Révolution bauderlairienne* (Paris: Flammarion, 1979).

—— *The Critical Difference* (Baltimore: Johns Hopkins University Press, 1980).

JOHNSTON, J. H., *The Poet and the City* (Athens, Ga.: University of Georgia Press, 1984).

JOLLES, A., *Formes simples* (Paris: Seuil, 1972).

JONES, L. E., *Sad Clowns and Pale Pierrots: Literature and the Popular Comic Arts in Nineteenth-Century France* (Lexington Ky.: French Forum, 1984).

JOUVE, P. J., 'Le Spleen de Paris', *Mercure de France*, 321 (Sept. 1954), 32–9.

KANT, I., *Critique of Practical Reason and Other Writings in Moral Philosophy*, trans. and ed. Lewis White Beck (Chicago: University of Chicago Press, 1949).

KAPLAN, E. K., *Baudelaire's Prose Poems: The Esthetic, the Ethical and the Religious in the Parisian Prowler* (Athens, Ga., and London: University of Georgia Press, 1990).

—— 'Solipsism and Dialogue in Baudelaire's Prose Poems', in Barbara T. Cooper and Mary Donaldson Evans (eds.), *Modernity and Revolution in Late Nineteenth-Century France* (Newark: University of Delaware Press, 1992), 88–98.

KERBRAT-Orrecchioni, C., 'Problèmes de l'Ironie', in *Linguistique et sémiologie*, 2, (1976), 10–46, repr. Presses universitaires de Lyon, 1978.

KIERKEGAARD, S., *The Concept of Irony, with Constant Reference to Socrates*, trans. Lee M. Capel (London: Collins, 1966).

KING, R., 'De-Marginalizing a Throw-Away Line: Baudelaire's Heroic Soldier', *Nottingham French Studies* 23/2 (Oct. 1984), 9–16.

KLEIN, R., '"Bénédiction"/"Perte d'auréole": Parables of Interpretation', *Modern Language Notes*, 85/4 (May 1970), 515–28.

KRISTEVA, J., *La Révolution du langage poétique: L'Avant-garde à la fin du dix-neuvième siècle* (Paris: Seuil, 1974).

LANG, C. D., *Irony/Humor: Critical Paradigms* (Baltimore: Johns Hopkins University Press, 1988).

LAVATER, J. C., *L'Art de connaître les hommes par la physiognomie*, ed. Moreau de la Sarthe (Paris, 1806–9).

LAYTON, L., and SCHAPIRO, B. A., *Narcissism and the Text: Studies in the Literature and the Psychology of Self* (New York: New York University Press, 1986).

LEAKEY, F. W., 'Baudelaire: The Poet as Moralist', *Studies in Modern French Literature presented to P. Mansell Jones* (Manchester: Manchester University Press, 1961).

—— 'Les Esthétiques de Baudelaire: Le "Système" des années 1844–47', *Revue des sciences humaines*, 127 (July–Sept. 1967) 481–96.

—— *Baudelaire and Nature* (Manchester: Manchester University Press, 1969).

—— *Baudelaire: Collected Essays 1953–1988* (Cambridge: Cambridge University Press, 1990).

LEBOIS, A., 'Prestiges et actualité des *Petits Poëmes en prose* de Baudelaire', *Archives des lettres modernes*, 18 (Dec. 1958), 1–32.

LEJEUNE, P., *Je est un autre: L'Autobiographie de la littérature aux médias* (Paris: Seuil, 1980).

LENTRICCIA, F., *Criticism and Social Change* (London and Chicago: University of Chicago Press, 1983).

LEVITINE, G., 'Some Emblematic Sources of Goya', *Journal of the Warburg and Courtauld Institutes* (1959), 110–17.

LICHT, F., *Goya: The Origins of the Modern Temper in Art* (London: J. Murray, 1980).

LLOYD, R., *Baudelaire et Hoffmann: Affinités et Influences* (Cambridge: Cambridge University Press, 1979).

—— *Baudelaire's Literary Criticism* (Cambridge: Cambridge University Press, 1981).

—— 'Taking the Cake: Some Aspects of Children and Food in 19th-Century Literature', *Romance Studies*, 13 (1987), 81–8.

—— 'Dwelling in Possibility: Encounters with the Other in Baudelaire's *Le Spleen de Paris*', *Australian Journal of French Studies*, 29/1 (1992), 68–77.

LOPEZ VASQUEZ, J. M. B., *Los Caprichos de Goya y su significado* (Santiago de Compostela: Universidad de Santiago, 1982).

LUCIE-SMITH, E., *The Art of Caricature* (London: Orbis, 1981).

LYOTARD, J.-F., 'On the Strength of the Weak', *Sémiotexte*, 3/2 (1978), 204–12.

MACINNES, J. W., *The Comic as Textual Practice in Les Fleurs du Mal* (Gainesville: University of Florida Press, 1988).

MACLEAN, M., *Narrative as Performance: The Baudelairean Experiment* (London: Routledge, 1988).

McLEES, A. A., 'Baudelaire and Caricature: Argot plastique', *Symposium*, 38/3 (Fall, 1984), 221–33.

—— 'Baudelaire's "Une Charogne": Caricature and the Birth of Modern Art', *Mosaic*, (Fall 1988), 21/4, 111–22.

—— *Baudelaire's Argot plastique: Poetic Caricature and Modernism* (Athens, Ga., and London: University of Georgia Press, 1989).

MADON, J.-P., 'Ironie socratique, ironie romanesque, ironie politique', *French Literature Series*, 14 (1987), 62–73.

MAINARDI, P., *Art and Politics of the Second Empire* (London and New Haven: Yale University Press, 1987).

MAURON, C., *Le Dernier Baudelaire* (Paris: José Corti, 1966).

—— 'Le Rire baudelairien', *Europe*, 45/456–7 (Apr.–May 1967), 54–61.

MERCER, C., 'Baudelaire and the City: 1848 and the Inscription of Hegemony', in F. Barker (ed.), *1848: The Sociology of Literature* (University of Essex, 1978).

MEYER, N., 'Flaubert's Irony in *L'Education sentimentale*', *French Literature Series*, 14 (1987), 161–9.

MONNIER, H., *Les Mémoires de M. Joseph Prudhomme*, 2 vols. (Paris: Librairie nouvelle, 1857).

MONROE, J., *A Poverty of Objects: The Prose Poem and the Politics of Genre* (London and Ithaca, NY: Cornell University Press, 1987).

MOREAU, P., 'La Tradition française du poème en prose avant Baudelaire', *Archives des lettres modernes*, 19–20 (Jan–Feb. 1959), 19–20.

MOUQUET J., and BANDY, W. T., *Baudelaire en 1848: La Tribune nationale* (Paris: Émile-Paul Frères, 1946).

MUECKE, D. C., *The Compass of Irony* [1969] (London: Methuen, 1980).

MURPHY, S., '"Le Mauvais Vitrier" ou la crise du verre', *Romanic Review*, 82/3 (1990), 339–49.

—— 'Le Complexe de supériorité et la contagion du rire: 'Un Plaisant' de Baudelaire', *Travaux de Littérature*, 7 (1994), 257–85.

NANCE, J. L., 'Le Rire, la présence', *Critique*, 488–9 (1988), 41–60.

NERVAL, G. DE, *Œuvres* (Paris, 1974).

NIES, F., *Poesie in prosaicher Welt: Untersuchungen zum Prosagedicht bei Aloysius Bertrand und Baudelaire* (Heidelberg: Carl Winter, 1964).

NOAKES, S., *Timely Reading: Between Exegesis and Interpretation* (Ithaca, NY: Cornell University Press, 1988), esp. 157–204.

OEHLER, D., 'Le Caractère double de l'héroïsme et du beau modernes', *Études baudelairiennes*, viii (Neuchâtel: La Baconnière, 1976).

—— *Pariser Bilder I (1830–1848): Antibourgeoise Ästhetik bei Baudelaire, Daumier und Heine* (Frankfurt am Main: Suhrkamp, 1979).

—— *Le Spleen contre l'oubli: Juin 1848. Baudelaire, Flaubert, Heine, Herzen*, trans. Guy Petitdemange (Paris: Payot, 1988).

—— *Ein Hollenstürz der Alten Welt: Zur Selbsterforschung der Moderne nach dem juni 1848* (Frankfurt am Main: Suhrkamp, 1988).

PARENT-DUCHÂTELET, A., *De la prostitution dans la Ville de Paris* (Paris: Baillière, 1836).

PÉRICAUD, L., *Le Théâtre des Funambules, ses mimes, ses acteurs et ses pantomimes depuis sa fondation jusqu'à sa démolition* (Paris: Léon Sapin, 1897).

PEYRE, H., (ed.) *Baudelaire: A Collection of Critical Essays* (Englewood Cliffs, NJ: Prentice Hall, 1962).

PICH, E., 'Pour une définition de la poésie comme phénomène social au XIXe siècle', *Romantisme*, 39 (1983), 85–95.

PICHOIS, C., 'Baudelaire en 1847', *Revue des sciences humaines* (1958), 121–38.

—— *Iconographie de Charles Baudelaire* (Geneva: Cailler, 1960).

—— 'Baudelaire ou la difficulté créatrice', in *Baudelaire: Études et témoignages*, ed. C. Pichois (Neuchâtel: La Baconnière, 1967).

—— *Vitesse et vision du monde* (Neuchâtel: La Baconnière, 1973).

—— 'Baudelaire devant la sociocritique ouest-allemande', *Études baudelairiennes*, ix (Neuchâtel: La Baconnière, 1981).

—— and CREPET, J., *Baudelaire et Asselineau* (Paris: Nizet, 1953).

—— and ZIEGLER, J., *Baudelaire* (Paris: Julliard, 1987).

PICHON YANN LE, and PICHOIS, C., *Le Musée retrouvé de Charles Baudelaire* (Paris: Stock, 1992).

PIZZAROSSO, A., '"Le Mauvais Vitrier", ou l'impulsion inconnue', *Études baudelairiennes*, viii (Neuchâtel: La Baconnière, 1976).

POMMIER, J., *La Mystique de Baudelaire* (Paris: Les Belles-Lettres, 1932).

POULET, G., *La Poésie éclatée: Baudelaire / Rimbaud* (Paris: Presses universitaires de France, 1980).

POULET-MALASSIS, A. DE, *Sept Dessins de gens de lettres, MM. Victor Hugo, Prosper Mérimée, Edmond et Jules de Goncourt, Charles Baudelaire, Théophile Gautier, Charles Asselineau* (Paris: Rouquette, 1874).

PRATT, M.-L., *Towards a Speech Act Theory of Literary Discourse* (Bloomington and Indianapolis: Indiana University Press, 1977).

PRENDERGAST, C., (ed.), *Nineteenth-Century French Poetry: Introductions to Close Reading* (Cambridge: Cambridge University Press, 1990).

—— *Paris and the Nineteenth Century* (Oxford: Blackwell, 1992).

PRÉVOST, J., *Baudelaire: Essai sur la création et l'inspiration poétiques* [1953] (Paris: Mercure de France, 1968).

PROPP, V., *Morphology of the Folktale* [1928] (Austin and London: University of Texas Press, 1968).

RABATÉ, D., (ed.), *Figures du sujet lyrique* (Paris: Presses universitaires de France, 1996).

RAHUT, F., *Das französische Prosagedicht* (Hamburg: Friedrichsen & de Gruyter, 1929).

RAITT, A. W., 'On *Le Spleen de Paris*', *Nineteenth-Century French Studies*, 18 (1989–90), 150–64.

RAPHAEL, L. N., 'Semiotics, Nihilism, Mimesis: Baudelaire's "Un Plaisant"', *Romanic Review* 75/4 (Nov. 1984), 453–68.

RASER, T,. 'Barthes and Riffaterre: The Dilemmas of Realism in the Light of Baudelaire's "Le Soleil"', *French Review*, 59 (Oct. 1985), 58–64.

RATTIER P. -E. DE, *Chants prosaïques* (Paris: Dentu, 1861).

REBEYROL, P., 'Baudelaire and Manet', *Les Temps modernes*, 48 (Oct. 1949), 707–25.

REDFERN, W., *Puns* (Oxford: Blackwell, 1984).

RIEUSSET-LEMARIÉ, I., 'Stéréotype ou reproduction de langage sans sujet', in Alain Goulet (ed.), *Le Stéréotype: Crise et transformations*, Actes du colloque de Cerisy-la-Salle, 1993 (Caen: Presses universitaires de Caen, 1994), 15–34.

RIFFATERRE, M., *Essais de stylistique structurale* (Paris: Flammarion, 1971).

—— *Semiotics of Poetry* (Bloomington and Indianapolis: Indiana University Press, 1978).

—— *La Production du texte* (Paris: Seuil, 1979).

RIMMON-KENAN, S., *Narrative Fiction: Contemporary Poetics* (London: Methuen, 1983).

ROBB, G. M., '"Les Chats" de Baudelaire: Une nouvelle lecture', *Revue d'histoire littéraire de la France*, 85/6 (1985), 1002–10.

—— 'Le Salon de 1846: Baudelaire s'explique', *Nineteenth-Century French Studies*, 15/3–4 (Spring–Summer 1987), 415–24.

—— 'Les Origines journalistiques de la prose poétique de Baudelaire', *Lettres romanes*, 44 (1990), 15–25.

—— 'The Poetics of the Commonplace in *Les Fleurs du Mal*', Modern Language Review, 86/1 (Jan. 1991), 57–65.

—— *La Poésie de Baudelaire et la poésie française 1838–1852* (Paris: Aubier, 1993).

ROSE, M. A., *Parody: Ancient, Modern and Post-Modern* [1993] (Cambridge: Cambridge University Press, 1995).

ROUSSEAU, J.-J., *La Nouvelle Héloïse, Œuvres complètes* (Bibliothèque de la Pléiade; Paris: Gallimard, 1964), vol ii.

RUFF, M., *L'Esprit du mal et l'ésthétique baudelairienne* (Paris: Armand Colin, 1955).

—— *Baudelaire* (Paris: Hatier, 1966).

—— 'Baudelaire et le poème en prose', *Zeitschrift für französische Sprache und Literatur*, 77 (Jan. 1967), 116–23.

—— 'La Pensée politique et sociale de Baudelaire', in *Littérature et société: Recueil d'études en l'honneur de Bernard Guyon* (Paris: Desclée de Brouwer, 1973), 65–76.

SACKS, S., (ed.), *On Metaphor* (Chicago: University of Chicago Press, 1979).

SAHLBERG, O., *Baudelaire 1848: Gedichte der Revolution* (Berlin: Wagensbachs Taschenbücherei, 1977).

—— *Baudelaire und seine Muse auf dem Weg zur Revolution* (Frankfurt am Main: Suhrkamp, 1980).

SAINTSBURY, G., 'Charles Baudelaire', in *Miscellaneous Essays* (London: Percival, 1892).

SARTRE, J.-P., *Qu'est-ce que la littérature?* (Paris: Gallimard, 1947).

SCHOFER, P., '"Une Mort héroïque": Baudelaire's Social Theatre of Cruelty', *French Literature Series*, 15 (1988), 50–7.

—— 'You Cannot Kill a Cloud: Code and Context in "L'Étranger"', in Barbara T. Cooper and Mary Donaldson Evans (eds.), *Modernity and Revolution in Late Nineteenth-Century France* (Newark: University of Delaware Press, 1992), 99–107.

SCHÖRER, C., *Les Petits Poëmes en prose von Baudelaire, eine Gedankendichtung, als Zeit- und charakterdokument*, unpublished diss. (Jena University, Leipzig, 1935).

SCOTT, DAVID, *Pictorialist Poetics: Poetry and the Visual Arts in Nineteenth-Century France* (Cambridge: Cambridge University Press, 1988).

SIMON, R. K., *The Labyrinth of the Comic: Theory and Practice from Fielding to Freud* (Tallahassee: Florida State University Presses, 1985).

SMITH, B. H., *On the Margins of Discourse: The Relations of Literature to Language* (London and Chicago: University of Chicago Press, 1978).

SOUCY, A.-M., 'Le Rire dans l'œuvre de Baudelaire', *Thalia*, 9/2 (1987), 32–9.

SPERBER, D., and WILSON, D., 'Les Ironies comme mentions', *Poétique*, 36 (Nov. 1978), 399–418.

STALLYBRASS, P., and WHITE, A., *The Politics and Poetics of Transgression* (London: Methuen, 1986).

STARKIE, E., *Baudelaire* (Harmondsworth: Penguin, 1971).

STAROBINSKI, J., 'Sur quelques répondants allégoriques du poète', *Revue d'histoire littéraire de la France*, 67 (Apr.–June 1967), 402–12.

—— *Portrait de l'artiste en saltimbanque* (Geneva: Skira, 1970).

STARR, W. T., 'Irony and Satire: A Bibliography', *French Literature Series*, 14 (1987) 183–209.

STEINMETZ, J.-L., 'Essai de tératologie', in Max Milner and Martine Bercot (eds.), *Les Fleurs du mal: L'Intériorité de la forme* (Paris: SEDES, 1988), 161–76.

STENZEL, H., 'Quelques souvenirs socialistes dans l'œuvre de Baudelaire', *Bulletin baudelairien*, 12/1 (1976), 3–13.

STEPHENS, S., '*Argot littéraire, argot plastique*: Caricature in Baudelaire's Prose Poetry', *Australian Journal of French Studies*, 30/2 (1993), 197–206.

—— 'L'Expérience urbaine et l'évolution d'un genre: Le Cas du poème en prose baudelairien', in Keith Cameron and James Kearns (eds.), *Le Champ littéraire 1860–1900. Études offertes à Michael Packenham* (Amsterdam: Rodopi, 1996), 39–47.

—— 'Boundaries, Limits and Limitations: Baudelaire's *Poèmes-Boutades*', *French Studies*, 70/1 (Jan. 1998), 28–41.

—— 'Voices in the Night: "A Une Heure du matin"', in P. Ford and G. Jondorf, *The Art of Reading: Essays in Memory of Dorothy Gabe Coleman* (Cambridge: Cambridge French Colloquia, 1998), 143–53.

STIERLE, K., 'Identité du discours et trangression lyrique', *Poétique*, 32 (Nov. 1977), 422–41.

STILL, J., and WORTON, M. (eds.), *Intertextuality: Theories and Practices* (Manchester: Manchester University Press, 1990).

STOREY, R., *Pierrots on the Stage of Desire: Nineteenth-Century French Literary Artists and the Comic Pantomime* (Princeton: Princeton University Press, 1985).

STREIT, G., *Die Doppelmotive in Baudelaires 'Fleurs du mal' und 'Petits Poëmes en prose'* (Zurich: Heits, 1929).

SULEIMAN, S. R., and CROSMAN, I. (eds.), *The Reader in the Text: Essays on*

Audience and Interpretation (Princeton: Princeton University Press, 1980).

SUSINI, J.-C., 'Liszt/Analyste: Dimension rhétorique du jeu de mots dans "Le Thyrse"', *Bulletin baudelairien*, 32/2 (Dec. 1997), 53–62.

SZONDI, P., *On Textual Understanding and Other Essays* (Theory and History of Literature, 15; Manchester: Manchester University Press, 1986).

TABARANT, A., *La Vie artistique au temps de Baudelaire* [1942] (Paris: Mercure de France, 1963).

TADIÉ, J.-Y., *Le Récit Poétique* (Paris: Presses universitaires de France, 1978).

TENER, R. L., *The Phœnix Riddle: A Study of Irony in Comedy* (Salzburg Studies in English Literature; University of Salzburg, 1979).

TERDIMAN, R., *Discourse/Counter-Discourse: The Theory and Practice of Symbolic Resistance in Nineteenth-Century France* (Ithaca, NY, and London: Cornell University Press, 1985).

TEXIER, E., *Physiologie du poète* (Paris: J. Laisné, 1842).

—— *Tableau de Paris*, 2 vols. (Paris: Paulin and Le Chevalier, 1852–3).

THÉLOT, J., *Baudelaire: Violence et poésie* (Paris: NRF, Gallimard, 1993).

THOMPSON, A. R., *The Dry Mock: A Study of Irony in Drama* (Berkeley: University of California Press, 1948).

THORÉ, T., *Dictionnaire de la phrénologie* (Paris: Librairie usuelle, 1836).

TODOROV, T., *Genres du discours* (Paris: Seuil, 1978).

—— 'Poetry without Verse', in Mary Ann Caws and Hermine Riffaterre (eds.), *The Prose Poem in France: Theory and Practice* (New York: Columbia University Press, 1983).

TRAHARD, P., *Essai critique sur Baudelaire poète* (Paris: Nizet, 1973).

TRILLING, L., *Sincerity and Authority* (Cambridge, Mass.: Harvard University Press, 1971).

VALÉRY, P., *Œuvres* (Bibliothèque de la Pléiade; Paris: Gallimard, 1957).

VAN SLYKE, G., 'Dans l'intertexte de Baudelaire et de Proudhon: Pourquoi faut-il assommer les pauvres?', *Romantisme*, 45 (1984), 57–77.

—— 'Les épiciers au musée: Baudelaire et l'artiste bourgeois', *Romantisme*, 55 (1987), 55–66.

VIVIER, R., *L'Originalité de Baudelaire* [1926] (Brussels: Palais des Académies, 1952).

WAUGH, P., *Metafiction: The Theory and Practice of Self-Conscious Fiction* (London and New York: Methuen, 1984).

WECHSLER, J., *A Human Comedy: Physiognomy and Caricature in 19th-Century Paris* (London: Thames & Hudson, 1982).

WELSFORD, E., *The Fool: His Social and Literary History* (London: Faber & Faber, 1935).

WILDE, A., *Horizons of Assent: Modernism, Postmodernism and the Ironic*

Imagination (Baltimore and London: Johns Hopkins University Press, 1981).

WING, N., 'The Poetics of Irony in Baudelaire's *La Fanfarlo*', *Neophilologus*, 59/2 (Apr. 1975), 165–89.

—— *The Limits of Narrative: Essays on Baudelaire, Flaubert, Rimbaud and Mallarmé* (Cambridge: Cambridge University Press, 1986).

—— 'Poets, Mimes and Counterfeit Coins: On Power and Discourse in Baudelaire's Prose Poetry', *Paragraph*, 13 (1990), 1–18.

WOHLFARTH, I., '"Perte d'auréole": The Emergence of the Dandy', *Modern Language Notes*, 85 (1970) 529–71.

WRIGHT, B., and SCOTT, DAVID H. T., *La Fanfarlo and Le Spleen de Paris* (London: Grant & Cutler, 1984).

YAGUELLO, M., *Alice au pays du langage* (Paris: Seuil, 1981).

ZALECKI, J., *Communicative Multivocality: A Study of Punning, Metaphor and Irony* (Cracow: Nakladem Universytetu Jagiellonskiego, 1990).

ZIMMERMAN, M., 'La Genèse du symbole du thyrse chez Baudelaire', *Bulletin baudelairien*, 2/1 (1966), 8–11.

Index